AF228447

THE 28TH INFANTRY DIVISION AND THE BATTLE OF THE BULGE

COMBAT, FAITH, AND PERSEVERANCE

WALTER S. ZAPOTOCZNY JR.

Cover image: American infantrymen of the 290th Regiment fight in fresh snowfall near Amonines, Belgium, January 4, 1945. While this image does not show men of the 28th Infantry Division, it accurately depicts the conditions in which they fought in the Battle of the Bulge.

First published in Great Britain in 2025 by
Fonthill
An imprint of
Pen & Sword Books Ltd
Yorkshire – Philadelphia
www.fonthill.media

ISBN 978-1-78155-928-4

A CIP catalogue record for this book is available from the British Library.

Typeset in Sabon LT 10/13
Typeset by Fonthill
Printed and bound in the UK by CPI Group (UK) Ltd, Croydon, CR0 4YY

The Publisher's authorised representative in the EU for product safety is Authorised Rep Compliance Ltd., Ground Floor, 71 Lower Baggot Street, Dublin D02 P593, Ireland.
www.arccompliance.com

For a complete list of Pen & Sword titles please contact
PEN & SWORD BOOKS LIMITED
47 Church Street, Barnsley, South Yorkshire, S70 2AS, England
E-mail: enquiries@pen-and-sword.co.uk
Website: www.pen-and-sword.co.uk

Or
PEN AND SWORD BOOKS
1950 Lawrence Rd, Havertown, PA 19083, USA
E-mail: Uspen-and-sword@casematepublishers.com
Website: www.penandswordbooks.com

Preface

In December 1944, Hitler's Germany was besieged on every front. Germany was working on superweapons and needed to buy some time to fight off the Red Army and the Allies. Until his superweapons could turn the tide, Hitler opted for a major counteroffensive in the west to split the Allied coalition. Hitler would launch his last military reserves in a desperate gamble aimed at driving to the port of Antwerp through Luxembourg and Belgium. Such a blow, Hitler believed, would wreck the coalition. One of the divisions facing the main German offensive was the American 28th Infantry Division, occupying a 25-mile front that extended along Belgium and Luxembourg's borders with Germany. The actions by the soldiers of that division combined to slow and finally stall the German offensive, robbing it of its momentum and, most of all, the precious time upon which the operation relied for success.

While this book follows the battles of the 28th Infantry Division soldiers, it is not a battle chronicle, nor is it intended to list all of the actions taken by the 28th Infantry Division or other American units during the Battle of the Bulge. Many books have been written that account for those actions. However, those books have not examined the reasons the men fought. This work explicitly explores the reasons why the soldiers of the 28th Infantry Division fought so fiercely to delay the German advance: the specific actions taken to delay the Germans, the spectrum of religious beliefs and practices soldiers brought with them as they went to war, and the motivating factors that contributed to the actions by the brave soldiers in the Ardennes.

Contents

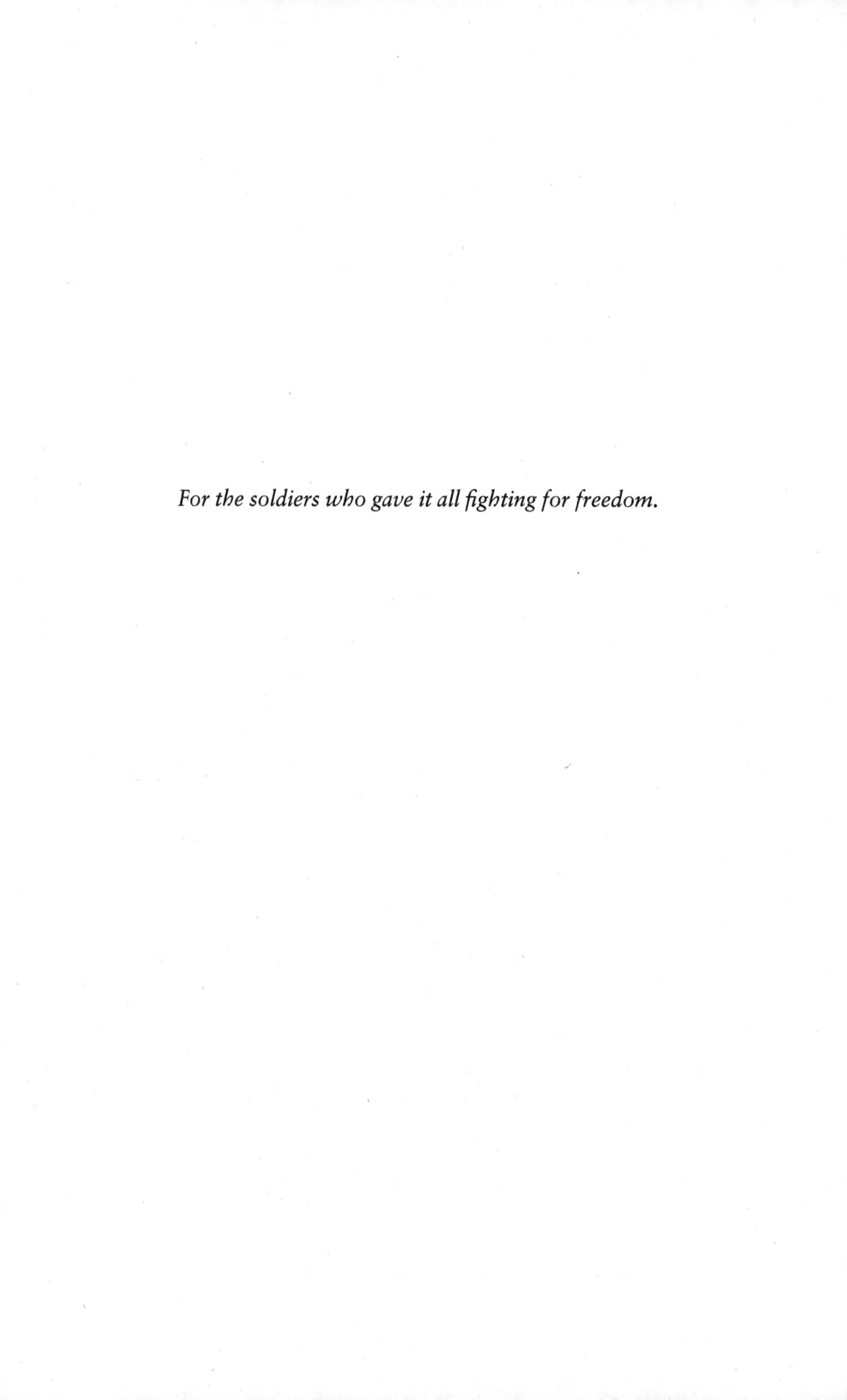

For the soldiers who gave it all fighting for freedom.

Introduction

The purpose of this study was to determine what motivated the soldiers of the 28th Infantry Division, in the face of overwhelming odds, to take action during the first few days of the Battle of the Bulge (Ardennes Offensive) to delay the German plan of attack. Challenging the conventional ideas about the contribution of the 28th Infantry Division and the motivations that cause men to fight, this study concluded that the soldiers fought for the American way of life. The aim of this study was to answer three research questions:

1. What forces beyond camaraderie and cohesion influenced soldiers to resist the German offensive in the Battle of the Bulge?
2. How did faith factor into the nexus of ideas that inspired the perseverance of the soldiers?
3. How significant was the delaying action of the 28th Division to the Allied success in the Battle of the Bulge?

The Allies thought the end was near for the German Army by mid-September 1944. The success by the Russians in the east added to their optimism. In an attempt to secure the Roer River and a complex of dams on the same river near Schmidt in Germany, the U. S. command transferred a number of units to include the 1st, 8th, 9th, and the 28th Infantry Divisions and the 4th Armored Division into the Hürtgen Forest. The 28th Division moved into position on October 26, replacing the weakened 9th Infantry Division. While the 28th Division was promised lavish air and artillery support, the weather virtually negated close air support and the terrain prohibited observed artillery fire. After bitter fighting from November 2–14, the division was withdrawn from the Hürtgen Forest and was moved to Luxembourg, with casualities of over 6,100.

The division needed a rest and a chance to refit. The Ardennes Forest in Belgium and Luxembourg was thick, and the Allied Command believed it to be impenetrable.[1]

The 28th Division was stretched over a 25-mile front facing the German lines. Since the entire front could not be occupied, the division established strongpoints at various villages and at key road intersections. By mid-December 1944, the division had been recuperating in Luxembourg for several weeks. Shortly after 5:00 a.m. on the morning of December 16, 1944, their recuperation ended as the German attack began. The 28th Infantry Division was the only major fighting force that stood between the German onslaught and Bastogne, Belgium—a key road network that led to the deep-water port of Antwerp. Taking the brunt of the German assault were three regiments of the division: the 109th, 110th, and 112th.

The initial actions carried out by the division's soldiers worked together to gradually impede and ultimately halt the advancement of the German attack. This hindered the attack's momentum and, most importantly, disrupted the crucial timeframe that the operation depended on for achieving its goals. The actions of the soldiers represent an element often overlooked by historians and is exemplified in the fighting spirit exhibited by the soldiers in delaying the German armies and buying time for the Allies to send reinforcements to Bastogne. Despite overwhelming odds, the soldiers managed to hold out as German assault forces began to work their way into and around the soldier's positions. Many of the defenders recognized that they were surrounded and that no relief or escape, save as prisoners, was possible. Yet despite this realistic assessment, they continued to resist until there were simply no other means to resist. In two days of heavy fighting, the men of the 28th Infantry Division had inflicted heavy casualties on the attacking German forces and upset the German timetable.[2]

History is full of desperate historic battles that are idolized and provide lessons for future soldiers and military leaders. Once such battle was the Ardennes Offensive, or Battle of the Bulge. It took place from December 16, 1944, to January 25, 1945, and it stands as a testament to resolve against a determined enemy. Movies have been made and books written about the stand of the 101st Airborne Division at Bastogne, Belgium, and their relief by General Patton's 4th Armored Division. World War II would probably have produced more casualties and lasted longer had it not been for the strong resolve of Brigadier General Anthony McAuliffe and the men of the 101st Airborne and other units around Bastogne. While the achievements of the 101st Airborne have been championed, the actions of the 109th, 110th, and 112th Regiments of the 28th Infantry Division during the first few days of the offensive get little attention from historians.

By December 1944, the war in Europe seemed to be drawing to a conclusion. Beginning in the fall of 1943, the Soviet Army had launched a relentless advance which, by the fall of 1944, had permitted their armies to occupy East Prussian soil and to be poised for a final advance to Vienna, Prague, and Berlin. The Western Allies, after landing in Normandy, France, on June 6, 1944, had broken through German defenses and pushed to the German border for a final thrust into the heartland of Hitler's Germany. By this time, the question was not so much could the Allies win the war, but how much longer could the battered German armies hold out. Hitler's Germany was besieged on every front. Germany was working on superweapons and needed to buy some time to defend against the Russian Army and the Allies. Until his superweapons could turn the tide, Hitler opted for a major counteroffensive in the west to split the Allied coalition. Hitler believed the Allied alliance to be weak.[3]

Throughout his political and military career, Adolf Hitler had shown an uncanny knack for surprising his opponents, confounding them by launching an unexpected offensive at the most unlikely place or moment.[4] For example, one of Hitler's first major foreign policy initiatives after coming to power in 1933 was to sign a non-aggression pact with Poland in January 1934. On September 1, 1939, Germany conducted a surprise invasion of Poland.[5] In another example, on August 23, 1939, Hitler signed the German-Soviet non-aggression pact. Nazi Germany conducted a surprise invasion of the Soviet Union on June 22, 1941.[6]

Hitler launched yet another unexpected offensive by committing his last military reserves in a frantic gamble aimed at driving to the port of Antwerp through Luxembourg and Belgium. If successful, the Allies could lose over thirty divisions. Such a blow, Hitler believed, would destroy the Allied coalition and cause them to negotiate an agreement with Germany to end the war. The area chosen by Hitler for the offensive was the Ardennes, that area of Belgium and Luxembourg which in late 1944 was considered to be a quiet sector by the Allied Command.[7] This was an area where the troops were sent for rest and refitting. Standing in the way were four U.S. divisions—two green units placed in a quiet sector to gain experience, and two badly shot-up units that were resting and training replacements, occupying a front that extended along the Belgium and Luxembourg's borders.

One of the badly shot-up divisions facing the main German offensive was the American 28th Infantry Division. This veteran division, originally a Pennsylvania National Guard unit, had been engaged in combat since arriving in France on July 22, 1944. It had participated in the breakout at Saint-Lô, fought through northern France, liberated sections of Belgium and Luxembourg, and then moved into Germany in early September, attacking the famous Siegfried Line, or West Wall.[8]

It was exceptionally cold, foggy, damp, and snow-covered when the Germans attacked on the morning of December 16, 1944. Without any sleep, often without food, the soldiers of the 28th Infantry Division fought nonstop, frequently until the last bullet and last man, to stop the German drive. Overall, the 28th Infantry Division would identify elements of nine German divisions in its sector before the battle was over.[9] The men fought like they were defending their own homes. The achievements of the soldiers, while facing overwhelming forces in the early days of the Battle of the Bulge, provide lessons for future soldiers and military leaders.

The questions of why men fight and what factors motivate them to fight even when death seems certain are ancient and complex. Despite the lack of a single unifying theory of combat motivation, military leaders strive to study, understand motivational factors, and cultivate them in their people to achieve the greatest chance for victory. Understanding combat motivation provides probable benefits to those who understand these factors and can instill them in soldiers. Both military historians and social scientists have studied how soldiers behave on the battlefield, including how they handle the stress of combat and what motivates them.

These studies have helped in understanding how war affects soldiers. One such motivating factor is camaraderie. Camaraderie is most socially expressed within military culture. It is a deep and abiding bond among soldiers within a small, interdependent unit. Other than being in the general vicinity of one another as in an aggregate social group, soldiers need to be organized toward a concrete, common goal. The military organization, with its bureaucratic objectives, lends itself to forming such concrete goals for the units. "The goal is the survival and close teamwork with others in the outfit. The life of each depends as much on the feeling of close mutual dependence which has been seen to be so important as a basis for other aspects of combat motivation," argues Samuel and Edward Stouffer.[10]

The literature about combat motivation supports the general belief that soldiers exclusively fight because of cohesion. For example, William D. Henderson, retired U.S. Army colonel, believes cohesion is the primary motivational factor.[11] A similar finding was found in *Cohesion and Disintegration in the Wehrmacht in World War II* by Edward A. Shils and Morris Janowitz. They studied the motivation of German soldiers during World War II and also concluded that cohesion as a combination of organizational integrity, fighting effectiveness, and tenacity is what motivated the German soldiers.[12]

In a contrasting view, Omer Bartov maintained that the German soldier was motivated by ideology.[13] Bartov maintains that ideology and indoctrination were really the German soldiers' prime motivating factors.

The key point, according to Bartov, is that unit cohesion was not maintained throughout the war, especially on the Eastern Front, and therefore could not have been the main reason the Germans fought desperately until the end of the war. The story of the German *Einsatzgruppen* offers insight into a fundamental Holocaust question of what made it possible for men, some of them ordinary men, to kill so many people so ruthlessly. The members of the *Einsatzgruppen* had developed a special motivation to kill. The *Einsatzgruppen* grew out of a Germany that was economically crippled by World War I reparations, global depression, and a national sense that the Jew was significantly to blame for their problems. Fostered by the ideals of National Socialism, the naivety of youth, and the sense of pride and accomplishment that military service gave them, the members of the *Einsatzgruppen* became fully indoctrinated into the beliefs of Adolf Hitler.[14]

Unit cohesion and camaraderie undoubtedly are strong motivators when soldiers are together and have a chance to get to know each other and how they can count on each other. As the 28th Infantry Division confronted the Germans from one battle to the next, the number of casualties grew. The men who left the training in Wales were not the ones who fought the next major battle, and the attrition of war since the division landed in Normandy steadily thinned out the ranks. Lone replacements found themselves among groups of strangers with little chance to get acquainted before being flung into battle, so there had to be other factors that motivated the men to fight as they did.

Understanding what inspired the men of the 28th Infantry Division to fight and how they delayed the Germans is the purpose of this research. This research is significant as it can address the reasons soldiers, faced with overwhelming odds, chose to stand their ground to delay the advance of the enemy. The answers can provide military leaders with a better understanding of what motivates soldiers and can fill the gaps in the historiography of the Battle of the Bulge.

To address these issues, the research presented in this book is focused on what specific delaying actions the soldiers took, what were the spectrum of religious beliefs and practices soldiers brought with them and experienced during war, and what were other motivating factors that contributed to the actions by the soldiers in the Ardennes. For example, how much did their belief that they were fighting for the American way of life affect the decisions of the men of the 28th Infantry Division to fight so fiercely? For most soldiers, the American way of life meant freedom. That freedom often emphasized the freedom to worship. In *Protestant, Catholic, Jew: An Essay in American Religious Sociology*, sociologist Will Herberg describes the American way of life as "an organic structure of ideas, values, and beliefs that constitutes a faith common to Americans."[15]

In his book *On War*, Carl von Clausewitz states: "It is the interaction between physical and moral forces that determines the victor in warfare."[16] Clausewitz goes on to say: "… they [moral forces] are the spirits which permeate the whole element of war."[17] Contained within moral force, most certainly, is the courage, morale, and the religious faith of the soldiers. The literature presented by historians writing about the Battle of the Bulge largely focuses on presenting the physical components of the battle, neglecting the moral aspects.

According to Charles H. Coates and Roland J. Pellegrin, "the only thing rated more helpful than prayer was not wanting to let the other men down."[18] Their book brings together historical material with detailed organizational charts and tabular data. Coates and Pellegrin describe the relationship between military institutions and the American value system. The concept of bureaucracy is used to analyze management theory, leadership, and informal social systems in military organizations.[19] In the case of the military, men the soldier sees daily and associate with tend to fuse together into one force. If the men of a small unit properly blend together and function as a team, the smaller unit's cohesion can become the primary factor influencing a soldier's fighting spirit.[20]

In the years immediately after World War II, historians argued that social cohesion within the soldiers' primary group is essential to military effectiveness. William Darryl Henderson considers cohesion a vital aspect of combat motivation.[21] Unit cohesion, mutual self-sacrifice, teamwork, and covering for each other contribute to individual bonding, and ultimately creates camaraderie—something which may have contributed to the fighting spirit of the 28th Infantry Division soldiers when they first landed in France. In a November–December 2000 article for *Military Review*, Major Robert J. Rielly, U.S. Army, argues that "The strongest motivation for enduring combat, especially for U.S. soldiers, is the bond formed among members of a squad or platoon."[22] Rielly claims that "This cohesion is the single most important sustaining and motivating force for combat soldiers."[23]

Although in some ways linked to vindictiveness, the soldiers' feeling about the enemy as human beings that are evil or subhuman has been offered as motivating factors. There are examples of hatred of the enemy as a motivating factor among some soldiers in combat during World War II. One such example is contained in the book *Road to Huertgen: Forest in Hell* by Paul Boesch, who was a lieutenant in the U.S. Army. He had a deep hatred for the Germans; on one occasion, he watches a man he shot slowly die: "I could stand there and watch him die and feel absolutely no qualms of any kind."[24] Boesch compares his killing the German to a carpenter hammering in a nail. They both have jobs to do, and Boesch has no feelings for the dying man. Killing him provoked no more emotion than hammering a nail.[25]

Another example of vindictiveness can be found in Charles B. MacDonald's book *Company Commander*. MacDonald was an army captain who served in Belgium and Germany. While he does not specifically mention any factor as being a primary motivator, his hatred for the Germans is mentioned often in the book. He has no sympathy for the Germans, military or civilian. He blames them for starting the war and does not care when German civilians are kicked out of their homes or stolen from; "These people had asked for it," is his typical response.[26] When a German farmer and his wife cry as their farm is burned down, MacDonald laughs and says, "Thank Adolf."[27] While evidence has been found in the interviews of 28th Infantry Division soldiers that were conducted shortly after the war and in 1988 by the 28th Infantry Division Historical Section that would indicate many soldiers hated the Germans, this was not found to be a significant motivating factor.

Some men actually enjoyed combat. According to psychiatrist Eli Ginzberg:

> ... many of the outstanding combat soldiers were hostile, emotionally insecure, extremely unstable personalities who might well be termed clinically psychopaths, who fully enjoyed the opportunity of taking out hostilities directly in a socially acceptable setting of warfare and who in the absence of such an outlet not infrequently end up in penitentiaries.[28]

After reports of an SS atrocity, it was not uncommon for American troops to refuse to take prisoners for several days; they had an excuse to take out hostilities. Some would kill any German soldier they could, even those attempting to surrender.[29] No evidence in interviews, after-action reports, or official documents of 28th Division soldiers indicate that this was a significant motivating factor.

Inherent to war is the apparent contradiction of sacrifice. The impulse to self-sacrifice goes against both what our culture has engrained within us and oftentimes, too, the directives of our own human nature. Cultural standards impel us to think of our own well-being primarily, and our natural human instinct for self-preservation tells us to avoid death at all costs.[30] Yet, somehow, sacrifice on the battlefield is just as much a reality as are the bonds of camaraderie which form between soldiers.[31] Sacrifice contributed to the fighting spirit of the 28th Infantry Division soldiers as they knew it was necessary to defeat their enemy.

Another factor that has been studied is honor. Camaraderie and sacrifice are battle-dependent experiences, while honor, according to Martin L.

Cook, is a virtue which is teachable. Cook proposes that honor "is most often transmitted through the natural process of socialization."[32] Children are taught the difference between right and wrong and good and evil, and they learn what is socially acceptable behavior. Furthermore, the standards of correct conduct in war are transmitted to soldiers through their training and the leadership of their superiors.[33] In *The Greatest Generation*, Tom Brokaw argues that "the World War II generation developed values of personal responsibility, duty, honor, and faith. These characteristics helped them to defeat Hitler."[34] Honor certainly contributed to the fighting spirit of the 28th Infantry Division soldiers.

American soldiers found comfort and motivation through prayer on the front lines of World War II. Despite witnessing horrific acts, most soldiers remained steadfast in their religious beliefs. In his book *Serving God and Country*, Lyle W. Dorsett relates a story by Chaplain William R. Thierfelder. The chaplain wrote: "... today I'm crawling from foxhole to foxhole, and the men gobble up every word of encouragement. Some were reading their Bibles, others their prayer books."[35]

Originally administered in the immediate aftermath of World War II, the "American Soldier" studies were conducted by the Army's Information and Education Division. They included 163 surveys and records of the attitudes and behaviors of American soldiers during World War II. In 2013, Brian Wansink and Craig S. Wansink, using data collected during the American Soldier surveys and records, published their findings in the *Journal of Religion and Health*. They concluded that as combat became more frightening, the percentage of soldiers who reported praying rose from 42 to 72 percent. The results suggest that near the time of combat, the more fear infantry men felt, the more they were likely to rely on prayer as a motivation to continue to fight.[36] Religious behavior was generally high among the veterans of World War II and the men of the 28th Infantry Division were no different.

The value and importance of religion was promoted at the highest level of the U.S. government. President Franklin D. Roosevelt stated in his Labor Day address on September 1, 1941 that the "preservation of these rights [rights of free laboring men and women] is vitally important now, not only to us who enjoy them, but to the whole future of Christian civilization."[37] Religion played a part in helping individual soldiers survive terrifying combat situations. Chaplain William R. Thierfelder recalled being called to a soldier lying on a litter shaking so violently he could not stand up. He had received no physical wounds. The chaplain helped the man up, took him by the lapels of his jacket, and asked him if he was a Christian and if he believed in God's help for those who believed in him. After a few minutes, "I told him to repeat my words. And we recited the 23rd

Psalm together. The man learned the Psalm and eventually returned to duty."[38] Belief in God did help to prepare young men for battle and helped them during the stress of combat. Henderson points out that religion can promote cohesion.

Regarding Christianity in America, Henderson writes: "The broad umbrella of Christianity that covers most religions in the United States and followed the 28th Infantry Division soldiers to war offers some basis for common religious values, which in turn promote basic values."[39] Many American soldiers said that prayer helped them in combat. However, no specific religion or belief was identified as being helpful. According to Anthony Kellett, "Prayer is not of itself a sufficient indicator of religious faith; it may have been adopted as an instrument of psychological self-defense in much the same way as belief in talismans (e.g., a rabbit's foot) or in fatalism."[40] However, interviews of 28th Infantry Division soldiers suggest otherwise and insist that religious faith may have contributed to the fighting spirit of the men.

Ideology includes nationalism, racism, and or political convictions. According to Henderson, "ideology is effective for getting men to join the military or enter battle, but during the battle, ideology appears to have significantly less influence in controlling a soldier's behavior."[41] "The American soldier was typically, without deep personal commitment to a war which he nevertheless accepted as unavoidable. He gave little concern to the conflicting values underlying the struggle," submits Samuel A. Stouffer.[42] In several books, Stephen Ambrose has always presented the theme that the American soldier fought for their comrades due to the strong cohesion that developed between them.[43] Sociologist Charles Moskos has proposed that latent ideology plays a role in soldier motivation, albeit a secondary one.[44]

There are many examples of 28th Infantry Division soldiers performing heroic actions and displaying courage in demanding situations or in the face of imminent death and receiving the Silver Star, Bronze Star, or Distinguished Service Cross. Some soldiers even received battlefield promotions for their bravery and leadership. Displaying eagerness to participate in a worthy cause at any cost also inspires peers, and this eagerness might also be inspired by peers.[45] Marshall argued that "for some, heroism may not involve risk-taking for the sake of excitement as much as it involves the willingness to sacrifice oneself for the benefit of the cause."[46] That cause was fighting for the American way of life, which reflected the values of the society from which the soldiers came from. To understand what compelled the soldiers to fight, it is important to look at their involvement with the national socio-political system, national identity, and acceptance of the American national ideology. Each contributed to the action of the military units on the battlefield, and also to the enlisting and sustaining of the force.[47]

Many Americans viewed the issues at stake during World War II in terms of clearcut right and wrong, democracy against fascism, defense against aggression, good against evil. The soldiers who left the shores of America to fight did not define what the American way of life meant, but their understandings of it reflected the overall views of American society. They knew they were fighting for—what President Franklin D. Roosevelt called in his address to Congress in 1941—four freedoms: freedom of speech and expression, freedom of every person to worship God in his own way, freedom from want (which meant economic understandings that would secure to every nation a healthy peacetime life for its inhabitants), and freedom from fear (meaning a worldwide reduction of armaments to such a point and in such a thorough fashion that no nation would be able to commit an act of physical aggression against any neighbor). While the soldiers may not have repeated Roosevelt's words, or invented the ideas, they did, by their comments and actions, demonstrate that they knew what the American way of life meant. Stephen Ambrose captured these feelings:

> Although the GIs were and are embarrassed to talk or write about the cause they fought for ... they were the children of democracy and they did more to help spread democracy around the world than any other generation in history. At the core, the American citizen soldiers knew the difference between right and wrong, and they didn't want to live in a world in which wrong prevailed.[48]

The overarching beliefs and values that unified Americans during World War II revolved around the ideology of the American way of life. This encompassed political, economic, and social elements. Politically, freedom and democracy were the guiding principles that appeared on virtually every war poster. These catchwords served as easy phrases for the public to rally around and an ideology for the soldiers to commit to. Stephen Wesbrook argued that the great majority of individuals exhibited a commitment to the national socio-political system. He wrote: "Although the person with such a commitment is not an ideologue, ideology still plays a major role in his motivations. From the individual's point of view, the significance of the national ideology is not that it directly causes him to do what is demanded, as in the case of the ideologue, but that it gives him a cause for doing."[49]

To fully understand what the American way of life meant to the American soldier, we have to examine the historical context of the society from which he came. Americans of the World War II generation experienced the full brunt of the Great Depression, and many harbored cynical memories of the unfulfilled idealism of World War I. Roosevelt's freedom from want resonated with many who had struggled during the Great Depression and were just beginning to work and recover when the Japanese attacked Pearl Harbor in December 1941. Roosevelt's freedom of every person to worship God in his own way resonated with many Americans as children born in the 1930s were raised during a time in which Americans were more rooted and less mobile. Tradition and institutional loyalty were important. People tended to go to church, and they tended to continue going to church as the years wore on. By the time the Japanese attacked Pearl Harbor, over 70 percent of Americans identified themselves as Christians or Jews.[50] Roosevelt's freedom from fear resonated with many Americans as they had seen and read what the Nazis had done in Germany and in the countries they conquered. Roosevelt's freedom of speech and expression reverberated with many Americans as they witnessed the burning of books and the censorship of Jews in Germany.

An analysis of the historiography surrounding the Battle of the Bulge reveals notable gaps in the existing scholarship. While brief acknowledgments are made of the division's holding actions, the accounts swiftly pivot to highlight the forces in the Bastogne region. Unfortunately, the specific actions and experiences of the 28th Infantry Division soldiers remain shrouded in obscurity, their stories often left untold. Within the prevailing literature, there exists a palpable absence of detailed depictions of the soldiers' actions, leaving much to be desired in terms of a comprehensive understanding of their contributions to the battle. Furthermore, the motivations that spurred these soldiers to undertake their actions are seldom expounded upon. The intricate tapestry of their decisions, shaped by factors such as religious beliefs, camaraderie, honor, and sacrifice, remains largely unexplored within these narratives.

While historiography has its limitations, it is crucial to recognize that the motivations, beliefs, and values that underpinned the soldiers' actions are integral to comprehending the Battle of the Bulge in its entirety. Their actions were more than mere tactical maneuvers; they were a reflection of the soldiers' commitment to their nation, their comrades, and their principles. Amid these gaps in the scholarly discourse, there lies an opportunity to delve deeper into the experiences and motivations of the 28th Infantry Division soldiers. By delving into the intricacies of their decisions, beliefs, and relationships, a more nuanced and comprehensive narrative can emerge. This approach not only honors the sacrifices of these soldiers but also enriches our understanding of the broader context of the battle and the human dynamics that shaped its course.

This research fills the gaps in the historiography by illustrating the comments made by soldiers while they were fighting and after. Those comments reflect their understanding and commitment to fight for the American way of life cause. This book follows the combat narratives of the 28th Infantry Division units which demonstrate the soldiers' commitment to the cause by acts of heroism and stubborn resistance to the German attacks. The soldiers' experience fighting across France, at the Siegfried Line, and in the Hürtgen Forest is a testament to their willingness to endure against demanding circumstances. This research fills additional gaps in the historiography by recording the determined effort of the 28th Infantry Division to delay the Germans from achieving their goals during the Battle of the Bulge and buying time for the Allies to reposition forces to eventually halt the German advances.

There are several books that were consulted to assist this research in determining what the overall situation was prior to the German attack, the disposition of forces, and the specific actions taken by the men of the 28th Infantry Division. Some examples include *Bastogne: The Story of the First Eight Days* (1946), in which Samuel Marshall describes the beginning of the German attack, briefly mentioning the 28th Infantry Division. His book provides a combat history of the critical battle during the Allied liberation of Europe in World War II. After a brief discussion of the events of December 16–18, he jumps to the encirclement of Bastogne and the deployment of the 101st Airborne Division to Bastogne.[51]

At the time John Toland was researching *The Story of the Bulge* (1959), the official after-action reports and documents were just becoming available to scholars. As a result, his book was based largely on interviews rather than official documents. He describes the events that occurred at Clervaux, Luxembourg, with the 28th Infantry Division's 110th Regiment.[52]

First published as CMH Pub 7-8-1, *The Ardennes: Battle of Bulge* (1965) by Hugh M. Cole was written for the U.S. Army Center of Military History. His publication tells the story of how the Germans planned and executed their offensive, how the Allies planned to defeat them, and some stories of the soldiers involved with the battle. Cole's work provides significant details about the 28th Infantry Division's maneuvering, artillery support, and movement of equipment to delay the German advance. This volume represents an exhaustive collection of personal memoirs by leading participants of the campaign. The memoirs contain interviews with American participants and written accounts prepared immediately after the end of the war by the German officers who took part in the Ardennes Campaign.[53]

In determining the German plan for the Battle of the Bulge, this study looked at works from the U.S. War Department collection, U.S. Army Center of Military History, *Bundesarchiv* (German Federal Archives), and the Imperial War Museum.

Napier Crookenden's *Battle of the Bulge 1944* (1980) presents some enlightening photographic and documentary information. The book provides more details about the German Fifth Panzer Army attack of the 28th Infantry Division, including counterattacks and door-to-door fighting. Napier's work looks at the German strategy, Allied positions, and tactical maneuvering that took place during the battle, with an explanation of the weapons used.[54]

Charles B. MacDonald's *A Time for Trumpets: The Untold Story of the Battle of the Bulge* (1985) presented the most definitive account of the Ardennes Offensive. His book incorporates personal accounts and official documents to examine the plans and preparations for the attack, the first days, the American resistance, the German penetrations, the American stand at Bastogne and American counterattacks. Regarding the 28th Infantry Division's sector, MacDonald offers more details about the stationing of troops, the movement of armor, emplacement of mortars and the maneuvering of squads then previous writing.[55] MacDonald's work is a traditional military history of the battalion level. The author attempts to demonstrate the valor of American troops and rebut the contention that some fled in disarray.

Citizen Soldiers: The U. S. Army from the Normandy Beaches to the Battle of the Bulge to the Surrender of Germany (1997) by Stephen E. Ambrose is about the junior officers, and enlisted men of the European theater of operations. Ambrose covers the period from D-Day through the German surrender. *Citizen Soldiers* includes maps and many accounts of the soldiers involved. Ambrose incorporates the most information to date of specific actions taken by soldiers to delay the Germans, but what he includes is limited.[56] Promoted as a story from the perspective of the men and women who fought it, Ambrose talks about the courage of the defenders but does not include any information about religious beliefs or why the soldiers were courageous.

Sir Antony James Beevor does not offer a new interpretation of the Battle of the Bulge. He does, however, provide a look at the ordinary soldiers on both sides of the battle in his book *Ardennes 1944: The Battle of the Bulge* (2015). The book includes maps of the German and American position throughout the battle and offers a detailed account of the German advance and the maneuvering of American units.[57] In Beevor's book, we get to see the big picture of grand strategy as generals on both sides devise plans to outwit and outfight their opponents. He does not offer much specific detail about the 28th Infantry Division. What he does offer is more from a macro perspective. The book does not offer any insight into what motivated the soldiers who resisted the German advance or anything about their religious beliefs.

Robert E. Merriam's *Dark December: The Full Account of the Battle of the Bulge* (2017) was first published in 1947 and then in an abridged edition in 2017. It is an account of the Battle of the Bulge, presented from both the Allied and the German viewpoints. Merriam writes a great deal about the advance of the German units and the Allied Command efforts to stop their advance.[58] The book contains unique and critical information, including details gleaned from interviews conducted by the author with commanding officers on both sides, some of which are the only reports gathered from these sources. However, the 28th Division is barely mentioned, and no mention of religious beliefs or other motivating factors are offered.

George Wilson's *If You Survive* (1987) provides little information about motivation in combat. Wilson did not participate in the D-Day invasion of France. While not as popular or well-known as many other World War II memoirs, Wilson's work covers nearly the entire campaign from Normandy to VE-Day through the eyes of an infantry officer. Wilson's story describes his experiences through the Normandy Campaign, Siegfried Line, Hürtgen Forest, and the Battle of the Bulge. His memoir tells of ambushes and close calls, with a tone of detachment that showed how many officers had to separate their feelings from many of the events in order to command effectively.[59]

My own *The 110th Holds in the Ardennes: The Blunting of Hitler's Last Gamble and the Invasion of the Reich* (2017) contains many of the after-action reports and personal accounts of soldiers and civilians who lived through the Ardennes Offensive. The book also contains excerpts from the publications from the U.S. Army Centre of Military History and research conducted by *Cercle d'études sur la Bataille des Ardennes* or Study Group on the Battle of the Bulge in Luxembourg. Incorporated are previously unpublished accounts of the last stand of the 110th Infantry, and many previously unpublished personal accounts and stories.[60]

Most of the abovementioned writers and historians end up with attributing the stopping of the German advance to the heroic stand of the U.S. 101st Airborne Division and other attached units and the relief of Bastogne by General George S. Patton's 3rd Army punch behind the German lines to relieve the Bastogne fighters. As time went on and more reports, interviews, and accounts became available, scholars and authors still have not given credit to the soldiers of the 28th Infantry Division for delaying the Germans long enough to influence the outcome.

Research for this book in the 28th Infantry Division archives uncovered interviews of soldiers who fought in the Battle of the Bulge with references to their religious faith and, in many cases, how their faith sustained them. The interviews were conducted by the 28th Infantry Division Historical Section in December 1988. Other interviews, located at the

National Archives, were conducted at Moosburg, Germany, and Buzancy, Hachinette, Lapoutroie, and Montfaucon, France, between January and June 1945 by the 3rd Information and Historical Services, Headquarters U.S. III Corps. These beliefs and experiences have been excluded from the writings about the Battle of the Bulge and are historically significant as scholars examine the reasons why soldiers fought so courageously. An examination of soldier interviews and memoirs offers an intriguing look at why soldiers fought.

During an interview in 1996, George Durham, Company "A," 109th Infantry, said: "We all knew we had to fight. We were all part of the same generation. When we grew up, everybody's father had been in the war [World War I], I mean, having veterans around was about like having trees in a forest, there wasn't anything unusual."[61] In his memoir, Charles Haug, Company "B," 112th Infantry, writes: "Six small German tanks headed out of Lutzkampen in our direction. Behind the tanks came hundreds of Germans on foot. We bit our lips and prayed. We were scared and shaking, but we knew God would protect us."[62] Asked why he fought in a 1988 interview, Private First Class Robert Pocklington, Special Troops, 28th Division, stated: "Well, you know in the military we were always to fight and to hold. We were never to retreat. My dad said if you come home and you get beat up, I'm going to beat the hell out of you. So that was always on my mind."[63]

Norman Forde carried a copy of the New Testament in a pocket of his uniform and wore a cross with his dog tags as he fought the Battle of the Bulge as an eighteen-year-old army private. "I was never afraid for my soul," the World War II veteran said. "My body could've been blown up at any time, but my faith didn't waver."[64] William Smith always wrote a prayer in his letters to his grandma. He asked that she share the prayer with others. He recalled: "We certainly didn't have an altar in the Ardennes. The Padre served communion from the hood of his jeep." Another veteran said: "There wasn't usually a priest around, so I prayed and confessed directly to God." Yet another veteran commented that "a chaplain had once used a tree stump and wasn't even Catholic, but it didn't stop me from praying along with him. The priest wasn't there. It was just me and God in that foxhole. I prayed for God to spare me, and he did. I had a direct hotline to 'the Man' and believe me; I used it. We were scared!"[65]

The following sources were examined for statements about what motivated the soldiers: official records of the 109th, 110th, and 112th Regiments of the 28th Infantry Division and German military units involved in the Ardennes Offensive; letters and personal diaries of soldiers; historical studies; oral histories; biographies, autobiographies, and memoirs; literary writing; newspapers and other periodicals; archives, eyewitness accounts, official records of the military units involved, and other peer-reviewed articles; unit histories, personal accounts, and stories; and unit reports.

Additionally, secondary sources that assist in explaining the spectrum of religious beliefs and practices soldiers brought with them to war and the factors that motivated them to fight include Thomas W. Bohn's *Why We Fight* film essay (1977). Bohn explains the assumption that servicemen would be more willing and able fighters if they knew the events that led up to, and the reasons for our participation in the war.

Tom Brokaw's *The Greatest Generation* (1998) tells the stories of individual men and women, the story of a generation, America's citizen heroes and heroines who came of age during the Great Depression and World War II and went on to build modern America.

The religious beliefs of the soldiers are examined by looking at several publications. *Chappie: World War II Diary of a Combat Chaplain* (2007) by Alton E. Carpenter and A. Anne Eiland paints a vivid picture of the daily reality Chaplain Carpenter and his fellow chaplains experienced during their three years of serving along the front line. It provides a firsthand account of an army chaplain who kept a diary, making entries before battles, in the midst of battles, and afterwards, recording the joys, the humor, and the tragedies unfolding around him and his fellow soldiers. Written at the time the events occurred, the author shared his observations and expressed his opinions.

Lyle W. Dorsett's *Serving God, and Country: U.S. Military Chaplains in World War II* (2012) tells the story of chaplains armed only with Bibles, Torahs, and the tools of their holy trade; these men of God went wherever the troops went. They prayed over men about to march into combat, and they guided fallen fighting men of every faith as they breathed their last breath and gave up their lives in the fight against tyranny.

Battlefield Chaplains: Catholic Priests in World War II (1994) by Donald F. Crosby offers a look at soldiers from the chaplain's perspective. Father Donald Crosby chronicles the little-known but crucial wartime role of Catholic chaplains and celebrates their compassion, courage, good humor, and humility. Their wartime efforts saved lives, provided comfort and hope, and renewed lost faith in a dark time.

Glenn J. Gray's *The Warriors: Reflections on Men in Battle* (1998) is a philosophical meditation on what warfare does to us and an examination of the reasons soldiers act as they do. Gray explains the attractions of battle, the adrenaline rush, the *esprit de corps*, and analyzes the many rationalizations made by combat troops to justify their actions.

Michael Snape's *God, and Uncle Sam: Religion and America's Armed Forces in World War II* (2015) shows how religion played a crucial role in helping more than 16 million uniformed Americans through the ordeal of World War II. Snape explains how America's armed forces were the products of one of the most diverse and dynamic religious cultures in the western world and were the largest ever to be raised by a professedly religious society.

The research method employed in this study involved locating and analyzing appropriate sources for the reconstruction of the first few days of the Battle of the Bulge. Each source was examined and their value to the study determined. Eyewitness testimony is problematic and sometimes inaccurate, especially decades after an event. Therefore, the outlook of the source was considered when using it as evidence. Statements made by veterans long after the event are corroborated by comparing them to after-action reports, official documents of the period, and interviews conducted shortly after the event.

Most of the interviews used in this study were conducted by members of the historical sections of army organizations while the soldiers were still in Europe. The accuracy of the interviews conducted decades after the events and other oral interviews many decades after the war were corroborated by comparing them to the unit histories, unit journal entries, and accounts written during the Battle of the Bulge. The major types of sources used for this study can be classified as archived, primary published and unpublished, secondary sources, and scholarly articles.

Primary sources such as memoirs, diaries, and interviews are the earliest available accounts of the Battle of the Bulge which have been used by later writers to interpret that event. They are the raw material used by other writers to provide them with information and data. In using primary sources, the value judgement was made by the people who wrote them and the intent of the author in writing the original document was analyzed. Secondary sources provide interpretations and make judgements about primary sources. When using secondary sources, this study considers that the account they give, even when it involves lengthy quotations from primary sources, may not be accurate or contain bias. Secondary sources are used to understand primary sources and provide supporting information.

In the early 1940s, America stood between the struggles of the Great Depression and the storm clouds of war in Europe and in the Pacific. The American people began to understand the magnitude of the challenge, the importance of an unparalleled national commitment, and the certainty that only one resolution was acceptable. The nation turned to its young to carry the heaviest burden: to fight the enemies of freedom in their own lands to keep the home front secure and free.

Fighting for freedom was a popular refrain in letters and interviews of veterans. While unit cohesion and fighting for one's buddy certainly were a factor in why soldiers fought, it is clear from interviews and personal accounts that the overriding reason why the men of the 28th Infantry Division fought so fiercely was to protect the American way of life.

While soldiers may not have used the exact words "fighting for the American way of life," their diaries, journals, and interviews shortly after the Battle of the Bulge and years later contain common threads that reflect the refrain. The veterans' comments echo President Roosevelt's appeal to the sensitivities of Americans as defenders of freedom. They clearly understood and stated the need to defend their own liberties, while simultaneously defending and restoring the liberties of other victims of the Nazi onslaught in Europe. They knew there would be sacrifices and repeatedly stated they knew what they were fighting for. The soldiers frequently commented that they had to beat the Nazis and they knew why they were there. Many reflected when writing home about stopping the Germans and having confidence that God was on their side and would protect them. They stated the reasons they went to war was to defeat a monstrous animal, a Nazi dictator, enslaving the people of Europe, who had his eyes on enslaving Americans. They commented that the Germans could not be allowed to strip anyone of their freedom, and if left unchecked, they would bring their terror to American shores. Some exhibited extreme bravery that earned them battlefield promotions and awards for valor. They felt so strongly about their convictions to fight for the American way of life that they were willing to risk all for the cause. Their bravery motivated others to continue to fight and exemplified their commitment to fight for freedom and stopping the Germans.

This research was intended to analyze the factors that contributed to the actions of the 28th Infantry Division's 109th, 110th, and 112th Regiments during the first days of the Battle of the Bulge and add to the historiography by offering a comprehensive explanation of why they fought so bravely in delaying the German advance. Although well-motivated troops would be expected to perform well in battle, assuming all other factors (like weapons technology) were equal to the enemy's, motivational factors also influenced or predicted casualty rates and can explain the reasons for unit success. The result of this research will provide military leaders and soldiers with the source of motivational factors and good military strategies that can be applied to a tactical situation like defensive positions using less strength to overcome superior numbers.

Subsequent chapters analyze and explain the results of examining the research questions. Chapter 1 analyzes the American culture and the definition and promotion of the American way of life by the U.S. government, civilian organizations, and by military leaders and trainers of recruits. It provides an understanding of the concerted effort that was taken to promote the idea of fighting for the American way of life. Chapter 2 looks at how churches, chaplains, and the military promoted and supported the religious practices of soldiers. It identifies the efforts that were taken to promote and support the religious beliefs and practices soldiers brought with them and experienced during war and how much they influenced them to fight. Chapter 3 describes the training the soldiers received and how that training prepared the men to fight for the American way of life. Chapter 4 outlines the Allied and German strategic setting, and the combat experience of the 28th Infantry Division and their movement across France up to and including their attack on the German Siegfried line. It shows how the soldiers confronted the Germans and continued to fight for their values. Chapter 5 is a description of the 28th Infantry Division involvement in the U.S. First Army plan to launch an attack aimed initially at the crossing of the Roer River, the capture of Duren, and then drive to Cologne and into Germany, and the 28th Infantry Division fighting in the deadly Hürtgen forest. This chapter identifies the struggles the soldiers faced in one of their deadliest battles and how their resolve was tested. Chapter 6 answers one of the research questions describing the specific delaying actions the soldiers took to delay the German advance between December 16 and 18, 1944. The tactics used by each of the elements of the three division regiments, beginning with the unit operational reports, after-action reports, and eyewitness accounts to determine the specific measures that were taken to delay the German troops are detailed. Chapter 7 contains vignettes in the words of veteran describing answering the third research question identifying the predominant reason the soldiers fought so fiercely to delay the Germans advance. The Epilogue concludes the research by summarizing the results of the study and answering the research questions of why the soldiers fought as they did during the first days of the Battle of the Bulge, discusses the research contribution to the historiography, and provides recommendations for future military leaders and soldiers as they consider the actions that will bring a successful outcome to defense against stronger force.

As far as can be determined, no studies have been conducted to identify motivational factors that contributed to the soldiers of the 28th Infantry Division action during the Battle of the Bulge. Therefore, this is original research intended to show that specific factors played a significant role in the motivation of the soldiers. This research proceeded in several phases. In the first exploratory phase, a literature review was conducted to produce a list of accounts of the Battle of the Bulge. An attempt was made to determine if there was any research done on the factors that motivated the 28th Infantry Division soldiers in combat. The second exploratory phase involved selection of the combat narratives to be analyzed.

Autobiographical accounts, memoirs, and diaries of the soldiers involved were considered. In the third exploratory phase, all books and documents were analyzed for references to factors that motivated the soldiers to fight. In the fourth explanatory phase, the conclusions of the research were formulated.

As the last major German offensive of the war, and the United States' largest land battle of World War II, the Battle of the Bulge is frequently examined in literature. Despite this, historians continue to focus primarily on physical aspects, suggesting that physical forces were the single influence on the final result. This research employs primary and secondary sources to conduct the historical analysis and provide an interpretation of the motivating factors that caused the soldiers of the U.S. Army 28th Infantry Division to delay the German advance during the first few days of the Battle of the Bulge. By analyzing the various interpretations presented in the literature and personal accounts, this research produced a reinterpretation of the first days of the battle through the perspective of combat motivating factors.

1

American Culture and the American Way of Life

As war raged in Europe and the Pacific theater in the years leading up to Pearl Harbor, many Americans suggested that what had happened politically in Germany might also happen in the United States. Educating American citizens in the ways of democracy, many felt, was an important response to the world crisis. In the late 1930s, the National Education Association inaugurated its Educational Policies Commission, a Washington-based group that devoted much of its time to pondering the role of education in democracy and the actions American educators could take to improve citizenship and save the American way of life from foreign and domestic foes.[1] An appeal to American military history or the insistence that the United States fought only because it had been attacked were frequently invoked in educational materials.[2]

The invasion of Poland had not yet happened when, in his 1938 State of the Union Address, President Franklin D. Roosevelt outlined the threat posed by Germany and its allies as an attack on religious freedoms. In the speech, he associated the defense of religion with the defense of democracy. He explained: "There comes a time in the affairs of men when they must prepare to defend, not their homes alone, but the tenets of faith and humanity on which their churches, their governments and their very civilization are founded. The defense of religion, of democracy and of good faith among nations is all the same fight."[3]

The economic policies rooted in capitalism that the United States embraced fostered a distinct level of social mobility, opening doors to upward progression and igniting a sense of hope and potential. This phenomenon gave rise to the iconic notion known as the American Dream. While the economic climate during the 1930s cast shadows over the exuberance linked to available prospects, the underlying spirit persisted undeterred. Notably, servicemen during this era emphasized the tangible economic advantages that America held in abundance. In a noteworthy publication,

The Saturday Evening Post showcased a compelling series authored by those in military service, entitled "What I Am Fighting For." Among the contributors, a recurrent theme was evident: aspirations encompassed not only notions of familial bonds, freedom, and democratic values, but also material aspirations such as houses, automobiles, and other tangible possessions. This compilation served as a testament to the enduring allure of the American Dream, where diligent effort and dedication were believed to hold the potential to enhance one's life circumstances significantly. This philosophy propagated the compelling idea that anyone, through diligence and hard work, could uplift their standing in society, a notion that held within it a profound motivator to uphold allegiance to the American way of life. Despite the trials of the times, this intrinsic promise of advancement and self-improvement echoed resiliently, cultivating loyalty and conviction in the ideals that defined the nation.

Soldiers' attitudes undoubtedly reflected American culture, as officials, privately and publicly, often spoke of the need to preserve the American way of life. In Roosevelt's annual State of the Union Address to Congress on January 6, 1941, also known as his "Four Freedoms Speech," he presented his reasons for American involvement, making the case for continued aid to Great Britain and greater production of war industries at home (see Appendix VI for the entire speech). He told Congress:

> ... In the future days which we seek to make secure, we look forward to a world founded upon four essential human freedoms: the first is freedom of speech and expressing—everywhere in the world, the second is freedom of every person to worship God in his own way—everywhere in the world, The third is freedom from want, which translated into world terms, means economic understandings which will secure to every nation a healthy peace time life for its inhabitants—everywhere in the world, and the fourth is freedom from fear, which translated into world terms, means a world-wide reduction of armaments to such a point and in such a thorough fashion that no nation will be in a position to commit an act of physical aggression against any neighbor—anywhere in the world...[5]

President Roosevelt appealed to the sensitivities of Americans as defenders of freedom. Roosevelt, who was an Episcopalian, believed religion was a distinct strength of America and emphasized faith in the nation's war effort, especially in the armed forces. Under his leadership, the military incorporated religion into the fabric of soldiers' lives by assigning clergy to the troops based on percentages of the religious affiliations of the nation's population. The goal of this strategy was to have soldiers' religious needs served by ministers of their own faiths. During the course of the war, American soldiers increasingly found motivation through prayer, especially at times of combat engagement.[6]

The soldiers' attitudes during this period were significantly influenced by the prevailing belief that the U.S. had been compelled to engage in the conflict as an act of self-defense. The watershed moment of Pearl Harbor, followed by Hitler's swift declaration of war, shattered the once-prevailing isolationist notion that the U.S. could remain aloof from the global turmoil. The isolationist stance crumbled under the weight of these events, compelling the nation to recognize its inescapable entanglement in the global conflict.

The history of Nazi aggression and domination played a pivotal role in shaping the collective realization that war was no longer a matter of choice, but an imperative for safeguarding national survival. The American public, bearing witness to the brutal expansionism and oppressive subjugation perpetrated by the Nazis, recognized that this war was a vital necessity for the preservation of their nation and its cherished values. In the face of a direct and imminent threat, a common realization took root within the hearts and minds of all individuals. The aggressors, Germany and Japan, had to be confronted and defeated in order to secure a future free from their tyranny. The aggression and encroachment perpetrated by these nations left little room for ambiguity; the fight against them became synonymous with the defense of American ideals and the preservation of freedom.[7]

The soldiers on the front lines shared a common understanding—that they were engaged in a battle that transcended individual interests. Samuel Stouffer proposes that "the American public understood the need to defend their own liberties, while simultaneously defending and restoring the liberties of the other victims of the Nazi onslaught."[8] With all aspects of American life devoted to victory, there was a constant personal and communal urging that all citizens play some part in the war effort. It was socially unacceptable for men to refuse service and those very few that did were effectively ostracized.[9]

The creators of comic books encouraged their readers to contribute to the American war effort and fostered a sense of patriotism and political obligation. *Captain America* burst onto the American comic books stands in March 1941. The cover of Issue #1 featured Captain America mid-fight, punching Adolf Hitler squarely in the nose. In Figure 1, Hitler is shown in his German headquarters surrounded by Nazi soldiers. Plans to destroy a U.S. munitions factory are in plain sight.[10]

Among the initiatives to foster a sense of patriotism and obligation was the *Why We Fight* film series. The films were developed to win the confidence of the citizen soldiers. Intended as a series of orientation films for all army troops before they went overseas, the *Why We Fight* series consisted of seven separate films produced between 1942 and 1945 by the U.S. Army Signal Corps, with the task of maintaining morale and instilling loyalty and

Figure 1: *Captain America*, Issue 1, March 1941. (*U.S. National Archives and Records Administration*)

discipline into the civilian army.[11] *Prelude to War* (1942) explains the rise of fascism in Germany and Italy as well as Japan's aggression in the Far East. The film examines the differences between the U.S. and the fascist Axis states of Mussolini, Hitler, and Hirohito by portraying the latter countries working together as gangsters to conquer the world. This was done through footage from *Triumph of the Will*, a propaganda film produced by the Nazi regime in Germany. Directed by Leni Riefenstahl, the film was released in 1935 and documents the 1934 Nazi Party Congress in Nuremberg. The purpose of the film was to showcase the power, unity, and grandeur of the Nazi Party and its leader. *Prelude to War* offered a different narration designed to support the Allied cause. It emphasized that after the Nazis smashed the opposing political parties and labor unions, they turned their attention to their last remaining obstacle: the church. In one scene, a stained-glass window is shattered by several bricks to reveal a "*Heil* Hitler!" poster behind.

The Axis aim of total world conquest is shown in *Prelude to War*. The Axis is depicted as seeking total world conquest. An animated map first shows Mussolini's ambition to recreate the Roman Empire, complete with the Mediterranean as the Italians' sea, then Japan's ambition to conquer Manchuria, China, Indochina, Siam, Burma, the East Indies, India, Australia, New Zealand, and Russia east of Lake Baikal, before moving east to crush the United States. The Nazis are shown as first claiming Europe, then moving east through Iraq and Iran into India, then south to conquer Africa. Once this is accomplished, the Nazis would cross the Atlantic Ocean from Dakar to Brazil, meeting up with the Japanese who would have crossed the South Pacific. Simultaneously, the Nazis would cross the North Atlantic Ocean from Scandinavia into Canada, meeting the Japanese forces crossing from Siberia. The combined Axis armies would then overrun the United States.[12]

The Nazis Strike (1943) covers appeasement, the Munich Crisis, and the years leading up to the German invasion of Poland. This second army orientation film in the series focuses on Hitler's early political and military achievements. After first describing Germany's inborn love of conquest, manifested by such leaders as Otto von Bismarck and Kaiser Wilhelm II, the film discusses Hitler's specific scheme for reshaping the world through the spread of national socialism. Recalling the twelfth-century invasions of Genghis Khan, the film defines Hitler's strategy in terms of geopolitics.

The principal focus of the film is the softening-up of the western democracies using fascist organizations such as the Belgian Rexists, the Sudeten German National Socialist Party of Konrad Henlein, the British Union of Fascists, and the German American Bund. Meanwhile, within Germany, the Nazis were beginning an enormous process of rearmament. Germany then began its territorial expansion with the first target being Austria, Hitler's full-scale invasion test. He used his Sudeten stooges under Konrad Henlein to soften up Czechoslovakia and annex the Sudetenland with the help of a Britain and France desperate to avoid war. Hitler's use of the concept of self-determination as a justification for these annexations was ridiculed by reference to prominent German Americans thoroughly loyal to the Allied cause, including Admiral Chester Nimitz, Henry J. Kaiser, Wendell Willkie, and Senator Robert Wagner.

Divide and Conquer (1943) focuses on the Blitzkrieg of Europe in 1939 and 1940. The film begins immediately after the fall of Poland. Of the two major Western Allies of 1940, the United Kingdom is first to be mentioned. The role of the Royal Navy in blockading Germany is highlighted, in that it means that Germany must overcome British resistance in order to clear the way for its world conquest. The film begins immediately after the invasion of Poland. Of the two major Western Allies in 1940, the United Kingdom is first to be mentioned. The role of the Royal Navy in blockading Germany is highlighted with Germany being forced to overcome British resistance to clear the way for its world conquest. Hitler's treachery towards the small neutral countries of Europe is exposed: "To Denmark, we have concluded a non-aggression pact," "To Norway, Germany never had any quarrel with the Northern States and has none today," "To the Netherlands, the new Reich has always endeavored to maintain the traditional friendship with Holland," and "To Belgium, the Reich has put forth no claim which may in any way be regarded as a threat to Belgium." Those quotes are repeated after the conquest of each of those countries is shown.[13]

The Battle of Britain (1943) explores the lethal contest for the skies above England. This fourth documentary in the *Why We Fight* propaganda series, shown in theaters across America during World War II to inform the public and rally support for the Allied troops, focuses on the harrowing bombardment of England by the Nazis in 1940. Using a combination of staged and real footage, director Frank Capra details the exploits of the heroic RAF pilots who fought the German Luftwaffe over the skies of London and celebrates the courage of the British during their darkest hour.

The narrator describes the fall of France, which leaves Britain almost defenseless. British forces are vastly outnumbered, but the British people are calm. The narrator explains that is because in a democracy, the people as a whole are involved in the decision to fight. Hitler's masterplan to subjugate Britain is described. Hitler begins by attacking convoys and ports but fails to destroy them. The RAF is outnumbered but knocks out far more planes than the Germans do. Also, baled-out British pilots can return to the air, but German pilots are lost. Unlike the Dutch and Polish Air Forces, Britain does not make the mistake of bunching its planes on the runways.

Losses force Hitler to take time out. Britain deploys improved listening posts to identify the coming attacks. In August and September, German losses are far more severe. However, the German mind cannot understand why free people fight on against overwhelming odds. The Germans now aim to crush the British spirit by attacking London and destroying homes, hospitals, and churches, but the people adapt and survive. Enraged, Reich Minister of Aviation Hermann Göring takes personal command and sends a massive attack on September 15, to which the British respond with everything they had. In the battle, the Germans suffer severe losses. Despite many losses and the destruction of historic buildings, the Germans cannot break Britain. They switch to night attacks in the hope of terrorizing the people to make them "cry for mercy" and "die of begging," but the people show great resilience. The British also counterattack and bomb key German factories.[14]

The Battle of Russia (1943) covers Hitler's 1941 attack on the USSR. The film stitches together newsreel and archival film to explore relations between Russia and the United States. The film also recounts Russia's military history through the use of stock footage and clips from Sergei Eisenstein's *Alexander Nevsky* (1938). Particular attention is paid to the Battle of Stalingrad, during which Soviet forces fended off Nazi troops attempting to seize control of the Russian city. The film begins with an overview of previous failed attempts to conquer Russia: by Teutonic Knights in 1242; by Charles XII of Sweden in 1704 (footage from Vladimir Petrov's film *Peter the Great* [1937] was used); by Napoleon I in 1812; and by the German Empire in World War I.

The vast natural resources of the Soviet Union are then described, showing why the land is such a hot prize for conquerors. To give a positive impression of the Soviet Union to the American audience, the country's ethnic diversity is covered in detail and elements of Russian culture that are familiar to Americans, including the musical compositions of Pyotr Ilyich Tchaikovsky and Leo Tolstoy's book *War and Peace*, are also mentioned. Communism is never mentioned in the film, but the Russian Orthodox Church is described as a force opposing Nazism. The start of the film includes a quote from U.S. General Douglas MacArthur, who commends the Russian people's defense of their nation as one of the most courageous feats in military history.[15]

The Battle of China (1944) shines the spotlight on Japan's genocide in Manchuria. This documentary examines the full and rich Chinese culture and history, while highlighting the Japanese invasion of China and the reasons Japan sought to conquer the country. Depicting numerous atrocities inflicted upon the Chinese people, the film brought to light the need for U.S. involvement in the war effort. Capra also captured the determined will and spirit of those already fighting for freedom. Using maps, cartoons, and film footage, this army orientation film documents the history of the Chinese people and the invasion of China by the Japanese. The cultures of China and Japan are compared, and aspects of China's pacifist history and the buildup of the military in Japan are highlighted. Japan is determined to fulfill the tenets of the Tanaka Memorial (a document describing Japanese world conquest).

Phase one of Japan's plan for world conquest began with the invasion of China. Various invasions are shown, including the conquests of Manchuria in 1931, Shanghai in 1931 and 1937, and Jehol in 1933. Graphic scenes of bombing, death, and mutilation accompany the footage of the Japanese invasion of Nanking, during which 40,000 men, women, and children died. The film shows how China finally unites its disparate states in a desire to resist the Japanese and develops a plan to yield territory slowly to create time in which to build up their forces. Thirty million people dismantle the cities and travel by boat, train, and on foot 2,000 miles to Chungking, where a new capital is established.

Not available to the soldiers during their training before the Battle of the Bulge and produced in 1945, *War Comes to America* is the climax of the series and depicts the United States' entry into the war.[16] The "*Why We Fight* series stands among the most ambitious and successful film projects ever undertaken by the U.S. government. Over the course of seven films, released from 1942 to 1945, director Frank Capra and his team argued forcefully for American service-people and civilians to unite in the massive labor of defeating the Axis Powers and defending American values," wrote Ashley S. Behringer for the National Archives Blog *The Unwritten Record*.[17] The films played a positive role in mobilizing millions to fight for freedom and tolerance against brutal enemies.

The American soldiers had read news accounts and seen films about life in Nazi Germany and military leaders reminded them of what and who they were fighting against before they even started the first days of training. The reasons they were fighting were emphasized by their military leaders. Eddie Pfannenstiel joined the 130th Field Artillery, Kansas National Guard, on September 25, 1939. In August 1940, he was sent to training camp at Camp Ripley, Minnesota. He remembered his superiors talking about what was happening in Germany. Officers would lecture the men about how the Nazis seized Austria, the campaigns against the Jews, the campaign to destroy all Jewish business, the Japanese war in China, and the Spanish Civil War. "They would remind us of what we would be fighting for," recalled Pfannenstiel.[18]

The soldiers of that time could vividly imagine the potential realities of existence under the rule of the Nazi regime. This apprehension and speculation about the consequences of such governance were later encapsulated by Philip K. Dick in his 1962 novel *The Man in the High Castle*. In this literary work, Dick skilfully channelled the anxieties of those years. Within the narrative, a haunting depiction emerged: a world in which the United States had lost the war and had been subjected to the dominance of both Japanese and German forces. Dick's novel painted a bleak portrait of this alternative reality, where cherished freedoms had been profoundly curtailed. Fundamental liberties like the freedom of movement and the freedom to practice one's faith were tightly controlled. Set against the backdrop of a fictional 1962 America, the narrative unfolded with unsettling facets such as the re-legalization of slavery. Moreover, the Jewish community, those who had managed to survive, were forced into hiding, using assumed identities to protect themselves from persecution.[19]

American's attitude toward getting involved in war slowly began to change. In his 2007 article for *Diplomatic History*, David Zietsma wrote: "Whereas American foreign policy before 1938 emphasized a more passive good neighbor approach rooted in the biblical parable of the Good Samaritan, Americans increasingly interpreted international events in terms of good and evil. Thus, Americans concluded that the United States should intervene as a righteous nation."[20] Many propaganda posters stressed the continuity between civilian employment and the military, such as the one in Figure 2, showing a soldier, a factory worker, and a sailor, published in 1941 by the Office of Emergency Management.

Figure 2: Men working together. (*Northwestern University Library*)

2

Churches, Chaplains, and Religious Practices Promoted by the Military

One of the research questions for this book was to explore how faith factored into the nexus of ideas that inspired the perseverance of the soldiers. In 1941, President Roosevelt argued for the escalation of American involvement by supplying the Allies with munitions. He maintained the aid was necessary to defend freedom. Incorporating worship into his conception of freedom, President Roosevelt created a channel through which Americans could perceive the war as a possible challenge to their religious beliefs. This approach allowed the nation to frame their engagement in the conflict not just in terms of physical threats, but also as a safeguard against potential encroachments on their spiritual convictions. By defending the nation, one could also defend one's faith. Military leaders also adopted such language. For example, General Douglas MacArthur described the war as a "crusade of personal liberty" in a speech in Australia soon after leaving the Philippines in March 1942.[1] In Europe, General Dwight D. Eisenhower adopted similar language. On the eve of the D-day invasion into France, a statement by Eisenhower was released in which he proclaimed the start of a "Great Crusade" and urged troops to "beseech the blessing of Almighty God upon this great and noble undertaking."[2] On D-Day, June 6, 1944, President Roosevelt asked the nation to join him in prayer:

> Almighty God: Our sons, pride of our Nation, this day have set upon a mighty endeavor, a struggle to preserve our Republic, our religion, and our civilization, and to set free a suffering humanity. Lead them straight and true: give them strength to their arms, stoutness to their hearts, steadfastness in their faith.[3]

Religion and faith were tremendously important to American soldiers in World War II. Religious beliefs and practices and ideas of freedom of religion were basic elements in American culture and this ethos naturally extended to the U.S. military.

Fighting for the American way of life was an idea that was promoted by churches, chaplains, and the military. For most, the American way of life meant freedom. That freedom often emphasized the freedom to worship. It also meant fighting so good would prevail over evil. In *Protestant, Catholic, Jew: An Essay in American Religious Sociology*, sociologist Will Herberg describes the American way of life as "an organic structure of ideas, values, and beliefs that constitutes a faith common to Americans." He points out that "the interfaith movement has emerged as one of the most vigorous and extensive enterprises on the American scene; above all, the interfaith idea has become one of the accepted aspects of the American Way of Life."[4]

Herberg is of the opinion that most Americans, over and above their adherence to one of three particular religious groups, have a notion of an underlying religious unity. This unity, he thinks, results from the fact that people believe each of the three major religions to be a different representation of the same "spiritual values"—the values which are sometimes sloganized as "the American Creed." What Herberg is suggesting is that we have a national religion with three creedal variants. One demonstrates his loyalty to the national religion by identifying with one of the creeds. According to Herberg, "being a Protestant, a Catholic, or a Jew is understood as the specific way, and increasingly perhaps the only way, of being an American and locating oneself in American society." Herberg goes so far as to claim that these basic values and ideals highlight the same fundamental commitment to the American way of life. This common faith was influenced by the organized religions in the U.S. during the war. In March of 1941, Congress authorized the expenditure of over $12 million to build chapels for army personnel.[5]

The challenges of helping keep morale strong and courage high required that the religious and spiritual needs of military personnel also be met. During World War II, a Jewish and Christian world view exercised a dominant influence over American thought and behavior. Military leaders recognized that training men to kill the enemy and sustaining them in this dreadful task required chaplains who could help combatants maintain their humanity and religious convictions in the worst of times.[6] It also required churches to emphasize to their congregations that fighting for the American way of life included freedom to practice religion.

During the tumultuous era of World War II, an array of challenges emerged for those responsible for maintaining the morale and courage of military personnel. Beyond the physical demands and psychological strains of warfare, it became evident that addressing the religious and spiritual needs of servicemen and women was crucial to their well-being and resilience. This undertaking was not without its difficulties, as the prevailing Jewish and Christian worldviews played a substantial role in shaping American thought and behavior during that time.

The profound impact of religious and spiritual beliefs on individuals' lives was particularly pronounced during World War II. Recognizing the gravity of preparing soldiers for combat and sustaining their spirits amid the horrors of war, military leaders acknowledged the significance of chaplains. These spiritual leaders were tasked with guiding combatants through the moral dilemmas posed by their roles, helping them reconcile the act of taking lives with their religious convictions, and providing solace during the darkest moments. Chaplains acted as pillars of support, offering counseling, religious services, and a sense of camaraderie that transcended the battlefield's turmoil.

Moreover, religious institutions and leaders took on a pivotal role in reinforcing the link between faith and patriotism. With the prevailing backdrop of a conflict driven by ideals of democracy and freedom, churches recognized the importance of emphasizing that fighting for the American way of life also encompassed the freedom to practice one's religion. By aligning religious values with the broader goals of the nation, congregations were instilled with a sense of purpose and unity that bolstered both morale and courage. This alignment also served as a reminder to service members that their sacrifices were in pursuit of a higher cause, making their experiences more meaningful and their sacrifices more bearable.

However, navigating the intersection of religious beliefs, wartime duty, and the inherent violence of combat was far from straightforward. The challenge lay in striking a balance between the demands of duty and the dictates of faith. Chaplains had to provide guidance that was sensitive to the complexities of warfare while remaining steadfast in their commitment to the spiritual well-being of the troops. Likewise, religious institutions faced the delicate task of promoting the principles of liberty and democracy without overshadowing the importance of preserving individual religious identities.

The challenges of upholding morale and courage among military personnel during World War II were deeply intertwined with addressing their religious and spiritual needs. The dominant Jewish and Christian worldviews of the time necessitated a delicate balance between the demands of combat and the convictions of faith. Chaplains emerged as essential figures, guiding soldiers through the ethical and spiritual dilemmas they faced and providing much-needed solace. Concurrently, churches and religious institutions played a vital role in reinforcing the connection between faith, patriotism, and the American way of life. Ultimately, the concerted efforts to meet the spiritual needs of service members contributed significantly to their resilience and ability to endure the hardships of war with their humanity and convictions intact.

Prior to the Japanese attack on Pearl Harbor, there was a strong anti-military and anti-war sentiment among Episcopalians and Quakers. The Presbyterian Church's General Assembly had declared that "war was a violation of human personality and is repugnant to the Christian conscience."[7] In the immediate wake of Japan's attack, many of America's young men stood in long lines to volunteer for military service. Before December 7, 1941, 80 percent of Americans believed that America should stay out of the war. Public opinion shifted nearly 180 degrees by early 1942 and religious institutional leaders quickly, albeit cautiously, joined the American public in changing their attitude toward war.[8]

In 1942, a partnership between civilian producers, the War Department, and the Army Chaplain Corps resulted in *Chaplain Jim*, a weekly radio show that followed the adventures of a fictional and religiously ambiguous chaplain. As Ronit Stahl has argued, "the show served to unite Americans under an umbrella of generic monotheism."[9] Civilian organizations, such as the National Conference of Christians and Jews and the Anti-Defamation League, promoted the idea of interfaith cooperation. For example, in early 1941, an official with the Jewish Welfare Board proposed that the Army Chaplain Corps should cooperate with the National Conference of Christians and Jews to sponsor a program in army camps promoting interfaith cooperation and to support the ideas of fighting for religious freedom.[10] As Kevin Schultz noted, "this partnership flourished during the war.[11] Catholic priests, Jewish rabbis, and Protestant ministers maintained regular contact with the men and women in uniform and could also assure families and friends at home that their sons and daughters were attending worship services and finding spiritual guidance and counseling."[12]

Lyle Dorsett reasoned: "Chaplains were absolutely essential to America's victory because they cultivated courage and morale among U. S. troops that allowed them to make needed sacrifices."[13] According to Dorsett, chaplains filled a very practical role for the U.S. military. They helped develop more effective soldiers and built support at home; Dorsett explained that during training, chaplains functioned to "help civilians become combatants, adjust spiritually and psychologically to a radically different way of life, and at the same time assure families and communities back home that military life would not destroy the moral values and souls of their loved ones in uniform."[14]

The sheer number of U.S. troops and the nature of military deployment made formal religious leadership challenging in the U.S. Army during

World War II. Consequently, "military chaplains sought to encourage lay leadership to expand religious coverage for smaller religious traditions as well as those located in remote locations," reasoned Karl H. Hertz.[15] "Recognizing the challenge of providing religious coverage, the U. S. military cautiously encouraged lay leadership as an extension of the religious work of chaplains."[16]

For lay leaders, the army included basic worship aids for them in their official songbooks. In 1941, the U.S. military printed a revised edition of the *Hymnal, Army and Navy*, first published in 1920.[17] Designed for use in chapels, this hymnbook included distinct sections devoted to Protestant, Catholic, and Jewish worship, but it was too bulky for common use when deployed overseas. Consequently, the U.S. military developed a second, shorter songbook in 1941 titled *Song and Service for Ship and Field.*[18] This book contained worship services with responsive readings divided among the three dominant traditions followed by a selection of popular hymns.

In addition to materials produced by the military, civilian organizations provided resources designed to equip soldiers and sailors for lay leadership. For example, four cooperating Protestant agencies launched the Service Men's Christian League in November 1942. Designed to supplement and support the work of chaplains, the league published the *Link Magazine*, a monthly periodical for soldiers and sailors that included daily devotional Bible readings as well as plans for weekly discussion meetings intended for use by self-organized lay people.[19]

Chaplains distributed the *Link Magazine* widely, with over 2.6 million copies printed during the first year alone. Similarly, the Jewish Welfare Board distributed over 1 million copies of an abridged prayer book that included dozens of services and prayers. The preface explained that the book was "designed to be used where the exigencies of life in the army or the navy do not permit attendance at regular synagogue services."[20]

Many soldiers during World War II practiced a private spirituality. One of the most private, but also devoutly religious soldiers in the American military, was General Matthew B. Ridgway, commander of the XVIII Airborne Corps who helped stop and push back German troops during the Battle of the Bulge. In his memoirs, he wrote about what many felt. He admitted that in the darkness, after he had gone to bed, alone with his God, his thoughts inevitably turned inward and with whatever resources of the spirit he possessed, he prepared himself as best as he could for whatever test may lie ahead. He found great comfort in the story of the anguish of Jesus in the garden of Gethsemane. Ridgway figured that if He could face tribulations with calmness of the soul then Ridgway surely could endure.[21] Ridgway's biographer, George C. Mitchell, claims that "Ridgway's fearlessness in the front lines was founded on his solid religious base. Mitchell said Ridgway reads the Bible and firmly believes that God will not permit him to be hit before Germany is totally defeated."[22]

In an essay for *Link Magazine* stating what he was fighting for, Private Henry Johnson mentioned freedom of worship and freedom from fear. He concluded: "I am fighting for what I consider to be the American way of life. That great ideal is high enough and fine enough to challenge me to fight, and, if need be, to die to guarantee its realization."[23] There were many who believed as Johnson did. In a letter to his mother, Morris B. Redmann wrote about the death of his brother on Tarawa. "He died fighting for an ideal, the American way of living," he reflected. "He died so that the squealing babies I saw baptized in church this afternoon may live in peace, speak their mind, and worship God in the true religion."[24]

While military chaplains and religious organizations sought to encourage and equip chaplains and lay leaders, some soldiers took the initiative to fill what they perceived as a vacuum of religious leadership. For example, Louis Gehr reported to the editor of *Wheaton Alumni*: "I actively participated in a unit of the Service Men's Christian League that met on Wednesday nights when I was training in England."[25]

Because of the tough conditions that prevailed during the war, chaplains and others had to compromise on some traditional worship practices.[26] Jewish chaplains concluded that dietary laws may be violated in extenuating circumstances, but they encouraged troops to obey them whenever possible.[27] Similarly, the Roman Catholic Church reduced and eventually omitted the required time of fasting before one could participate in the Eucharist under pressing conditions.[28] Because of the limited number of priests and the very real potential for death, Catholic chaplains occasionally practiced general absolution where they would absolve an entire group from their sins.[29]

Aside from spiritual edification, some soldiers and sailors turned to religious readings to remain connected to familiar aspects of home. In letters to his mother, Private Roger Houtz, a committed Presbyterian, often mentioned reading his Bible regularly while in the army. "The act of reading seemed to comfort me both spiritually and emotionally in that it sustained a connection with mother."[30] From basic training, he sent home a pocket testament exactly like his own as a Mother's Day gift, hoping that it would make up for his inability to get anything else. Five months later, he reflected on the significance of he and his mother reading from duplicate testaments: "God joins us together tho we are miles apart."[31]

Soldiers participated in organized programs for religious study when the circumstances permitted. The Service Men's Christian League made available information for weekly Bible lessons in the *Link Magazine*.

While the league was essentially a product of the Protestant establishment, other organizations emerged. Most significantly, the "Navigators" provided templates and resources to equip soldiers to study the Bible both alone and with others. Organized by Dawson Trotman in the mid-1930s, Navigators focused on military personnel, initially as an outreach to sailors.[32] Evangelistic in nature, the organization sought to help new Christians grow through intensive Bible study.

The soldiers of the 28th Infantry Division, like most other soldiers in World War II, took with them their religious beliefs and practices. Civilian organizations and the military provided materials and support for soldiers to practice their faith. Some men gained revelations and strengthening of their religious convictions. Still others believed that pleading to God provided a sense of calm and strength in an otherwise difficult situation. Jon Butler suggested:

> Many believed that God would protect them in battle. Regardless of perceived effectiveness, some soldiers sought supernatural intervention in order to preserve their lives and the lives of those around them. Many made such appeals out of desperation or as something they could do when nothing else could be done. Some solidified their commitment to a faith they had previously held only loosely.[33]

The soldiers drew from the religious beliefs and practices they brought with them to petition God for protection as they fought for the American way of life.

The federal government and military leaders celebrated the idea of interfaith cooperation and religious practices, soldiers believed that the freedom to practice their religion as they saw fit was an integral part of the American way of life and were willing to and ready to fight for it. The spiritual mindset of the 28th Infantry Division soldiers who entered combat can be reflected and summarized in a poem written by an anonymous World War II soldier:

No shell or bomb can on me burst,
Except my God permits it first.
Then let my heart be kept in peace,
His watchful care will never cease.
No bomb above, nor mine below
Need cause my heart one pang of woe
The Lord of Hosts encircles me,
He is the Lord of earth and sea.[35]

3

The Military Trained Men to Fight for the American Way of Life

Fighting for the American way of life was an idea that was promoted by military leadership. Prior to the Japanese attack on Pearl Harbor on December 7, 1941, the general attitude about America getting involved in war was passive. Michael Snape suggested: "Army Chief of Staff, General George C. Marshall had a shrewd understanding of the character of America's non-professional soldiers. He was also acutely aware of the likelihood of political and public relations problems arising from the idea of American becoming an army of democracy."[1]

The U.S. plan was to annihilate the enemy. "The prevailing view was that victory would be accomplished through the utter destruction of evil, often going beyond moral boundaries and evoking moral qualms," argued Thomas W. Zeiler.[2] This was a necessary fight against genocide and aggression. Military leaders would defend fighting a supposedly "good war," as commentators later called it, against murderous ideologies.[3] There was no broad national plan of using military threats to effect political ends, engage in international politics, or base military strategy on national security, principles, values, and defense interest. Russell F. Weigley noted: "[Rather, for the U.S.,] war was the strategy. Its objective was to eviscerate the enemy, military and civilian alike, through industrial technology and an insistence of unconditional surrender that amplified the killing by promising total defeat."[4]

World War II had a profound and far-reaching impact on virtually every facet of American society. Its influence extended beyond the battlefields, seeping into the very fabric of the nation, leaving an indelible mark on government, the economy, entertainment, and the societal landscape. In the realm of governance, the war necessitated a significant expansion of governmental powers and intervention. As the nation mobilized its resources for the conflict, government agencies were tasked with coordinating war efforts, rationing essential goods, and managing wartime production. This heightened government involvement reshaped the relationship between the state and its citizens, creating a more centralized and directed approach to national affairs. The economy underwent a dramatic transformation as well. Wartime production demands led to an unprecedented surge in manufacturing and industrial output. The production of war materiel not only pulled the nation out of the Great Depression but also facilitated the rise of the U.S. as a global economic powerhouse. Additionally, the workforce experienced a shift as women and minorities were increasingly integrated into the labor force to fill the gaps left by men deployed overseas.

Entertainment, a cornerstone of American culture, was also deeply influenced by the war. Hollywood, recognizing its capacity for influence, collaborated closely with government agencies like the Office of War Information's Bureau of Motion Pictures. This partnership aimed to ensure that the messages conveyed in films were aligned with the government's objectives and values. Thus, even before new military recruits embarked on their basic training, efforts were made to shape public opinion through the silver screen, promoting patriotism, sacrifice, and unity.

Society as a whole underwent a profound transformation during the war years. Communities rallied around the common cause, fostering a sense of national identity and solidarity. Women's roles evolved as they assumed responsibilities outside traditional gender norms, taking on jobs and roles previously reserved for men. The war also prompted societal reflection on issues of civil rights and equality, laying the groundwork for the social movements that would emerge in the decades that followed. In essence, World War II was not confined to the battlefronts; it permeated every aspect of American life. The war's impact on government, the economy, entertainment, and society at large was profound and lasting. From influencing government policy to reshaping economic structures and cultural norms, the war left an enduring legacy that continues to shape the trajectory of the U.S. to this day.

In *Hollywood Goes to War*, Clayton R. Koppes and Gregory D. Black assert that the Office of War Information's supervision of Hollywood filmmaking was "the most comprehensive and sustained government attempt to change the content of a mass medium in American history."[5] The Office of War Information wanted movies to extol the virtues of the American way of life and to portray the Allies as models of righteousness and the Axis as embodiments of evil.[6] This was the exposure the new recruits faced as the entered the military. The ideas of fighting for the American way of life were continually promoted by the soldiers' leaders.

In training and morale materials for American soldiers and in representations of soldiers created for civilian audiences, depictions of the military emphasized the continuing individuality and autonomy of each

American serviceman. By describing the most regimented elements of military life as analogous to civilian life, emphasizing the moral autonomy of men even in a military situation, and attempting to train Americans to fight for empirical, rational reasons, the military leadership attempted to construct, in word and action, an army ready to fight for the American way of life. The military leadership realized, as Roy R. Grinker and John P. Spiegel argued, "In order to become an effective soldier, he must learn to adapt himself to a completely undemocratic group, which required of him submission and fixation in a dependent position and ideology."[7] The potential soldier and sailor was constantly reminded of what America had to do to protect freedom.

Government representatives saw knowledge as essential to the morale of American troops. Troop morale had to be based on a knowledge of the facts if this was to be a war against fanatical belief systems. Thus, from very early in the forming of military strategy, key figures stressed the importance of knowledge on the good morale of the troops. Secretary of War Henry L. Stimson, addressing a conference of army public relations officers held in Washington, D.C., in March 1941, argued: "The success of the army depends upon its morale.... Nothing can undermine this morale."[8] A later memo from the War Department's Information and Education Division laying out the objectives of the morale program emphasized, among other goals, fostering both a "belief in the cause for which we fight and a resentment, based on knowledge of the facts, against our enemies who have made it necessary to fight."[9]

Technical Sergeant Glenn M. Girardat, Company "C," 112th Infantry Regiment, wrote in his diary that he had enlisted on November 11, 1940 after seeing the war movies. He enlisted in the National Guard and was mobilized at the Meadville, Pennsylvania, armory on February 17, 1941. He left for training the night of February 27. He said the entire time, "I was itching to get into the fight."[10]

Staff Sergeant Robert F. Sessoms wrote in his diary that "Uncle Sam interrupted my happy-go-lucky days and inducted me into service at Fort Bragg, North Carolina, along with a group of sad-faced guys. We were not slackers and put our shoulders to the wheel and pushed forward our aims for victory, just as we had seen in the movies."[11]

Mrs. Mabel Smith wrote about her son Staff Sergeant Robert L. Smith, Company "C," 112th Infantry Regiment. She said he was training at Camp Lee, Virginia, when the Japanese attacked Pearl Harbor, and he was sent to Company "F," 112th Infantry. Robert was nineteen years old then. He came home on furlough and that was the last time his mother saw him. He was killed on September 19, 1944. While he was home, he told her that he wanted to fight. He had seen the movies and read about what the Germans and Japanese were doing. He knew it was his duty to fight.[12] Staff Sergeant Smith received the Distinguished Service Cross for his actions near Percy, France.

General Marshall knew that duty, honor, and country encompassed feelings of duty, both to country and fellow soldiers, a sense of honor, patriotism, and a love for the individual's home country and all it represents. Richard Holmes defined honor as "concerned with the obligation of a soldier, and in part it is a reflection of the manly honor which encourages so many young men to enlist and buoys them up before their first battle."[13] The concept of honor for soldiers is based primarily upon moral standards of his culture and what values and virtues his society upholds. Martin L. Cook argues that "it is the value system of his culture which will form the soldier's concept of honor and will inform the soldier's conduct in battle."[14]

Marshall understood that the army had to motivate men who were highly individualistic, democratic, and even anti-military. In 1942, the U.S. government established the Office of War Information to serve as the U.S. propaganda branch during World War II. The office created thousands of posters (like the ones in Figure 3), books, pamphlets, radio broadcasts films, and other media that were used at home and abroad. Enlistment and worker posters were placed in public places.

Figure 3: Recruiting posters. (*U.S. Department of Defense*)

"The soldier's idea of honor is based upon the training he has received to instruct him in the right conduct of war," argues Johnson.[15] In the Army, fresh recruits soon realized physical training was focused on their survival and psychological training was focused on why they were fighting. The purpose of the transformation from a civilian into a soldier was to teach men what they needed to know to stay alive on the battlefield. They also needed to be reminded of the reasons they were fighting. Along with instilling teamwork, and learning the basics of survival, drill sergeants stressed the importance of winning to preserve the American way of life. The Germans and the Japanese could not be allowed to win or America would be a different place.[16] New recruits were issued *FM 21-100—War Department Basic Field Manual: Soldier's Handbook, July 23, 1941*. It covered everything from how to assemble a field pack and address officers to how to react in a mustard gas attack. The first paragraph of the forward reads:

> You are now a member of the Army of the United States. That Army is made up of free citizens chosen from among a free people. The American people of their own will, and through the men they have elected to represent them in Congress, have determined that the free institutions of this country will continue to exist. They have declared that, if necessary, we will defend our right to live in our own American way and continue to enjoy the benefits and privileges which are granted to the citizens of no other nation. It is upon you, and the many thousands of your comrades now in military service, that our country has placed its confident faith that this defense will succeed should it ever be challenged.[17]

Along with movies produced exclusively for the military, such as training and orientation films, the *Why We Fight* films were shown to American soldiers during basic training. Beyond basic training, about 160 technical bulletins were produced with combat footage. These movies played a significant role in the lives of American soldiers from the moment they entered the military.[18]

Senior military leadership understood that if soldiers could believe that America was the place for them to practice Judeo-Christian traditions, they would die to defend it. Military leaders and chaplains emphasized that Communism in the Soviet Union, Fascism in Italy, National Socialism in Germany, and the rise of the Showa in Japan represented totalitarian regimes that limited freedom—particularly, religious freedom.[19]

A speech was delivered during an "I am an American Day" gathering in New York's Central Park on May 18, 1941 by Harold L. Ickes, President Franklin Roosevelt's secretary of the interior; the speech served to define what it meant to be a free American and is indicative of the message the government wanted to get out to its citizens. It came at a perilous moment in history, May 1941, when Hitler and the Nazis seemed headed toward possible world domination. (See Appendix VI for the entire speech.) Ickes said:

> ... what constitutes an American? Not color nor race nor religion. Not the pedigree of his family nor the place of his birth. Not the coincidence of his citizenship. Not his social status nor his bank account. Not his trade nor his profession. An American is one who loves justice and believes in the dignity of man. An American is one who will fight for his freedom and that of his neighbor. An American is one who will sacrifice property, ease and security in order that he and his children may retain the rights of free men. An American is one in whose heart is engraved the immortal second sentence of the Declaration of Independence. Americans have always known how to fight for their rights and their way of life. Americans are not afraid to fight. They fight joyously in a just cause...[20]

During his fireside chat on December 28, 1941, President Roosevelt warned: "at this moment the forces of the states that are leagued against all peoples who live in freedom are being held away from our shores. The Axis powers represented the revival of the oldest and the worst tyranny. In that there is no liberty, no religion, no hope..."[21] In effect, Roosevelt framed the war as a momentous struggle for the preservation of human liberty and the American way of life. Roosevelt shared his "profound conviction that the American people are now determined to put forth a mightier effort than they have ever yet made to meet the threat to our democratic faith."[22]

The messages from the leaders of the U.S. were not lost on the men who would be part of the 28th Infantry Division. They entered the military with those messages fresh in their minds.

While the U.S. was still neutral at the start of World War II, and as the war clouds gathered over Europe, in August 1940, all U.S. National Guard regiments were called into Federal service for twelve months to bolster the strength of the Regular Army. The "28th Infantry Division Historical Summary" provides some information about the beginning of the division.

Before being federalized, the 28th Infantry Division was a unit of the Pennsylvania Army National Guard and is the oldest division-sized unit in the Department of Defense. Some of the units of the division can trace their lineage to Benjamin Franklin's battalion, the Pennsylvania Associators of 1747.[23] The division's storied history was not lost on many of the men who served in its ranks. When soldiers joined the division, they were given a card that outlined a brief history of the division. The journey of the 28th Infantry Division towards the pivotal Battle of the Bulge commenced on February 17, 1941, a date etched in the annals of history, as they were called into federal service at the Indiantown Gap in Pennsylvania, situated to the east of Harrisburg. This marked a momentous step on a path that would ultimately lead them to one of the most consequential battles of World War II.

As the calendar marched on towards June, the division anticipated a surge in its strength, with enough replacements projected to bolster its numbers to a formidable 12,947 soldiers. During this phase, the division remained stationed at Indiantown Gap, undergoing rigorous training, honing their skills, and forging bonds that would prove indispensable in the trials that lay ahead. With August 1941 came a new chapter as the division's journey took them to the A.P. Hill Military Reservation in Virginia, where their training continued with undiminished vigor. Amid the rustling leaves and rolling landscapes, the soldiers of the 28th Infantry Division dedicated themselves to the arduous preparation that would equip them for the challenges that loomed on the horizon. Their dedication bore fruit in the form of participation in maneuvers across the picturesque expanses of North Carolina, spanning from September to December 1941. These exercises not only tested their mettle but also solidified their cohesion as a fighting unit, a camaraderie that would be a wellspring of strength in times of adversity.

In January 1942, the division was dispatched to Camp Livingston, Louisiana, marking another waypoint in their transformative journey. Come March, a pivotal shift took place as the division fell under the aegis of the U.S. Army Ground Forces and found itself placed within the purview of the IV Corps of the Third Army. This realignment situated them on the path that would ultimately lead to their role in the historic Battle of the Bulge, an event that would test their training, resilience, and courage in ways they could scarcely imagine.[24]

According to Sergeant Albert W. Burghardt, Company "K," 110th Infantry Regiment, "the basic training was very tough at Camp Livingston, especially when most of the troops came into the Army without knowing what exercise was. It didn't take long to weed out the fellows who could not take the training."[25] The obstacle courses and the marches were tough on most soldiers. The calisthenics for forty-five minutes without stopping were very difficult, but most of the trainees made it.

In January 1943, the division moved to Camp Gordon Johnson, near Apalachicola, Florida, where the Amphibious Training Command was set up. This was a training school for all-weather, shore-to-shore assault training.

The tempo of the training increased. They went on many speed marches that consisted of 4 miles in forty-five minutes and 5 miles in an hour. Almost daily, the division participated in mock landings on islands in the Gulf of Mexico and beach landings on the coast of Florida. At that time, they did not know where they were going—the Pacific area or the European theater of operations. They did a lot of patrolling in the swamps and long marches in the sand. It looked like the South Pacific for the division. Frequent lectures reminded the men that they were going to fight for the American way of life.[26]

The barracks floors were sand, they slept on cots, and every morning the soldiers would hit the heel of their boot against the side of the cot to see what would fall out. Scorpions, giant ants, etc., crept into them over night. The men did a lot of swimming in the Gulf as part of their training, as everyone was expected to learn how to swim. During one of the night training exercises, the 112th Regiment lost several men when the ramp on an LCP (landing craft personnel) was lowered on a sand bar in the Gulf instead of on land.[27]

Howard J. Friedman talked about the living conditions in a 1975 interview: "The winter of 1942–1943 proved severe, and the barracks lacked adequate heating. The Army did not build mess halls for some time, requiring troops to eat outside with mess kits for several months. A permanent chapel was not completed until a month after the men arrived, and no recreation center existed for several months."[28] The men of the 28th Infantry Division did not realize it at the time, but they would experience these conditions many times as they fought their way across Europe.

At Camp Gordon Johnson, the tempo of the training continued to increase. To add realism to the training in the use of the bayonet, the instructors had the men leave the scabbard in place. The soldiers would pair off and go at it until one of the contestants was slashed, jabbed, or was touched with the scabbard over the bayonet. One of the more important parts of their training was street combat that took place in an abandoned town they called "Schicklgruber Haven." The men went through the town one at a time. Cardboard dummies popped up, and they fired at them, learning to fire from their hips.[29] In May 1943, while at Camp Gordon Johnson, the division went by truck to Camp Rucker, Alabama, for both qualification and familiarization of their weapons.

The men of the division were reminded of their mission by their leaders and in their unit newsletters. For example, in the May 30, 1943 issue of the *Trumpeter* (the 110th Infantry newsletter), there was an article entitled "Memorial Day 1963?" It read:

> Each year on May 30th, the nation honors the dead of the various wars. In later years some of us may be among those honored dead. Will we

have accomplished the objectives for which another crop of carnivorous Caesars be trying to dominate the world, subjecting minority groups and allegedly inferior peoples to Machiavellian abuse? To observe Memorial Day 1963 peacefully we have a big job to do. The war, which should be called a Peoples Revolution, must be won! The war is being fought to secure for men everywhere the freedoms which Americans have been taking for granted for many generations.[30]

On June 10, 1943, the division arrived at Camp Pickett, Virginia, from Camp Gordon Johnson by train, where the training continued. Troops were taken to an area, where there was a large platform, which was a replica of the side of a ship, about two and a half stories high. They had cargo nets secured to the top. The men went up one side hand over hand with a full pack and then down the other side—the way they would on a regular ship.[31] In August, the division moved by rail and trucks to Norfolk, Virginia, where they participated in ship-to-shore amphibious training at the Solomon Islands in Chesapeake Bay, Virginia. While at Camp Pickett, the 45th Infantry Division was alerted for an overseas assignment. The 28th Infantry Division was assigned to furnish 1,500 replacements to bring the 45th up to strength.[32]

The soldiers were able to get a short break from the grind of training. At Camp Pickett, they were able to visit the Red Cross Hospitality Center, participate in religious services, and leave the post on a three-day pass. Many went to Washington, D.C. Some of the men, whose hometowns were close, went home for a couple of days. This was the last time the soldiers would leave the confines of their camp before leaving the U.S. The men had some time to think about why they were there. In his diary, Tom Hickman, 109th Infantry, wrote: "I do believe that the war against Hitler was a proper one, but we were subject to a great deal of propaganda. We were told that Hitler was stamping out religion."[33]

On September 28–29, 1943, the division moved from Camp Pickett to Camp Miles Standish, near Taunton, Massachusetts. This was a type of security camp. No one was permitted to leave the area. Some of the men went to the wire fence that surrounded the camp and gave some kids money to get liquor for them. The soldiers were not at this camp very long. They had inspections and got ready to leave for their overseas assignment to the European theater of operations. On October 6 and 7, they boarded troop trains and went to the port of Boston where they boarded the SS *Cristobal*. In October, the division set sail, arriving ten days later at Newport, Wales.[34]

The training continued in Wales, and none of it was easy. While they trained, they were exposed to hedgerows—long, deep walls of hedges that reached 15 feet in height. Little did they realize that these tremendous obstacles awaited them in Normandy, France, where they would cost the lives of so many men. During their stay in Wales, they were out of camp more than in. Rumors circulated that the camps might be the targets of German air raids. The more time spent in the field, the less likely the unit would suffer casualties from such raids before embarking for Normandy. There were German planes overhead most nights.[35]

While in Wales, the men went to the Assault Training Center near Barnstable, Devonshire. The English had a large area set up to resemble the type of fortifications that the soldiers would encounter when they hit the beach in Normandy. Trainee soldiers were young, fit men but the Infantry Assault Teams had to be at the peak of physical fitness, and to monitor this they were subjected to strength and endurance tests known as burp-up exercises. Passing this earned them the Expert Infantryman's Badge and an extra $10 in their monthly pay, failure resulted in a transfer to a non-combat unit. To qualify for this coveted badge, the 100-yard run had to be made in twelve seconds and they had to do thirty-five pushups and ten chin-ups, complete the obstacle course within the target time, and qualify on pistol, rifle, and machine-gun ranges. Some found this relatively easy to achieve and a limited amount of cheating was ignored to retain suitable men.

The obstacle course was over 800 yards long and stretched over sand dunes in the shape of a horseshoe; it began by heading south, taking a semicircular turn to the right, before heading north so that the beginning and end of the course were only 100 yards apart. The course was 10 yards wide and ran in teams of five abreast. Originally it was designed to acquaint soldiers with obstacles that may be encountered on crossing the beaches, but later additions included obstacles to be found on board a ship, such as ladders and cargo nets. Not only was it a test of the troops' physical condition, but it encouraged teamwork as well as individual proficiency and brought into play muscles neglected by the general physical training of an infantry division as arm, chest, and stomach muscles were strengthened by tugging and pulling on walls, ladders, and ropes. The division would later use the tactics learned as they approached the Siegfried Line in Germany. They formed into assault teams, with each team made up of sergeants, riflemen, flame throwers, demolition teams, bazooka teams, light machine gun squads, 60-mm mortar squads, and men with Bangalore torpedoes. Each assault team was assigned a pillbox to attack and destroy. Umpires judged their efforts.[36]

On one of the amphibious exercises, they went by troop transport to the Irish Sea. They disembarked down the cargo nets into small assault crafts and, after circling around, made for the beach. The surf was very high, and one could look over the side of the boat and see the sand in front. Albert

W. Burghardt recalled: "the waves in the surf must have been around twenty feet high. The surf was deep, and as usual everyone was wet. There was never a change of clothing."[37] The Irish Sea was very cold, but after the original shock, the woolen long johns gave them a measure of warmth.

In June 1944, Lieutenant General George S. Patton was given command of the Third United States Army, a field army which was newly arrived in the United Kingdom and was composed largely of inexperienced troops. Patton began delivering speeches to his troops in the United Kingdom in February 1944. The speeches were made available to other units training at the time. Patton's speech to the Third Army was a series of speeches given by Patton to troops prior to the Allied invasion of France. The speeches were intended to motivate the inexperienced Third Army for its pending combat duty. In the speeches, Patton urged his soldiers to do their duty regardless of personal fear, and he exhorted them to aggressiveness and constant offensive action. Patton's profanity-laced speaking was viewed as unprofessional by some other officers, but the speech resounded well with his men. This is an excerpt from his June 5, 1944 speech, also known as his "Blood and Guts" speech (see Appendix VII for the entire speech):

> ... Sure, we all want to go home. We want to get this war over with. But you can't win a war lying down. The quickest way to get it over with is to get the bastards who started it. We want to get the hell over there and clean the goddamn thing up, and then get at those purple-pissing Japs. The quicker they are whipped, the quicker we go home. The shortest way home is through Berlin and Tokyo. So keep moving...[38]

When the men had a break during their training in the field, they collected watercress. There were many streams in this mountainous area, and the watercress was fresh and crisp and a change from what was offered in the company mess. The occasional break in training gave the soldiers a chance to attend religious services and to write letters to loved ones at home. Although chaplains were not readily available everywhere in 1942, or present in all combat areas, by 1943 almost no soldier in uniform was without benefit of clergy care if he wanted it. The soldiers were able to go to the local town and frequent the pubs, which usually had better food than the mess halls. During the religious services, chaplains and lay personnel emphasized that the men were fighting for the freedom of all oppressed peoples.[39]

Infantry soldiers were not the only ones who experienced hardships and died for their beliefs. Chaplain Captain Clyde E. Kimball, who would die in combat in the Battle of the Bulge, left behind a diary that provided a glimpse of a chaplain who willingly made rounds in England to serve as many troops as possible. Chaplain Kimbell blessed many men by tirelessly traveling, speaking about why they were fighting, and passing out Bibles, stationery, and other useful items he would purchase in the post exchange. For his later actions during the Battle of the Bulge, he was posthumously awarded the Silver Star for displaying great personal bravery, volunteering to pass through fierce German machine-gun fire in an effort to render treatment and evacuate the wounded.[40]

On April 17, 1944, the 28th Infantry Division moved from Wales by motor transport to Chiseldon Camp and Rackley Park in Wiltshire on Salisbury Plains. The men were back to primitive living, assigned to pyramid tents that held between four and six men. They were not issued army cots, so they made stakes out of tree branches, drove the stakes into the ground, and laced twine between the stakes. This gave them a sort of hammock and kept them off the damp ground. They were issued mattress covers that were filled with straw. Training continued with marches and firing various weapons, including the bazooka anti-tank rocket.[41]

While at Rackley Park, the word came down that another move was imminent. On July 18, 1944, the division left Rackley Park and moved 60 miles south to Moorhill Camp, near the port of Southampton. Moorhill Camp resembled a security camp because it was surrounded by barbed wire and security troops were on patrol everywhere. No one could leave the camp, and the soldiers were billeted in very close quarters. Their stay in this camp was short. Equipment was checked and some replaced. They were issued items for combat, cigarettes, candy rations, water purification tablets, and pocket Bibles.

Chaplains accompanied the fighting soldiers throughout their training and into battle. In his book *Serving God and Country: U. S. Military Chaplains in World War II*, historian Lyle W. Dorsett describes the role of chaplains in various theaters of operation and the promotion of religion by military commanders. For example, he cites comments by Brigadier General F. B. Prickett who commanded regular habits of church attendance by soldiers under his command.[42] The general got specific about his expectation of chaplains:

> The chaplains are more than morale builders; morale building is every officer's Duty. The primary function of chaplains is to be ministers of religion to the officers and men of his command. In order to do this work most effectively, the chaplains are training with the men, going to the field, living with the troops, getting close to them, understanding their psychology.[43]

Dorsett explains that chaplains were also directed to provide sex and hygiene lectures to soldiers. Many chaplains used the Bible to make their case.[44] Chaplains also distributed steel-covered New Testament Bibles to soldiers as they prepared to go into battle. Advertised in newspapers and magazines as protection from bullets, the small books were designed to be carried in the pocket over one's heart as both symbol and shield.[45] On the first page was a printed message from the White House, with the printed signature of Franklin D. Roosevelt. Roosevelt's message encouraged the new recruit to use the Bible as a source of strength:

> To the Members of the Army: As Commander-in-Chief I take pleasure in commending the reading of the Bible to all who serve in the armed forces of the United States. Throughout the centuries men of many faiths and diverse origins have found in the Sacred Book words of wisdom, counsel, and inspiration. It is a foundation of strength and now, as always, an aid in attaining the highest aspirations of the human soul. Very sincerely yours, Franklin D. Roosevelt.[46]

The American Bible Society was producing 12,000 New Testament Bibles for soldiers per day by the end of 1943.[47] Chaplains were responsible for not only distributing the Bibles, but as Lyle Dorsett pointed out, "Chaplains were absolutely essential to America's victory because they cultivated courage and morale among U. S. troops that allowed them to make needed sacrifices."[48] Dorsett explained: "During training, chaplains functioned to help civilians become combatants, adjust spiritually and psychologically to a radically different way of life."[49]

Chaplain Alton E. Carpenter's vivid daily account of his travels with the 20th, 1340th, and 1171st Combat Engineers from November 1942 provides a look at the lives of the soldiers he ministered to and the emphasis and support of the military for chaplains in combat.[50] While records are not available of the number of soldiers who attended services conducted by chaplains, many soldiers attended services as they could. Some soldiers practiced their faith in private. Most men who fought in the war were fairly traditional Christians or Jews from childhood, though they expressed their beliefs in a variety of ways. Nicholas Pellegrino concluded that some soldiers faced enemy fire believing that God would protect them.[51] In *The Greatest Generation*, Tom Brokaw argues that "the World War II generation developed values of duty, honor, economy, courage, service, love of family and country, and, above all, responsibility for oneself. Coupled with their faith, these characteristics helped them to defeat Hitler."[52]

4

Fighting Across France to the Siegfried Line

After crossing the English Channel to the coast of France, everyone was apprehensive about what they would see. The 28th Infantry Division landed at Omaha Beach on July 22, 1944, where the first American troops landed on D-Day, June 6. The aftermath of the battle was evident, with debris everywhere. As the men went from the beach up a road to high ground, they saw to their left what looked like a cotton field in the distance. On putting the binoculars on the area, what they saw was not a cotton field; it was row after row of white crosses. These were the graves of the men of the U.S. invasion force that landed on Omaha Beach on D-Day.

Once they left the beach area, they began the march inland where there did not appear to be too much damage from the fighting. When they stopped periodically for one reason or another, and there were buildings nearby, they checked them out. The buildings were empty, but the soldiers found traces of bandages and dark stains, and assumed it was from troops that had been injured in the fighting in the beach area.[1]

While they waited for the orders to replace the 35th Division, there was a delay. During this waiting period, the 28th Division was several miles behind the front lines. They heard hundreds of Allied planes passing overhead. This was the start of the saturation bombing near Saint-Lô involving over 1,000 planes. This also was the start of the big offensive to breach the German lines, and even though they were miles from the bombing, the ground shook. During this devastating bombing, some of the planes dropped their bombs short, and they caused many casualties in the 35th Division while it awaited relief from the 28th. During the wait, the men of the 28th had time to think about their training and why they were in Europe. They thought about what President Roosevelt had told America about fighting for freedom and the American way of life.

They thought about their families back home and were determined that the Germans would not set foot on American shores. Private First Class Milton R. Downey, Company "C," 112th Infantry, wrote to his mom and dad on July 30: "The American flag means a whole lot to me. I am glad that when I do come home I can say I have a share in it. That is more than some people can say. I hope my son doesn't ever have to go through what I have and will go through. I am going to have a son when I come back home. That's what I am fighting for."[2] Map 1 shows the First Army Breakout, July 24 to August 4, 1944.

Within a few days after the Allied invasion of Normandy, the U.S. Army found itself facing a stubborn terrain that favored the defender. Units fought desperately for hills, towns, and bridges that had become of strategic importance. At every turn, the Americans faced the seasoned veterans of the *Wehrmacht* (German Army). The effects of weather and the terrain of the French countryside had a particularly strong influence on the conduct of operations. A significant tactical dilemma facing the U.S. Army in Normandy was the local terrain, called *bocage* in French. *Bocage* refers to farmland separated by thick hedgerows. These hedgerows are denser, thicker, and higher in Normandy than elsewhere along the French coast or in the British countryside on the opposite side of the English Channel. From a military perspective, they were ideal for defense, since they broke up the local terrain into small fields edged by natural earthen obstacles. They provide real defense in depth, extending dozens of miles beyond the coast. The *bocage* undermined the U.S. Army's advantages in armor and firepower, and the hedgerows gave the German defenders natural shelter from attack.

The *bocage* presented a substantial obstacle to tanks. While it was possible for tanks to charge the hedgerows and push over the top, this exposed their thin belly armor to German anti-tank weapons. Some hedges were so entangled with foliage and small trees that a tank could become trapped if attempting to push through, or could shed a track, effectively immobilizing it. The whole area was drained by the Taute and Vire Rivers, which empty into the English Channel near Carentan and Isigny, respectively. The marshlands were flat, and the ground was soft and moist, making travel by foot difficult, with vehicle traffic being almost impossible. Heavy rains made the marshlands even less trafficable, restricting movement to the few asphalt roads that traversed the bogs. On the American right, the terrain was more favorable. Between the marshes in the center of the sector and the coastline on the extreme right flank, a group of hills rises up to dominate the northern end of the Cotentin Peninsula.

As American units advanced inland, they had to conduct attacks to dislodge German units from the high terrain features on the rim of the

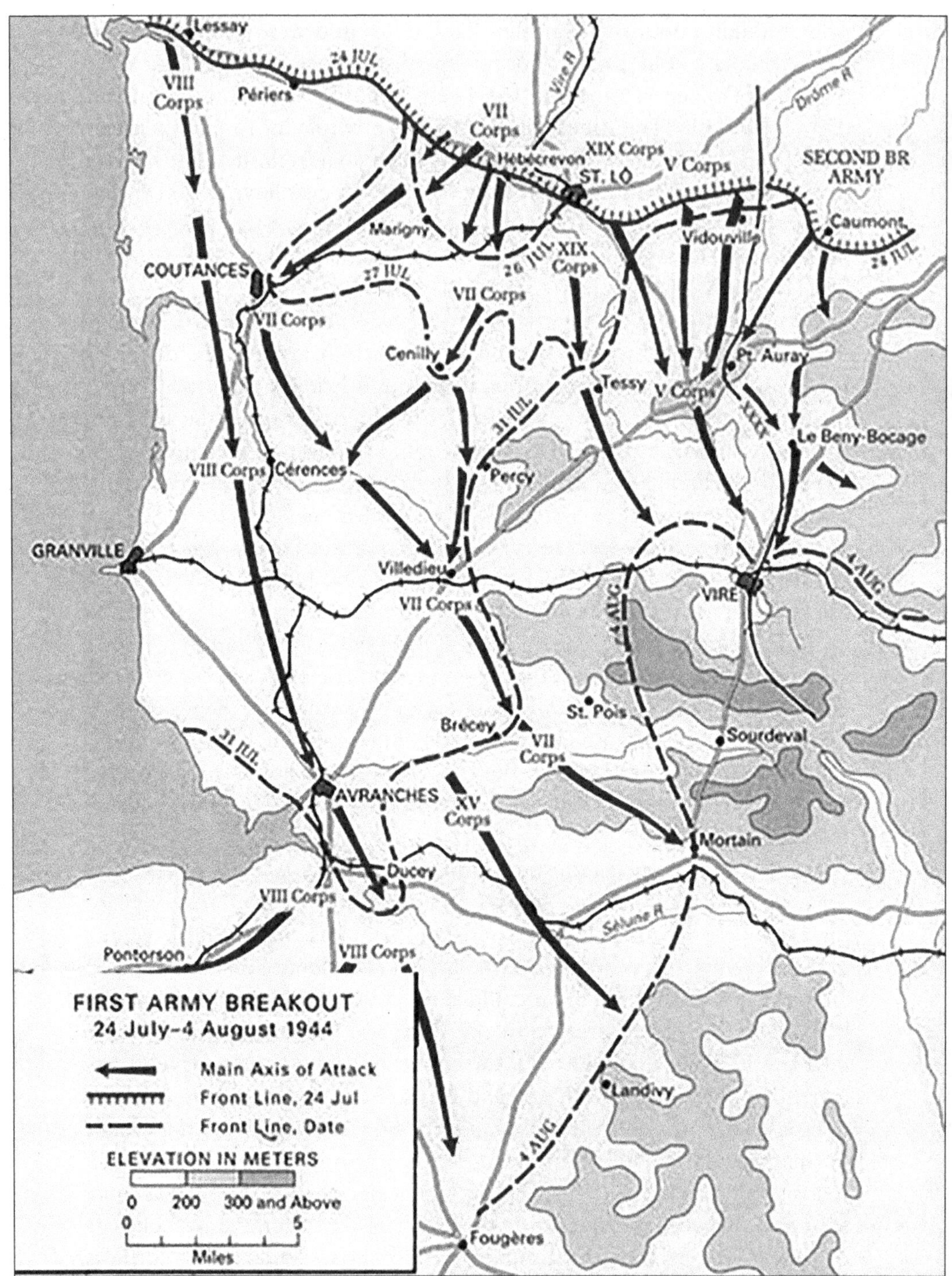

Map 1: First Army breakout, July 24 to August 4, 1944. (*U.S. Army Center of Military History*)

plateau. Some of the bitterest fighting of the Normandy campaign took place around Saint-Lô, as American units confronted German units, such as the 2nd SS Panzer Division, that held the high ground around the village. Several miles inland, the low terrain throughout the First Army sector rose into a plateau, with average heights of 200 meters above sea level. The swamplands restricted all cross-country maneuver, making the use and control of the road network a necessity for offensive operations. The natural, uneven lay of the land in the rest of the American sector made command and control of deployed combat forces extremely difficult. Despite these natural obstacles, the soldiers found ways to breach the obstacles.

On July 29, 1944, the men of the 28th Division rode trucks through Saint-Lô. It had been heavily bombed and shelled. There were bodies and parts of bodies visible in the debris, and there was the ever-present smell of death. Bloated bodies of draft horses and cows littered the area. After three and a half years of training, the men of the 28th now faced war: stench, decay, devastation, and death. Despite witnessing horrific acts, most soldiers remained steadfast in their religious beliefs and committed to why they were there.[3]

The division's first attack on July 31 was on the French town of Percy and Hill 210, south of Saint-Lô. It was a morning attack. The division assault teams took off reminiscent of Picket's charge at Gettysburg, with a lot of yelling and hollering. They entered Percy confused and disoriented. Eventually some of their troops who were in reserve took them back to the original lines. Displaying the usual symptoms of a unit new to combat, the troops of the 28th would need several days to overcome a natural hesitancy to advance under fire, to become accustomed to maneuvering in unfamiliar terrain, and to learn the techniques of advancing through hedgerow country.[4]

Hesitancy to advance under fire did not stop Staff Sergeant Walter R. Tauchert of Company "L," 110th Infantry Regiment, from doing what he came to do. During the attack on Percy at approximately 4 p.m. on July 31, Sergeant Tauchert and the 2nd Platoon were holding down the right flank of his company when they came upon a crossroad near the town. The crossroad was heavily defended by German machine-gun emplacements on either side of the road, by a machine gun and a sniper in the attic of a house on the right front, and by a half-track vehicle on the left front. This crisscrossed concentration of fire was supplemented by a heavy German artillery barrage that had succeeded in pinning down Tauchert's company.[5]

From his position at the side of the road, Sergeant Tauchert opened fire on the machine-gun emplacement menacing his right flank, knocking it out with his grenade launcher. Utilizing a machine gun nearby, he turned his fire upon the machine-gun emplacement on his left flank and silenced it. Although an airburst from a German 88-mm gun exploded with such force as to knock Tauchert to the ground and rip the clothing and equipment from his back, he turned his weapon on the machine gun and sniper in the attic and silenced them. He then directed his fire on the German half-track. but its fire forced him to withdraw. For his extraordinary heroism and courageous actions that day, Staff Sergeant Tauchert was awarded the Distinguished Service Cross.[6]

In an interview by the 28th Infantry Division Public Relations Section on September 28, 1945, Technical Sergeant Edward F. Schroder, Company "D," 112th Infantry, remembered Percy. It was Sunday, August 1, "when my battalion was initiated into combat. We suffered heavy casualties and at the end of that day, my platoon had eight of the original thirty-five men left. We knew there would be sacrifices, but we knew what we were fighting for. Those who were left knew what combat was and had gained some knowledge and combat experience at the expense of their buddies."[7]

The men of the division took their kindergarten training in hedgerow fighting at Percy and Hill 210. In the assault on Percy, their orders were to take Hill 210 and dig in at the top that overlooked the town below. As they started to dig their foxholes, they were ordered forward into the town. As they approached the town, they faced a hedgerow that crisscrossed a field of corn. The enemy was in and out of the hedgerows and the Americans had to dodge fire from the Germans as they made their way into town.

Their post-graduate work was at Gathemo and Hill 288, further south. Gathemo was a small town with a population of 500. When the battle smoke cleared away, German and American bodies lay everywhere. It was hot and dusty when the attack began on August 7. The infantry fought and sweated and clashed in hand-to-hand battle from morning until night for four days.[8]

The smell of death was all around when Private First Class Edward J. Sharkey, 109th Infantry, saw that his rifle company was pinned down by flanking machine-gun fire. He voluntarily crawled across an open field under heavy fire, leapt into a German emplacement, and fired his automatic rifle into the gun crew, killing three Germans and knocking out their weapon. His company then advanced a couple of hedgerows. Sharkey was awarded the DSC for his actions but was killed in a subsequent action.

Private Sharkey was not the only man who demonstrated brave action. Private First Class Frank Kielbasa, 112th Infantry, crawled to within 40 yards of a German position on Hill 288. Throwing his grenades, he killed six German riflemen supporting the position before he was fatally wounded by machine-gun fire. He received the DSC posthumously.[9] There were many heroes at Gathemo and Hill 288, who fought the Germans so that America could remain free. They battled and fell, and sometimes it was days before their bodies were found, surrounded by bodies of the green-gray-clad *Wehrmacht* (German Army). On the afternoon of August 10, Gathemo fell to the 28th Infantry Division men and Hill 288 was cleared of the Germans.

On August 12, Maj. Gen. Lloyd Brown left the division after completing a hard fight and seizure of Gathemo, France. The next day, Brig. Gen. James E. Wharton assumed command and was killed in action by a sniper's bullet as he went forward to the 112th Regimental Command Post. In his place, Brig. Gen. Norman Cota, who landed on Omaha Beach on D-Day, took command after returning to duty having been wounded in Saint-Lô.

After the bitter hedgerow fighting around Percy, and a brief respite to refit and receive replacements for the many casualties suffered, the 28th Infantry Division continued their advance across France in pursuit of the fleeing Germans. The Germans continued to fire artillery at the advancing Americans, but the division pressed on to accomplish their mission: to defeat the Germans. Martin Blumenson recalled: "for protection from German artillery shells, we would dig slit trenches, the length of our bodies and deep enough to protect us from shells that might fall close by."[10]

As the soldiers of the 28th Infantry Division traversed the French landscape, their journey was punctuated by both unwavering guidance from their leaders and the unwelcome intrusion of German propaganda. This barrage of information—delivered via artillery shells loaded with sinister messages—aimed not only to physically harm, but also to challenge the fortitude of the American fighters. Amid this tumultuous backdrop, the division's commitment to its mission remained resolute, bolstered by a deep sense of purpose.

Amid the chaos of war, the leaders and chaplains of the division undertook the vital task of constantly reinforcing the reasons behind their presence on foreign soil. Their voices rose above the cacophony of battle, reminding the men of the values they were upholding, the freedoms they were defending, and the imperative to stand united against oppression. This unyielding guidance served as a moral compass, guiding the soldiers through the darkness of conflict.

Yet, the enemy's attempts to sway the American fighters did not stop at mere rhetoric. The German forces deployed a sinister strategy: propaganda leaflets concealed within artillery shells, aimed at infiltrating the minds of the soldiers. One such leaflet—titled "Do You Remember—The Olympic Games in Berlin?"—carried a loaded message; adorned with an image of American athletes who had participated in the 1936 Olympic Games, the leaflet read: "Have you ever heard or seen in these reports [reports of the Olympic Games] that the German people then was unhappy, oppressed and enslaved by the Nazi bosses?—NO. You have seen a peaceful, sporting, gay people, at work and at festivals and contest. But today you are told to liberate the German people..."[11] Undeterred by the psychological warfare waged upon them, most soldiers reacted with a mixture of skepticism and determination. Many chose to repurpose these propaganda flyers, employing them as practical tools rather than succumbing to their intended impact. These sheets of deception often found themselves serving as makeshift toilet paper or as kindling for small gasoline stoves, used to brew coffee or warm C- or K-rations. The soldiers, acutely aware of the propaganda's deceptive nature, were steadfast in their conviction to remain focused on the cause of defending freedom.

In the face of dual assaults, one from German propaganda and the other from the harsh realities of war, the soldiers of the 28th Infantry Division demonstrated an unwavering commitment to their mission. Guided by the unwavering leadership of their officers and chaplains, and fortified by their shared determination, they persisted in their purpose of upholding the values that had brought them to the forefront of the conflict. Their resilience and unity not only prevailed over the psychological tactics of the enemy but also ensured that the flame of freedom burned brightly in the midst of darkness.[12]

On August 21, the 110th and 112th Infantry Regiments captured Verteuil, Breteuil, and Damville. The next day, they liberated Nogent-le-

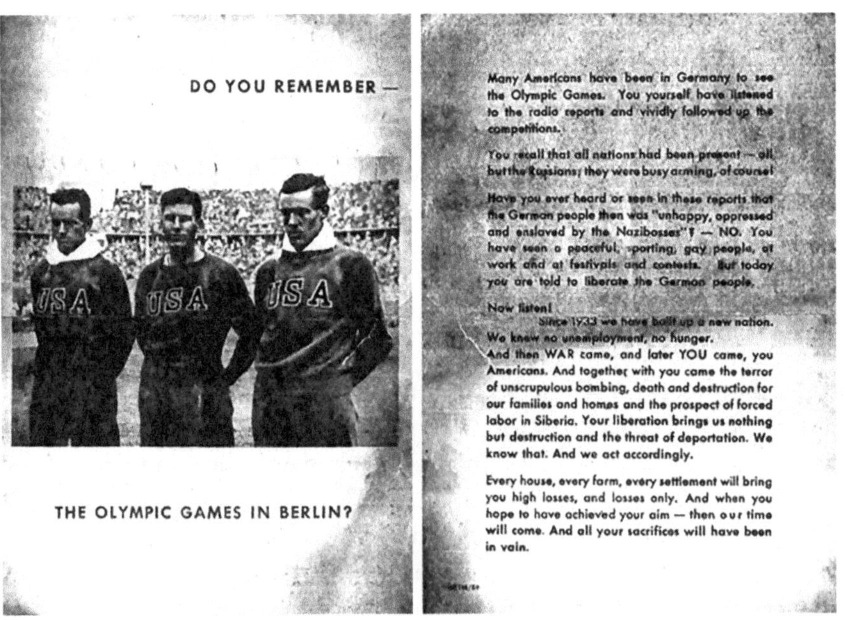

DO YOU REMEMBER —

THE OLYMPIC GAMES IN BERLIN?

Many Americans have been in Germany to see the Olympic Games. You yourself have listened to the radio reports and vividly followed up the competitions.

You recall that all nations had been present — all but the Russians; they were busy arming, of course!

Have you ever heard or seen in these reports that the German people then was "unhappy, oppressed and enslaved by the Nazibosses"? — NO. You have seen a peaceful, sporting, gay people, at work and at festivals and contests. But today you are told to liberate the German people.

Now listen!

Since 1933 we have built up a new nation. We knew no unemployment, no hunger.

And then WAR came, and later YOU came, you Americans. And together with you came the terror of unscrupulous bombing, death and destruction for our families and homes and the prospect of forced labor in Siberia. Your liberation brings us nothing but destruction and the threat of deportation. We know that. And we act accordingly.

Every house, every farm, every settlement will bring you high losses, and losses only. And when you hope to have achieved your aim — then our time will come. And all your sacrifices will have been in vain.

Figure 4: German propaganda flyer about the 1936 Olympic Games. (*28th Division Archives*)

Sec, Bonneville, Conches, Cleville, and Bacquipuis. The frantic Nazis put up a short, but stiff fight at Le Neubourg on August 24. But a task force composed of the 1st Battalion, 109th Infantry, the 107th Field Artillery Battalion, Company "C" of the 630th Tank Destroyer Battalion, and a small tank unit stormed and took the town.[13]

TSgt. Emerson W. Buckler, Company "C," 112th Infantry, wrote in his journal that after they landed on Omaha Beach, he joined the 1st Platoon. The platoon looked pretty rough at that point. As they started to push towards the Germans, he experienced his first combat and was plenty shaken up, but knew they were there to fight for the folks back home. They were not going to let the Germans win.[14]

After weeks of slow progress through hedgerows and cities, the men of the division found themselves in a fast advance east, liberating towns as fast as they could move forward. They encountered the occasional German resistance nest, detaching a regimental combat team or a battalion to deal with it, and kept the rest of the division moving. By August 25, the division's 110th and 112th Infantry Regiments had placed themselves on the Seine River to cut off German forces retreating from the Falaise pocket. The 109th Infantry Regiment captured Elbeuf on the Seine, cut off the last of the retreat route of the German Army in the area, and took 500 POWs.[15]

The Falaise pocket was the decisive engagement of the Battle of Normandy. Map 2 shows the Allied forces that formed a pocket around Falaise, Calvados, in which German Army Group "B," the 7th Army, and the Fifth Panzer Army were encircled by the Western Allies.[16] The battle resulted in the destruction of most of German Army Group "B" west of the Seine, which opened the way to Paris and the Franco-German border. On August 21, the Falaise pocket (Map 2) was sealed. Around 60,000 soldiers of Army Group "B" were trapped inside, 50,000 of whom were taken prisoner. The remainder were killed by artillery or air strikes inside the pocket.

While they spearheaded across France, every French town and village showed their appreciation for being liberated by bringing all kinds of things to drink—wine, champagne, brandy, calvados (apple brandy), etc. The calvados was supposedly 180+ proof and was used by the soldiers when there was a gas shortage. Albert Burghardt noted: "it made the jeeps backfire a little, but it worked."[17] The Americans were proud to have guaranteed the freedom of the French people while they fought to preserve their own.

The Germans constantly built roadblocks of several types. One was to put a two-man machine gun alongside a road, usually in a ditch, where they would wait until the division spearhead was close and would then open fire.[18] The men of the division walked and fought the Germans day after day across France. On August 27, the men were notified of a move by

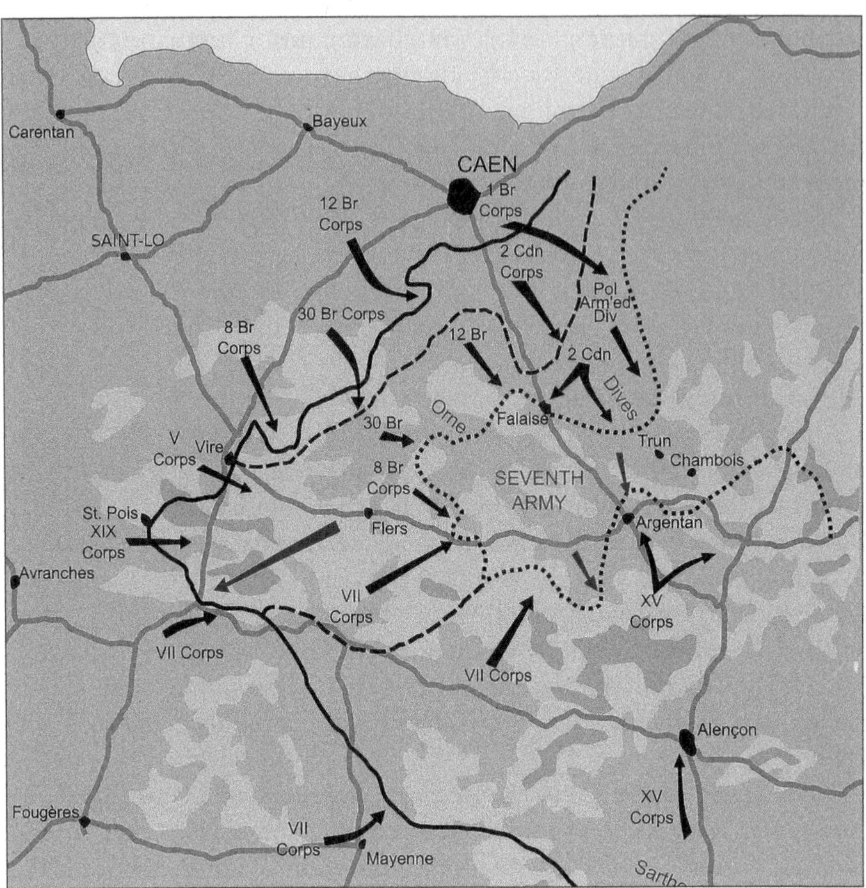

Map 2: The Falaise Pocket. (*U.S. Army Center of Military History*)

truck, but were not told the destination. The soldiers were surprised when they arrived at *Bois de Boulogne* (Boulogne woodland), a large public park in the outskirts of Paris, where they took their place in formation for the triumphal march through the French capital. The division marched down the Champs-Élysées and around the Arc de Triomphe as crowds of French people lined the street, several rows deep, and cheered them as they passed, twenty-four abreast.

The men had only been in combat for five weeks, and they were already being treated as heroes. Many soldiers thought that this war was not so bad after all. There was confident talk among the troops that the war would be over by Christmas, but they were wrong. The Germans still posed a serious threat. It would be no easy task, but the men knew what they had to do. They marched out of Paris and bivouacked near the city dump that night; the following morning, they were up and after the Germans once again.[19]

As they got farther from Paris, the division went through beautiful country, pursuing and engaging the Germans in short, sharp skirmishes as the Germans tried to slow the American advance. Having cleared the Compiègne Forest, at dusk on September 2, the 110th Infantry Regiment stormed into the streets of Saint-Quentin in Northern France. The Germans, overrun by the speed of the American advance, stumbled out of houses and shops, firing at the Americans. Within minutes, the gathering darkness was filled with rifle and machine-gun fire and the shouts of officers and the cries of the wounded. While moving through the city, they were suddenly engaged by a column of Germans of about a company size.[20]

The Nazis, aided by several armored cars, attempted to break the regimental column. Capt. Archie W. Stewart's jeep stopped and fired at the Germans coming up the street. The Germans overran the jeep, killed the driver, and shot Stewart, leaving him for dead, before capturing the vehicle and driving away.[21] The 110th Regimental S-2 (intelligence officer), Maj. Robert Gaynor, earned the DSC for his actions that day. He pursued the six Germans who were fleeing in the captured jeep, killed or wounded the entire group, and recovered the vehicle. While he was questioning one of the wounded, a German platoon advanced on foot toward his position. Despite overwhelming odds, he killed and wounded several of the German platoon before he was seriously wounded, and the Germans overran Gaynor's position and continued on. Maj. Gaynor crawled to his vehicle and reported the information to headquarters. Artillery fire was brought on the German platoon and most were killed.[22]

After they left Paris, the soldiers of the division had walked over 195 miles, an average of 18 miles a day. There was more walking and less leap frogging with trucks than before they arrived in Paris. German opposition was very light. There was an occasional roadblock or booby trap. The division continued to advance through La Fère, Saint-Quentin, Laon, Rethel, Sedan, Charleville-Mézières, and Bouillion, and on September 6, they crossed the Mouse River.

As they got close to the German border, word came down the line from headquarters that they were not to accept anything to drink from the German people. On September 10, they arrived at Binsfield, near the Our River, the geographical border between Luxembourg and Germany. That night, a patrol from the 109th Infantry Regiment crossed the border and became the first 28th Infantry Division troops to enter Germany. Two days later, the entire division dug in on German soil.[23]

The pillboxes that the division soldiers faced were 20–30 feet in width, 40–50 feet deep, and 20–25 feet high, with roofs and walls 3–8 feet thick of reinforced concrete. About half were underground, and most had two firing portholes for machine guns or light anti-tank weapons sited to cover

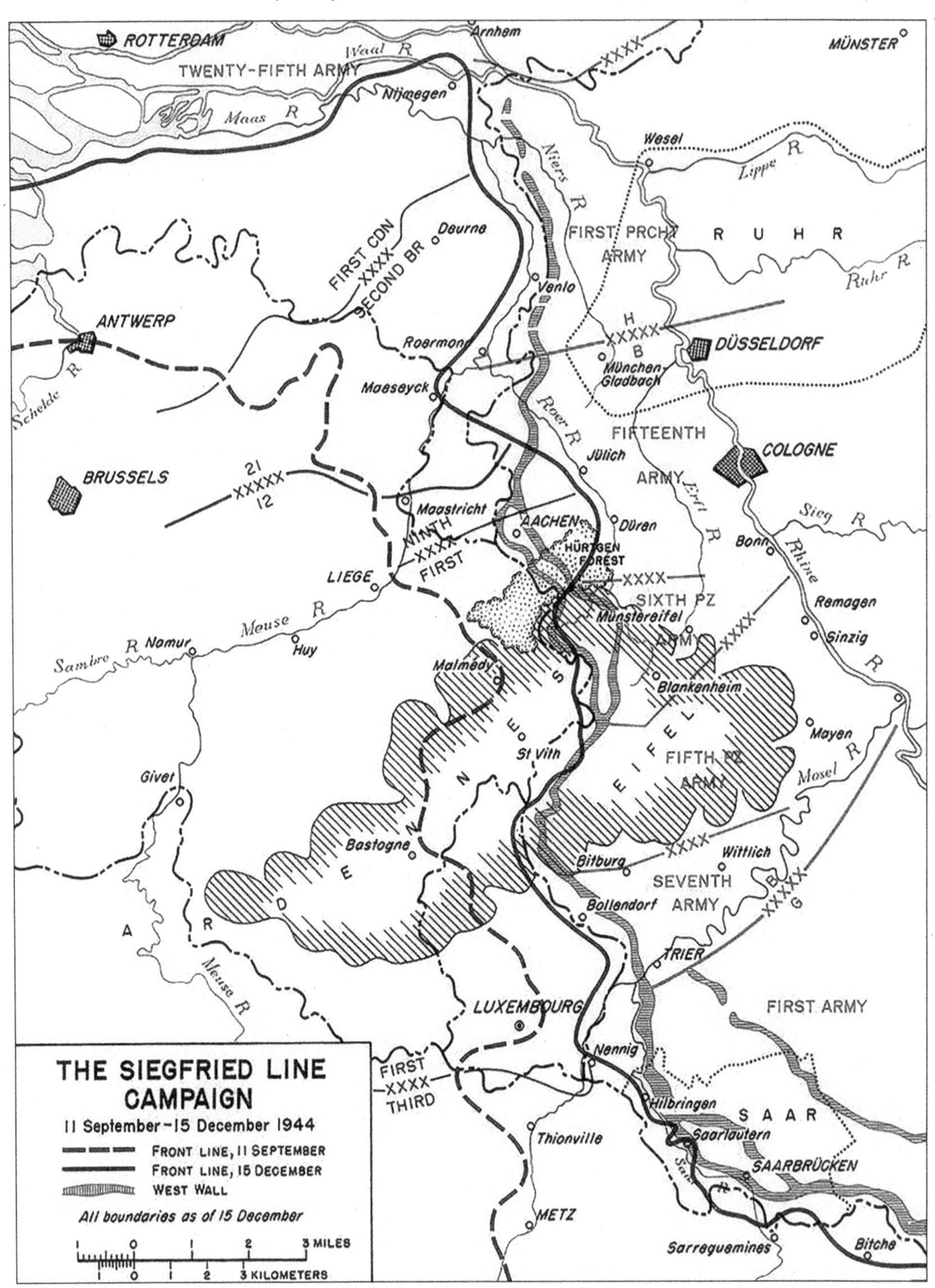

Map 3: The Siegfried Line, September 11 to December 15. (*U.S. Defense Mapping Agency*)

approaches and provide mutual support to other pillboxes. Each structure provided sleeping rooms for five to seven men. Concrete bunkers in the rear were designed to hold and protect reserves, counterattack forces, and command posts.[24] Most pillboxes were on the forward slope where they had longer fields of fire and observation. Map 3 illustrates the position of the Siegfried Line and the Allied front lines on September 11 and on December 15.

In this area of the Siegfried Line, good tank approaches were protected by lines of "Dragon's Teeth"—pyramid-shaped blocks of concrete in five rows rising in height from 2–5 feet; barbed wire was also strung in front of the blocks. There were trenches running between adjoining pillboxes to protect the troops when they moved from one box to another and to provide outside lookout and listening posts.[25]

Available intelligence gave no reason for concern. The V Corps G-2, Col. Thomas J. Ford, predicted that the corps would meet only battered remnants of the three divisions that had fled before the corps across Belgium and Luxembourg. These were the 5th Parachute, *Panzer Lehr*, and 2nd *Panzer* Divisions. It was possible, Col. Ford added, that the corps might meet parts of the 2nd SS *Panzer* Division, known to have been operating along the corps' north boundary. "There seems no doubt," Col. Ford concluded, "that the enemy will defend [the Siegfried Line] with all of the forces that he can gather." But, he intimated, what he could gather was open to question.[26]

On September 11, combat patrols of the 109th and 110th Infantry Regiments, moving under the cover of darkness, pushed into the Siegfried Line. Travelling down the roads leading to the Dragon's Teeth and the German fortifications, the soldiers came under intense German artillery fire. They reached the Dragon's Teeth and found that the engineers had blown a path large enough for tanks to go through; they proceeded very cautiously, waiting for the Germans to attack, but they never did. They penetrated a mile or two, clearing empty pillboxes stripped of any guns.[27]

On September 12, 1944, two platoons in Company "K," 109th Infantry, were crossing the Our River near Kalborn, Luxembourg, to get to higher ground on the other side. Thanks to an early morning fog, TSgt. Francis J. Clark and his platoon safely made it across. The fog lifted by the time the second platoon reached shore, though, and they were hit by gunfire, which killed the two men in charge and pinned the rest down.[28]

Clark saw what was happening and crawled across a field riddled with gunfire to reach the stuck platoon. He led the survivors to safety, then turned around and went back to rescue a wounded soldier, all while German gunfire continued to try to cut him down. Later, Clark led his squad and the men from the rescued platoon: "In dangerous sorties against strong German positions to weaken them by lightning-like jabs," the citation read.[29] During this time, Clark killed two German machine gunners with hand grenades. He continued to put himself in danger, running toward the fight, killing and wounding several Germans, scattering German patrols, and eventually forcing a full company of heavily armed Germans to withdraw.[30]

Five days later, on September 17, Clark's unit had moved northeast and across the border into Sevenig, Germany. Clark single-handedly killed an enemy machine gunner and forced another to flee before the Germans came at them hard, taking out a lot of the soldiers in Company "K." Seeing that they were left without leadership, Clark stepped up and took command. He was wounded the next day, but he refused to be evacuated. By daybreak on the 19th, Clark managed to kill three more Germans, one of whom was trying to set up a machine gun only 50 yards away. Later that day, he braved more gunfire to deliver food and water to an isolated U.S. platoon. Clark assumed leadership when it was desperately needed. His actions were essential to keeping up the spirits of the hard-hit troops of Company "K." For his efforts, Francis J. Clark received the Congressional Medal of Honor.[31]

As the 110th Infantry Regiment reached Germany, they found the outer reaches to be ill-defended. A reinforced patrol from Company "I" crossed the border and moved on to the town of Harspelt, where it was ordered to return to the battalion area on September 12. The same day, the 2nd and 3rd Battalions crossed the border at Stuppach, with Company "F" receiving slight resistance while the remainder of the group met no opposition and occupied the ground short of the Siegfried Line. At 8 a.m. on September 13, the 2nd Battalion launched an attack with the mission of driving through the Dragon's Teeth and to assault the town of Kesfeld after breaching the fortified area. The attack was launched without armor support and was not successful. The battalion was held up by automatic weapons fire from pillboxes and by artillery and mortar fire.

On the morning of September 14, the attack was resumed by the 2nd Battalion, this time using a company of medium tanks in support.[32] SSgt. Richard A. Dalton of Company "L" volunteered to lead a tank through a minefield in the face of German fire. It was necessary to get the tank into firing position against pillboxes, otherwise the pillboxes would have had to be taken without the use of tanks, potentially resulting in many casualties. The pillboxes were taken out by the tank, allowing the company to continue its attack. Sgt. Dalton was awarded the Bronze Star for his actions that day.[33]

At the same time, the 1st Battalion attacked with no armor support. They were unable to make any progress, as the men were slowed down by automatic weapons fire from pillboxes and considerable artillery and mortar fire. Company "F" was able to get through a gap that had been created by Companies "E" and "G" and succeeded in seizing six pillboxes but was hit by a counterattack supported by flamethrowing tracked vehicles. Very heavy casualties were inflicted on the Americans.

On September 15, the 2nd Battalion was unable to advance, but the 1st Battalion, supported by a company of tanks, was able to break through and capture a key hill after engineers had blown a second gap out of the Dragon's Teeth. The Germans counterattacked on the night of September 15, quickly destroying Company "F." A small German force from the 2nd SS *Panzer* Division, well-armed with automatic weapons and flamethrowers and supported by tanks, made quick work of the company. Units met with some success, but fierce German counterattacks quickly erased the gains.[34]

SSgt. Philip Columbus, HQ Company, 1st Battalion, 110th Infantry, was a member of an anti-tank squad. The squad had moved into a position covering the only road supplying the forward-line companies of the battalion. During the night, a German patrol tried to cut off the road, but small arms fire from the anti-tank squad drove the patrol off after the German patrol leader had been killed.[35] The following morning, three American tank destroyers moved into the anti-tank gun position and began firing on German troops on a nearby hill. The tank destroyers drew so much German mortar and 88-mm gunfire that the anti-tank squad was pinned down except for Gnr. Cpl. Paul G. Woodward, who was on outpost duty, protecting the flank of the gun position.

At about 10 a.m. Cpl. Woodward told Sgt. Columbus that two Germans were setting up a machine gun about 1,000 yards from the road, apparently trying to knock out the tank destroyer crews. Despite heavy mortar and artillery fire, Columbus led the squad in a rush for the German gun position. Fortunately, the Germans had not had time to put the gun properly into position and the rush caught them unprepared. They fired one burst when the squad was about 20 yards from them, then abandoned their gun and ran.[36]

On September 16, the 1st Battalion attacked and seized a key hill, after Company "A" and Company "C" attacked and seized yet another key hill. The 2nd Battalion was still unable to advance and the 3rd Battalion was committed in the gap created by the 1st Battalion and 3rd Battalion. The 3rd Battalion, with a patrol of tank destroyers, attacked and seized eleven pillboxes with a loss of one man killed and two men wounded. Then they silenced the opposition which had stymied the 2nd Battalion to that point. That same day, the 3rd Battalion closed the gap between battalions and the 1st and 2nd Battalions continued to occupy defensive positions. From

September 18–29, the 110th continued to occupy a defensive position in the vicinity of Kesfeld with a force of medium tanks to mop up pillboxes, some of which had been reoccupied by the Germans.[37]

Private First Class Thomas J. Ciccone, Company "M," 110th Infantry Regiment, was awarded the Silver Star for his action on September 25. Ciccone, ammunition bearer in a mortar squad, and four other men were given the mission to go back 3 miles to secure food and ammunition for their platoon. After successfully securing the needed rations and ammunition, Ciccone and his party were fired upon by Germans that had infiltrated friendly lines and established a machine-gun position. During the intense firefight that ensued, Ciccone crawled within close range of the gun position before the enemy discovered him. Disregarding the machine-gun fire directed at him, he continued to advance and killed three of the German crew with hand grenades, causing the remainder of the Germans to withdraw. After returning to the location of his companions, they secured the rations and ammunition and proceeded to their company lines.[38]

On October 1, SSgt. Herman B. Leff, Company "K," 110th Infantry Regiment, was in a group attempting to re-secure three pillboxes captured by counterattacking enemy forces. He volunteered to take dynamite charges up a rain-soaked hill under intense German machine-gun fire. Leff ran and crawled 200 yards to one of the fortifications, only to find that the Germans were holding three American soldiers inside. After a small wet charge failed to explode, he returned for additional explosives, and became seriously wounded on the return trip to the emplacement. Despite his wounds, he continued forward over fire-swept terrain until he placed the explosives around the door of the pillbox. Through his heroic actions, the door of the fortification was demolished, the three Americans were freed, and the pillbox eliminated as a threat. SSgt. Leff was awarded the Silver Star for his actions.[39] With no appreciable gains, the 110th Infantry Regiment received orders that they would be relieved by the 23rd Infantry Division and were sent back to Elsenborn, Belgium, for rest and reorganization.[40]

While in the Siegfried Line, the men were able to observe the famous German "buzz bomb." The launchers were about 10–15 miles in front of their position. One's watch could be set by when they went over the division positions, exactly every fifteen minutes. The range of these weapons was controlled by the amount of fuel they carried. They made a funny sound because they were rocket propelled. When the sound stopped, their nose dropped, and they came down. The Germans employed these V-1 rockets against the division's rear.

Russell M. Hark, Company "B," 630th Tank Destroyer Battalion, remembered one instance of a soldier's belief that he was invincible. Hark's unit was assigned to the 110th who had taken several pillboxes. Hark had just moved into one when the Germans started to fire mortars at the pillbox. Hark looked out the door and saw Private Stanley T. Masztzak making some hot chocolate on a small gasoline stove. Hark yelled: "You dummy, get in here." Masztzak replied: "Don't worry. They can't hit me. God is on our side."[41] Masztzak finished making the hot chocolate and shared his drink with the group inside.

Elements of the 112th Infantry, attached to the 5th Armored Division, crossed into Germany and captured the town of Wallendorf on September 15. In a small village near Wallendorf, the commander of Company "D," Lt. Frank L. Schmidt, had the men round up all the German villagers to look for German soldiers. They herded the people by an L-shaped rock wall for their protection as the Germans were shelling the town. The villagers, not knowing the motives of the Americans, thought they were being lined up against the rock wall to be machine gunned. The women and children were screaming, and the men were making gestures to the Americans not to harm them. Lt. Schmidt, who spoke German, informed the people that they were not going to be harmed. Sgt. Edward F. Schroder recalled that Lt. Schmidt was a quiet man but would constantly remind his men why they were fighting. After the incident with the frightened villagers, Schmidt told some of the men that they were fighting for the villagers' freedom too.[42]

Sgt. Charley S. Jordan, Company "C," 1st Battalion, 112th Infantry, was captured on September 17 at Bollendorf. In an interview by the 28th Infantry Division Public Relations Section on September 28, 1945, Jordan remembered:

> Most of the men were green, including myself, in combat. I had only been with the outfit about thirty days. Our company was put out in front that evening as outposts and most of the men had dug in when the Germans opened fire on us. My squad lasted all night until about 8:00 a.m. the next morning. When I was captured, I was completely out of ammunition, but I was not going to retreat. We had to resist the Nazis. That is why we came.[43]

For the 112th and for the other units of the 28th Infantry Division, a new kind of warfare had begun. Pressed against the border of their home country, the Germans fought desperately, not just the usual combat divisions that had survived the great retreat, but new units of former garrison troops, overage men, and youth forced prematurely into uniform. For both sides, including the 112th Infantry, the casualty rate was fearful and defeat bitter.[44]

As the 28th Infantry Division fought along the Siegfried Line, the soldiers and their commanders were unaware that Hitler was planning a counteroffensive through the Ardennes Forest. Hitler became convinced that after the Allies had broken out of their Normandy beachheads, he had to regain the initiative in the war or face certain defeat. It appears that the first idea of the Ardennes Offensive was discussed on September 16, 1944, during a second meeting after the daily *Führer* Conference that took place in the Wolf's Lair, Hitler's East Prussian headquarters. Present at this meeting were Field Marshal Wilhelm Keitel, Gen. Heinz Guderian, and Gen. Alfred Jodl.[45] Hitler is reported to have said: "I have made a momentous decision. I am taking the offensive. Their [the Allies] out of the Ardennes!" And smashing his fist down on a situation map, he shouted: "Through the Ardennes and on to Antwerp!"[46]

As German resistance stiffened, Maj. Gen. Leonard Gerow, the American V Corps commander, ordered all offensive operations at the Siegfried Line to end on November 13 and for most of the corps' forces to withdraw back across the Our River.[47] The 28th Infantry Division crossed into Belgium, where, after dark, they dug in. Within an hour, some troops came up to them and introduced themselves as Canadian artillery. They were in the field behind the 28th Infantry Division. They told the men that if they had to fire that night, they would blow their helmets off, so the 28th soldiers moved off to their right and out of their line of fire. After five days of attacks, the 28th had run out of steam. Only limited progress was made during the operation, and the cost was very high for the division.[48]

The shock of heavy casualties and tough resistance by a determined enemy had a demoralizing effect on the men. The chaplains had their work cut out for them. The total 28th Infantry Division casualties during the Siegfried Line attacks was more than 3,000. Included in this figure were 230 killed, 1,815 wounded, 141 missing, sixty-three captured, and 961 non-battle injuries.[49]

From the Siegfried Line, the division went to a rest area at Elsenborn, Belgium, to receive replacements and equipment and for continuous training. They bivouacked in a tree line with an open field in front of them. Russell M. Hark recalled: "the Red Cross and kitchen trucks were there. They offered the soldiers doughnuts and coffee; the doughnuts were two cents apiece."[50] Rest and recreation activities were extremely limited to the soldiers. Instead, V Corps ordered extensive training. The designated training priorities included assault of a fortified position, river crossing techniques, personal hygiene for winter months, patrolling, booby trap removal, defensive positions, and weapons familiarization.[51]

The strong personal bonds, comradery, and unit cohesion formed between the soldiers during their training and early fighting had dissolved.

The veterans were now surrounded by new soldiers with no combat experience whose motivation to fight was only to protect the American way of life. On September 29, the division received orders to move into Aachen, Germany, in preparation for a planned First Army attack to seize the Roer River Dams. The division's involvement in this campaign would take them into the Hürtgen Forest and once again test their commitment to fight for the American way of life.

5

The 28th Division's Mettle is Tested in the Hürtgen Forest

The commitment of the men was about to be tested as never before as they entered the dark, damp Hürtgen Forest in Germany. War correspondent Ernest Hemingway called it, "Passchendaele with tree bursts."[1] Not even Hemingway could quite capture the true description of this awful place. Under these conditions, morale suffered, and many found the psychological strain too much. Some soldiers broke and ran to the rear. Commanders were relieved of their command because they refused to carry out an attack or were unable to get their men to follow them. Men were put to the ultimate test. Yet, the majority of the men fought on, confident that they had to fight, not only for themselves, but for the folks back home. They may not have said the words, but they knew they were fighting for freedom, for their religious beliefs and from tyranny.

The 28th's harrowing experience in the Hürtgen Forest is etched in history as a testament to the unyielding resolve of both the German defenders and the American soldiers who found themselves embroiled in this grueling battle. The campaign unfolded amid a backdrop of severity, where the dogged determination of the German forces converged with the challenging terrain and relentless weather conditions, underscoring the brutal reality of warfare on foreign soil. Engaged on German territory, the American soldiers confronted an adversary who was equally steadfast in their defense. This clash of wills created a crucible of conflict, where each side was determined to hold their ground at any cost. The Hürtgen Forest became a crucible of close combat, where soldiers grappled with the adversities of the environment, relying on their resourcefulness and camaraderie to navigate the challenges that lay ahead.

The terrain itself added an additional layer of complexity to the battle. The forest was characterized by its dense undergrowth, punctuated by patches of woods that concealed both danger and opportunity. This environment turned each step into a potential hazard, with soldiers having to remain perpetually vigilant against ambushes and unexpected encounters. The forest concealed the intentions of the enemy, requiring the men to be prepared for sudden confrontations that could unfold at any moment. In this unforgiving landscape, the soldiers found themselves reliant solely on their skills, their weaponry, and their unity. The proximity of the combatants often necessitated engagements at remarkably short distances, pushing the soldiers to their physical and psychological limits. The battle took on an intensity that exceeded even the expectations of the seasoned veterans of the 28th Infantry Division, highlighting the ferocity of the struggle and the sacrifices it demanded.

While the fighting in the Normandy breakout was intense, nothing prepared the men for the Hürtgen Forest. The 109th and 110th Infantry Regiments faced the special problems of fighting in woods-separated formations, poor command and control, confusion, and the ability of small pockets of determined Germans to inflict heavy casualties and disrupt American attacks. Across the Kall River, the 112th Infantry Regiment was in Schmidt and on an otherwise open plain. They were simultaneously exposed to German gunners on the plain and isolated from their sister regiments. Many times, success depended decisively on a small number of audacious and bold men who knew they were fighting to defeat Nazism and protect the American way of life.

By the end of September 1944, the 60th Infantry of the 9th Division already had tested the forest, encountered small but resolute German units, and drawn back bloodied. Seeking to pass directly through the woods to capture the Hürtgen–Kleinhau road net along ridge-top clearings that characterize the eastern half of the forest, one regiment had proved no match for an enemy utilizing the defensive potentialities of the forest to advantage. As October opened and First Army prepared to clear up unfinished business before renewing a general offensive, the Hürtgen Forest still stood unconquered crossways along the path to the Roer River of the right wing of VII Corps. In early October, as the 9th Division prepared to attack, few within the American command appeared to appreciate the critical importance of another objective which capture of Schmidt might expose. This was a multiple objective, a series of seven dams near the headwaters of the Roer. Though three of the seven are on tributaries of the Roer, all came to be known collectively as the Roer River Dams. Map 4 shows the Roer dams.

The value of the Roer River Dams to German defense was outlined several days before the 9th Division's October attack by the division G-2, Maj. Jack A. Houston. "Bank overflows and destructive flood waves," Houston concluded, "can be produced [on the Roer River] by regulating the discharge from the various dams. By demolition of some of them, great destructive waves can be produced which would destroy everything in

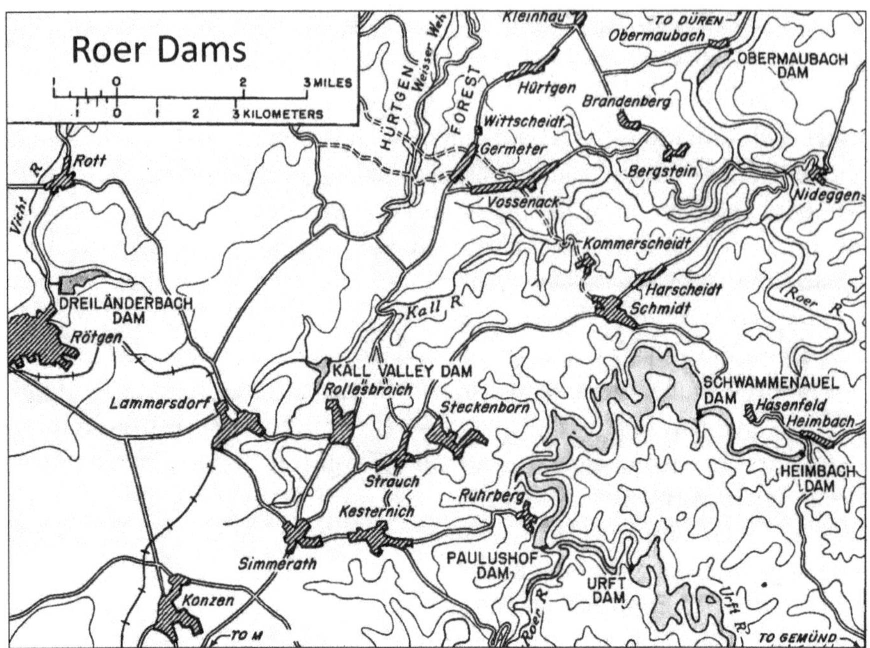

Map 4: The Roer Dams. (*U.S. Army Center of Military History*)

the populated industrial valley [of the Roer] as far as the Meuse and into Holland."[2] The intimation was fairly obvious: should the Allies cross the Roer River downstream from the dams, the Germans could release the impounded waters to produce a flood that would destroy tactical bridges and isolate any force east of the Roer. Allied troops beyond the river would be exposed to destruction in detail by German reserves.

The 9th Infantry Division, then operating under the VII Corps, commenced their attack on October 6 at 11:30 a.m., and from the outset, it became apparent that there was going to be a very stiff asking price. The attack commenced through the Siegfried Line in the vicinity of Roetgen, Germany. The towns of Rott and Zweifall were among those captured. As the division continued its attack towards Germeter, situated west of Vossenack and north of Simonskall in the North Rhine-Westphalia area of Germany, it suddenly met with a severe German counterattack from the north and northeast from Hürtgen.[3] Map 5 shows the first attack on Schmidt.

At least one battalion was cut off from the main body of the division, which during the entire action had suffered heavy casualties. The line was stabilized toward the end of the third week in October just west of the main road running north and south through Germeter to Hürtgen. As a result of its heavy casualties, plans were made to replace the 9th Division with the 28th Infantry Division, who had been resting and refitting at Elsenborn, Belgium.[4]

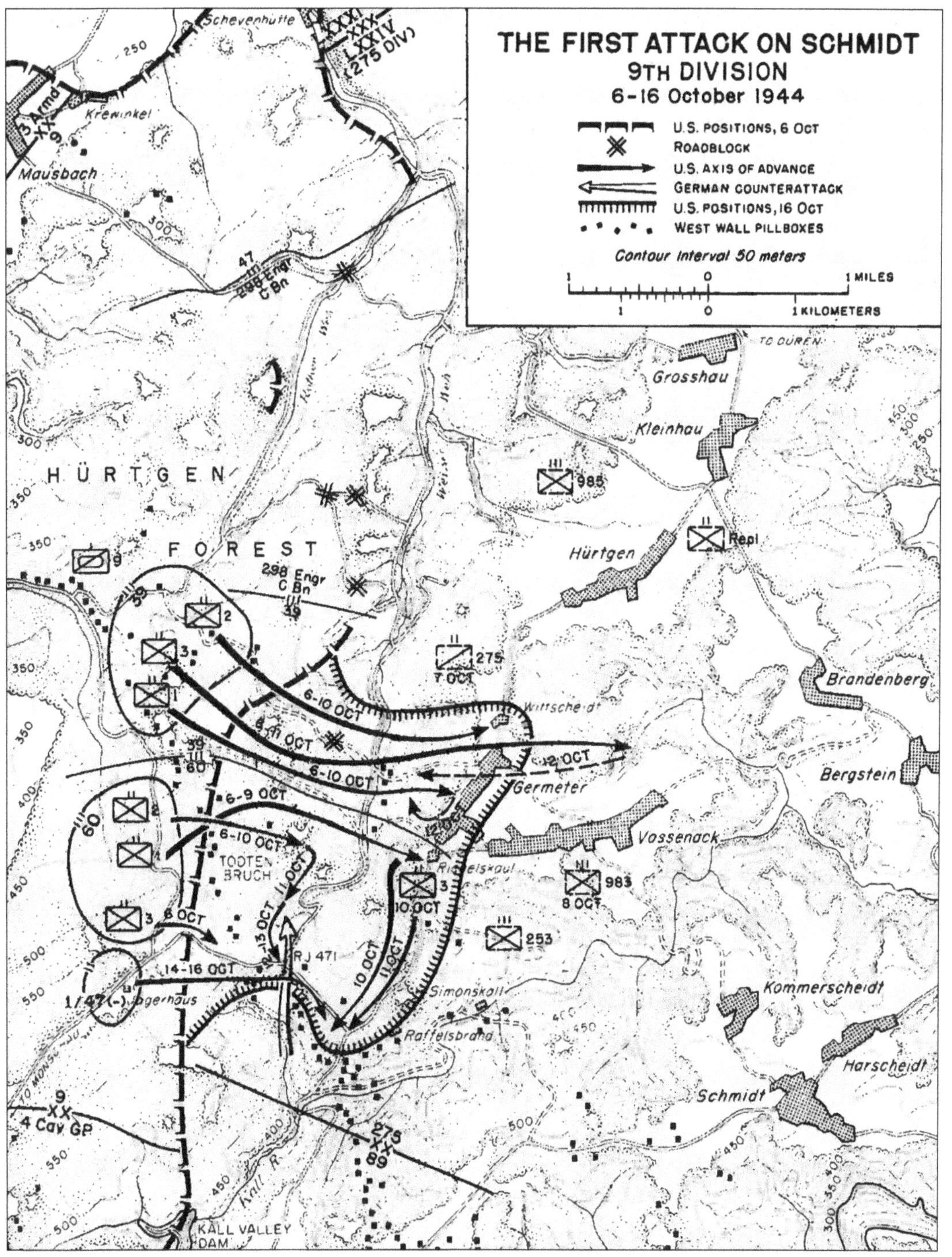

Map 5: The first attack on Schmidt. (*U.S. Army Center of Military History*)

On October 10, Private Kensler wrote in his diary to his wife, Cindy, explaining he had just received a lecture on how to handle POWs. He told her how he missed the things they had back home: "That is the honor and misery of war, I guess. We are here to make sure we keep those things."[5]

"Unrelenting German artillery and mortar fire had twisted the trees in the 9th Infantry Division sector into weird shapes," wrote Charles Whiting.[6] "Graves registration personnel were completely overwhelmed due to the number of deaths and the terrain. The bodies of 9th Infantry Division soldiers lay throughout the sector. Trash and equipment that had been discarded was everywhere."[7] The ragged appearance and the experiences related by the 9th Division soldiers were sufficient to unnerve many of the 28th Division men, especially those without combat experience.[8] Private First Class Albert Drapeau, Company "K," 3rd Battalion, 112th Infantry Regiment, recalled: "Approaching Germeter, we were brought into the grim reality of what may lie ahead. Dozens of vehicles were approaching us enroute to the rear. They were loaded with dead and wounded."[9]

In the overall plan, from which the V Corps and 28th Division attack stemmed, the U.S. First Army was to launch an attack aimed initially at the crossing of the Roer River, the capture of Duren, and then to drive to Cologne and into Germany. Preceding it by about a week, V Corps was to launch a strongly supported attack with the 28th Division to seize the important crossroad town of Schmidt. Upon its capture, the division was to drive to the south and southwest with the aim of clearing the towns of Straunch and Steckenborn.[10] In the second phase of the attack, elements of the 5th Armored Division were to launch a coordinated attack from the vicinity of Lammersdorf, and drive to the northeast to meet the elements of the 28th Division driving south.[11] The V Corps plan called for the attack to begin on October 31. However, bad weather prevented its launch until November 2, when under orders from First Army, the attack was launched despite bad weather, which almost completely prevented artillery observation and grounded air support until well after the attack had begun.[12]

In the V Corps sector, with a part of the lower portion of the VII Corps sector assigned to V Corps for this attack, the 28th Division entered the deadly forest. The entire Western Front was quiet when the 28th Division attacked. As a result, the Germans were unhampered in bringing in reserves, additional infantry, artillery, and armor to confront the 28th Division's advance. Opposing the 28th Division was the German 275th Infantry Division, 275th Fusilier Battalion, 1412nd Infantry Battalion, 89th Fusilier Battalion and the *Kampfgruppe* (Combat Group) Trier.[13]

Beginning about 5 miles southeast of Aachen, the Hürtgen Forest covered some 200 square miles, extending south to the village of Steckenborn. In the middle of the Hurtgen Forest, astride high plateaus and cut by gorges of the Kall and Roer Rivers, was open farming country. Three high ridges dominated the sector of Germany faced by the U.S. First Army. The entire eastern side of the Hürtgen Forest was faced by a chain of German fortifications stretching in a double line through the trees. Running parallel to one another, these defenses consisted of concrete pillboxes with interlocking fields of fire, camouflaged log and earth bunkers, reinforced concrete command posts, hidden machine-gun nests, and tall concrete pylons to prevent armored vehicles from penetrating its defenses. Minefields and booby traps were scattered within the defenses.

On November 1, the 28th Division was in a relatively inactive sector and was almost at full strength but was still attempting to integrate new replacements. The division had been in combat three plus months and had seen heavy fighting in France in August and at the Siegfried Line in September. The cumulative casualties to November 1 were 8,775, including 6,130 battle losses.[14] For the attack of Schmidt, the division had been reinforced by the 630th Tank Destroyer Battalion and the 707th Tank Battalion. The division also received forty-seven Weasels (M29 cargo carriers) in recognition of

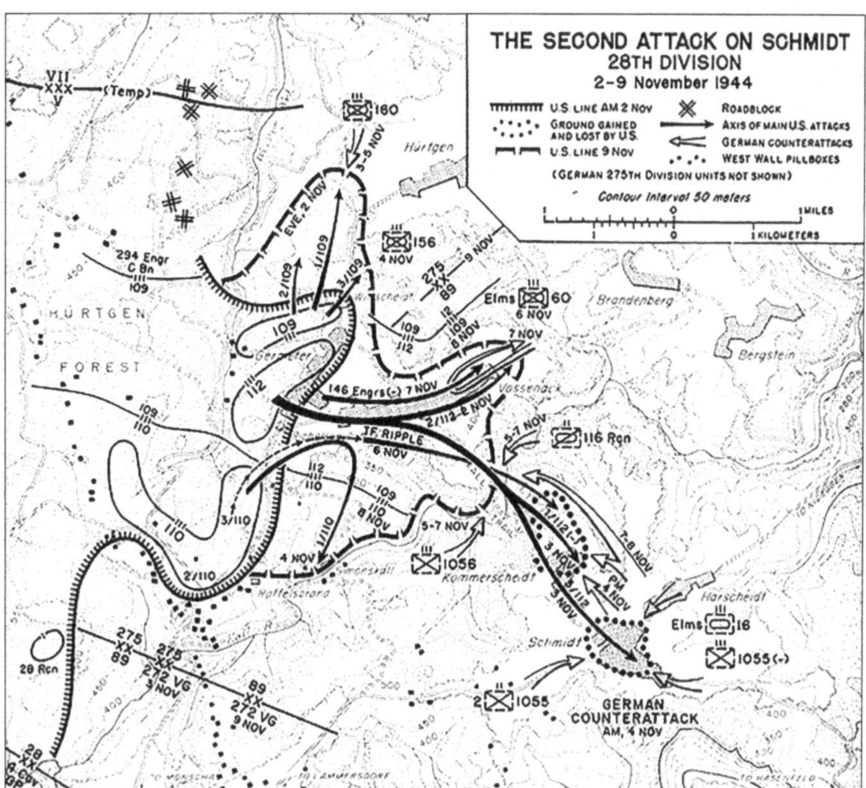

Map 6: 28th Division objectives in the second attack on Schmidt. (*U.S. Army Center of Military History*)

the rugged terrain in which resupply would have to be conducted. Eight battalions and a separate battery of V and VII Corps artillery were available for fire support. Map 6 shows the 28th Division's objectives in the second attack on Schmidt, November 2–9, 1944.

Upon arrival of the 28th Division in the Hürtgen Forest area, an estimate of the supply and evacuation situation showed that the mission assigned to the division could not be accomplished with their organic transportation assets. This left few alternatives: horses with pack saddles or M29 Weasel cargo carriers, or a combination of both. Suitable pack saddles were not available from the army quartermaster class II dump, so the plan for horses was discarded and forty-seven Weasels were requested.

For direct and general support, the corps placed eight battalions and a separate battery of artillery to support the 28th Division's attack. Using five fighter-bomber groups and a night fighter group, the IX Tactical Command was to direct its main effort toward air support of the division.[15] Following a heavy massed artillery barrage from six battalions of VII Corps artillery from 8–9 a.m. on November 2, in misty, cloudy weather, the attack began, with over 12,000 rounds of artillery fired. The 2nd Battalion, 112th Infantry, with Company "D," 707th Tank Battalion, attached, attacked through Germeter to Vossenack. At the same time, in the north half of the VII Corps sector, the U.S. 1st Division attempted to feint the Germans into thinking the attack might be along the entire front by firing mortars and artillery. The 2nd Battalion met light resistance in its drive eastward, reaching the northeast section of Vossenack by early afternoon. Two 2nd Battalion attacking companies set up defensive positions on the forward slope of the ridge while the reserve company mopped up the stragglers and snipers that were bypassed.

The German's well-observed artillery fire took a heavy toll on the American companies, reducing them considerably. It was already evident that the American artillery was unable to effectively neutralize the German observation posts and positions on the commanding ridges because the shells were coming into the town from three major points of the compass. The companies reported German armor in the town of Schmidt.[16]

First Lieutenant Eldeen H. Kauffman, Company "F," 112th Infantry, was awarded the DSC for his actions that day. While advancing through Vossenack, 1Lt. Kauffman personally directed fire of a tank in support of two platoons of infantry that had suffered many casualties and whose advance was slowing by the strong German resistance. Then, armed with a pistol, he stepped into the street, firing as he went and urging his men forward. He entered several houses and assaulted the Germans with his pistol, causing twelve of them to surrender, and thus clearing the German stronghold. Inspired by his actions, the company moved ahead to accomplish the mission they came for.[17]

After several days of fighting and crawling in and out of the basements of houses in Vossenack and Germeter, the 109th Regiment were ordered to launch an attack to the northeast of the town of Hürtgen. The attack was through heavy forest all the way, so they massed all of their .30-caliber and .50-caliber machine guns to throw interdictory fire on the roads near the town. They even took .50 -caliber guns from the kitchen trucks and had them operated by headquarters and kitchen personnel to increase the firepower. They also laid out a ladder-type barrage as they advanced through the forest.

The attack went well for a while, and they made good progress in their coordinated attack with the 112the Infantry and succeeded in knocking out fifteen pillboxes and capturing over 200 prisoners. The 1st Battalion had advanced 2,700 yards in a drive to the northeast toward the town of Hürtgen, but the other assault battalion attacking in the same direction could only gain 500 yards due to the thick minefields and wire obstacles that were covered by bands of grazing fire from German automatic weapons.[18]

The 109th Infantry partially succeeded. One battalion secured most of its objective by the end of the day. The other battalion failed to reach its objective because of encountering unexpected minefields and strong resistance from previously unlocated German strongpoints. An excerpt from the diary of Thomas W. Hickman, Company "I," 1st Battalion of the 109th Infantry, offers a picture of the situation facing the soldiers:

> 11/5—This place is just one big hell hole. You can't move. Death and devastation everywhere. By far this is the worse place we have been in. Our casualties are terrific. These Jerries [Germans] are pure SS.
>
> 11/6—Attacked at 0600 and took battalion objective—Germeter. Replacements pouring in. Casualties pouring out.
>
> 11/7—Attacked at 0600 and took the first of our division's objectives—a crossroad on Cologne–Aachen highway at Vossenack. We are really beat up now. Don't see how we can possibly hold this ground. Replacements come in and leave within an hour—either as litter cases or basket cases. We don't even have a chance to assign them to platoons or squads. The poor guys don't even know what division they are in.
>
> 11/8—Vossenack is leveled. Not a building standing. Wish I could get out of this place.
>
> 11/9—From 1000 to 1800, holding. Counted four thousand rounds coming in. Our dead are all over the place. Can't waste time with them—too many casualties that need help. No possible way to get them out unless you want to join them. Everyone has trench foot. Been snowing for more than a week now. Holes are full of ice and mud. Can't help but remain saturated. Have a bad case myself. Feet hurt. We only have shoes. I even lost my leggings.[19]

The 2nd Battalion, 112th Infantry Regiment, took their objective by 10:30 a.m. and proceeded to dig in. Opposition had been light. The rest of the 112th Infantry Regiment ran into unexpected opposition south of Vossenack and was unable to advance further on that day. Private First Class Raymond Carpenter of Company "M," 3rd Battalion, spoke for many of his buddies: "I never saw a wood so thick with trees as the Hürtgen. It turned out to be the worst place of any."[20] He could only blame himself for being there. In earlier service with the 45th Infantry Division, an Oklahoma Army National Guard outfit, Carpenter received a foot injury. After his recovery, he received assignment to a quartermaster service battalion, a relatively safe rear-area job: "But I still wanted to fight for our right to be free and be of service to my nation, so in Wales I requested transfer to Company M, 3rd Battalion, 112th Infantry Regiment, 28th Infantry Division—America's oldest division."[21]

That same day, the action of TSgt. Jacob Welc won him a battlefield commission. The soldiers were taking a beating at Vossenack: the roads had been converted into rivers and mud due to all the rain and snow, German artillery pummeled all routes to the advancing units, and the use of vehicles was limited. Hampered by these conditions, the wounded were only brought back as far as the most advanced aid station; further evacuation to the rear appeared impossible. Without orders, TSgt. Welc drove one of his trucks through the mud-choked roads in the dead of night. In the battered town of Vossenack, German artillery rained in constantly, but despite the incessant shelling, he brought his vehicle into the town, helped load the wounded, and then drove over the treacherous road to the rear medical station.[22]

SSgt. Conrad W. Johnson was with Company "D," 1st Battalion, 112th Infantry. In an interview by the 28th Infantry Division Public Relations Section on September 28, 1945, he recalled that after a few days rest from the fighting at the Siegfried Line, he was back in the fighting in the Hürtgen Forest. The fighting was tough because the land was hilly and there were thick woods. It was there that his unit was surrounded. Some of the men were able to escape but he was one of the ones who was taken prisoner by the Germans. He helped carry some of the wounded to a German aid station for treatment. Marching for several days, the group came to Bonn, Germany. There they were loaded into boxcars and sent to *Stalag* XII-A in Limburg, Germany. Even though he was captured, Johnson later wrote home that he did his best trying to stop the Germans. He knew that his side would eventually win.[23]

Private First Class Robert J. Esterly, Company "I," 112th Infantry, was awarded the Silver Star for his actions. He carried a Browning Automatic Rifle (BAR) and was picked to provide the chief means of fire power for a five-man reconnaissance patrol which had the mission of penetrating deep into German territory at night. The patrol had gone well into the Nazi lines when suddenly the stillness was broken by a German guard's order to halt. When the Americans failed to reply to the second challenge, burp gun and rifle slugs began to rip through the darkness. The patrol hastily deployed. Esterly lost contact with the rest of the patrol. All he could see were German gun flashes. Instead of retreating, he chose to stay and fight. Crouching low, he held his fire until he had spotted the muzzle flashes from ten burp guns and rifles, at which point he fired, killing all the Germans. When asked later why he did not retreat, he said he "came here to fight the Germans, not to retreat."[24]

The 110th Infantry Regiment attacked against deadly German positions and failed completely to achieve much success. During the attack, the assault battalions received heavy mortar and artillery fire from the Germans and found their advance slowed by heavily booby-trapped defensive positions, pillboxes, dug-in wooden bunkers, and other prepared defensive positions. They were only able to advance about 200 yards. On the morning of November 3, the 2nd and 3rd Battalion again launched an attack. The entire front received heavy American mortar and artillery fire. Even after the area had been saturated with artillery and mortar fire, the assault battalions were unable to breach the fortified positions.[25]

On November 3, the 112th Regiment resumed their attack. The 1st and 3rd Battalions of the 112th succeeded in reaching Kommerscheidt and Schmidt. The two battalions set up defensive positions in each town. The 109th Infantry Regiment renewed their attack, bringing into action the previously uncommitted reserve battalion, but they were still unable throughout the day to achieve success. In the morning, a sharp counterattack against the left flank of the regiment from the direction of Hürtgen forced a slight withdrawal.

In the November "28th Infantry Division Summary of Activity from Regiments," the G-2 Section reported: "The 2nd Battalion, 109th Regiment attack didn't get too far but their preliminary attack in the 109th area had sucked the Germans in..." Such daily summaries from the 28th Division headquarters might have confused riflemen in the battalions of the 109th Infantry Regiment. They did not feel they had sucked in the German counterattack or foiled their enemies. As they stumbled blindly through the battle area following inadequate maps, they might have marveled to know the divisional headquarters prided itself on letting every man know what he is supposed to do.[26] Yet, without good maps or clear guidance, the men did the best they could to fight for freedom. The 110th Infantry Regiment again attacked but suffered heavy casualties and gained no ground.[27]

TSgt. Gary M. Dix, Company "M," 109th Infantry, was awarded the Silver Star for his actions on November 3, 1944. He was left in command of his section when his platoon leader went forward to re-establish contact with his company. During an attack of German artillery and mortar fire, TSgt. Dix was seriously wounded by a shell fragment which completely pierced his body. When the artillery and mortar fire ceased, a force of approximately fifty Germans attacked his weapons platoon and heavy machine-gun section. Dix, though suffering with pain, and weakened from shock and loss of blood, directed the placing of machine guns and deployed his men. Moving about with an ammunition belt tightened around his stomach to contain the bandages he had applied, he gave the necessary fire orders. Dix refused to be evacuated until the hostile force had been completely dispersed, leaving behind many German casualties.[28]

On November 4, German artillery fire throughout the entire division area began to increase. A counterattack against the positions in Schmidt drove the 3rd Battalion, 112th Infantry Regiment, out. At first, the counterattack split the battalion in two. One company disappeared into the woods south of the town. The rumble of exploding artillery shells bombarding the town of Kommerscheidt and Schmidt sent the men of Company "L" into their foxholes. They dug feverishly in an attempt to enlarge their foxholes while there was still time. They were not planning on going anywhere. The artillery fire was especially heavy to their south. Because of a hill and sloping terrain between them, they could not fully prevent the problems Company "K" was facing. In addition to the artillery fire, they were also drawing German tank fire. The 2nd Platoon from Company "L" was dug in on a forward slope facing east with the town of Schmidt directly to their rear. Through the morning haze, the men could see about fifty Germans coming over a rise about 600 yards to their front.

Private First Class Albert E. Drapeau wrote in his journal: "the 2nd platoon was dug in on a forward slope facing east with the town of Schmidt being directly to our rear. Through an early morning haze, I discerned what appeared to be about fifty enemy coming over a rise about six hundred yards to our front."[29] "A rising crescendo of yelling and cussing was enveloping our rear," explained Drapeau, "along with increasing enemy fire. Company K was breaking, some units fleeing to our rear through Schmidt and toward Kommerscheidt. Orders to hold were being refused. I personally shouted and cussed some of these men. We came here to fight and defeat the Germans, not to run."[30]

Most soldiers just wanted the war to end, and many looked to God for protection. In his November 5 diary entry, Private Kensler wrote about a letter he sent to his wife: "I wrote to Cindy.... We are about two miles from the front and can hear the field artillery. This is it, my darling, this is what we've been trained for and we are here. What is in the future for me God only knows ... we can hope for the best and pray for the courage to carry on ... and a protector when the going gets tough."[31]

During this action, Captain Linguiti, the 112th Infantry Regiment's medical officer, moved his aid station by pack carry to a small, abandoned house overlooking Kommerscheidt to guarantee immediate medical attention for the wounded. As the fighting grew in ferocity, American infantry and tanks took up positions close to the house occupied by Captain Linguiti's aid station. On November 5, a resupply convoy for the 1st Battalion arrived in Kommerscheidt at 5 a.m. and dumped its load in front of the house used by medical personnel as its battalion aid station. For the next two hours, Captain Linguiti fumed as he watched company-carrying parties arrive to receive their distribution of ammunition and rations. He was terribly concerned that such activities would compromise his work and that German artillery batteries would fire on the site, unaware that an aid station lay in the midst of all of the activity.

The Germans on the far slope of the surrounding hills, spotting increasing activity around the house, laid down an artillery and mortar barrage on the aid station and surrounding vicinity.[32] Captain Linguiti realized the aid station had to be moved if he were to ensure safety for his people and the casualties who crowded their facilities. After dark, he evacuated his staff and patients along the road leading out of Kommerscheidt toward the river.

On three occasions, the Germans scored direct hits on the house, killing medical officers and two medical aidmen, as well as destroying all food and most of the medical supplies. Despite the continuous artillery, Captain Linguiti continued receiving, treating, and evacuating the wounded. When German artillery again hit the already shattered house, rendering it almost completely unusable, he withdrew to combine with the 3rd Battalion aid station in a log dugout bunker. Linguiti left eight litter bearers in Kommerscheidt. These men would collect casualties and carry them to the dugout.[33]

As the dugout became untenable and troops were withdrawing, both battalions' chaplains decided to stay within the dugout, where many of the wounded cried out for religious support. The men had fought for their religious freedom and wanted to exercise their faith even as they lay on the stretchers. Chaplain Alan P. Madden, 1st Battalion, and Chaplain Ralph E. Maness, 3rd Battalion, remained there until November 9, ministering as best they could to those who were brought to the bunker. They represented both major Christian faiths. Father Madden cared for Roman Catholics, while Reverend Maness cared for Protestants.[34] Father Madden was eventually captured by the Germans.

Captain Linguiti's decision to advance his aid station into the village enabled seventy-seven casualties to be given immediate medical treatment, a factor that saved the lives of many of them. Captain Linguiti was listed as missing in subsequent action against the Germans. He was posthumously awarded the Silver Star for his actions that day.[35]

The balance of the battalion drew back to the northern edge of Schmidt, where they were again hit by the Germans. They could not hold their position and withdrew to Kommerscheidt. There is some evidence that the soldiers refused to hold their positions. The 1st Battalion defensive position at Kommerscheidt was reinforced by some of the men from the 3rd Battalion, 112th Infantry Regiment, and held until the morning of November 7.

TSgt. Emerson W. Buckler was in Company "C," 1st Battalion, 112th Infantry. In an interview by the 28th Infantry Division Public Relations Section on September 28, 1945, he recalled that on November 8, the remainder of his platoon was withdrawing from the Kall River Valley. Besides being wet from dunking in the stream they crossed, he and the rest of his unit were lost. They were on the forward slope of a hill facing the Germans, while they tossed mortar and artillery fire on the men all night. Fortunately, no one was hit.[36]

When dawn broke Buckler gathered the eight remaining men from his platoon and found their way back to the company kitchen set-up. They found several more men from the platoon. From there, they went to Harcheidt to a holding position. This is where the German breakthrough occurred. Buckler said, "I never saw so many men in all my life." The enemy used searchlights to find the Americans. They held out until the enemy machine-gun fire ripped the top off of their dugouts. From then on, they fought a rearguard fight. Company "C" was split up and half of the men got lost.[37]

Maj. Howard L. Topping, commander of the 3rd Battalion, 109th Infantry, was assigned the mission of moving his battalion from the vicinity of Germeter to a position about two miles away. His troops were given the task of defending a road and heavily wooded draw from German infiltration, which would prevent the remnants of the 3rd Battalion, 112th Infantry Regiment, from an untenable position on high ground. With a small reconnaissance party, Major Topping moved out at the head. The nearest route to his destination led across an open field under German artillery fire. During the trip, the party was twice fired upon by German artillery. Reaching the woods on the opposite side of the field near his objective, Maj. Topping observed a five-man German patrol moving toward him. When they were about 100 yards away, he opened fire on the German with his M-1 rifle, mortally wounding two of them.[38]

Continuing to his objective, he observed another German patrol about 200 yards away. Again opening fire, he killed one of them and forced the others to flee. Despite a German mortar barrage, he remained at his position until he was thoroughly familiar with the ground he was to occupy. When he was about to leave, a German sniper from across the draw shot him through the left wrist. He returned to his battalion but refused to be evacuated until after he had led his men to their new positions. His action permitted the remnants of the 3rd Battalion, 112th Infantry, to safely withdraw. Maj. Howard Topping was awarded the Silver Star for his actions.[39]

The 110th Infantry Regiment again attacked but achieved no material success. As the daily German barrages began, men of the 110th ran for their foxholes. In the distance they could hear mortars firing. Usually, the Germans would fire about eighteen rounds; a moment or two later, the shells would land. As debris from explosions settled, someone would lift his head out of his hole and ask if anyone was hit. Soon the Germans found out that the Americans were counting shell rounds, so while the eighteen expected ones were landing, they dropped three more rounds in the mortar tubes. Private Robert C. Wells said: "those last three rounds blew the ass off more than one of our guys because we weren't expecting them."[40] Wells refused to be intimidated by the German efforts. As the noise faded from the bursting rounds, "I would always look out of my foxhole and call out, in imitation of President Roosevelt: I hate you. Eleanor hates you. Even Fala hates you. You sons will never step foot on our soil. And here we were, sitting just inside Germany. It helped to keep up the guy's spirits."[41] Another favorite comment was to call out to one's buddies, "Alright, I want to take a poll. All you confirmed atheists sound off. I want to see how many of you are left. There were never any responses."[42]

Private George Nikola, a scout in the 1st Platoon, Company "G," ran along a firebreak toward a shallow dip in the ground he thought might serve as a good field of fire for use against a pillbox. He carried a light machine gun. As he reached the hollow, he dropped to the ground and set the gun down beside him. As it touched the earth, it depressed a hidden plunger on a buried mine that then exploded, destroying the barrel of the machine gun and wounding Nikola in the face. Thrashing with pain, his right foot struck a booby trap, setting it off and injuring his foot. Refusing to crawl back to safety, he remained where he was for an hour in order to shout warnings to his buddies not to venture into the area with mines and booby traps. When asked later why he would not withdraw, Nikola said: "I came here to fight the Germans in their country and that is what he was going to do."[43] Private George Nikola was awarded the Silver Star for his actions.

On November 4, the 1st Battalion, 110th Infantry, which had been uncommitted up until that morning, succeeded in a flanking attack and managed to seize their two initial objectives. But they were then faced with the presence of the Germans in dug-in positions cutting them off from the rest of their regiment. Attempts to clear out the area were only partially successful during the following nine days. The regiment was finally pulled off the frontline on November 13.[44] The men of the division were grateful to be out of combat, if even for only a few hours or days. They talked about their fears to one another. Private Charles Hubner remembered such conversations: "At first we were petrified, really scared. But if we were lucky enough to live through a few skirmishes we weren't so much scared of a fight as getting maimed. Most of us said we would rather be dead than go home a cripple or, worse, go home to Germans running the country."[45]

On November 6, the Germans counterattacked in the town of Vossenack. The 2nd Battalion, 112th Infantry, had given up their positions, without evidence of strong attacks by infantry, in the face of extremely heavy artillery fire, some of which was direct. At the same time, the Germans captured the main supply route to Kommerscheidt and effectively isolated the 112th Infantry and the newly formed Task Force Ripple that consisted of the 3rd Battalion, 110th Infantry, a company of tank destroyers, and two tank companies.

Private Kensler made another entry in his diary on November 8, recording what he wrote to his wife that day: "During the night it snowed. It was damp and cold. I pray God that this may soon end and stop the killing and suffering. To me war is murder. Maybe others would not agree, but that's one nice thing about being an American, everyone can have his own thoughts and ideas. Thank God for that. This is why we are here. Good night my darling."[46]

While the situation seemed hopeless, the bravery of some continued unabated. During a barrage in which 600 German artillery rounds fell within a thirty-minute period, SSgt. Paul Kerekes of Company "M" dashed out from his hiding place to repair breaks in communication wire. As Army Air Forces planes flew in to bomb and strafe German attackers, SSgt. Arthur Johnson of Company "K" dragged panels marking American position into view so pilots would be able to differentiate between German and American troops.[47] Both men were awarded the DSC for their efforts.

As the German tanks worked their way towards the Americans, they drove them from their foxholes, forcing them to retreat as best they could. Sgt. Tony Kudiak of HQ Company was not one to give up easily. He knew the Germans had to be stopped at all costs. When German tanks tried to erase his position, he picked up a bazooka and blasted the tank. When the Germans crawled from the wreckage, Kudiak and his men picked them off with rifles, then chased away other German tanks that had pinned down the American infantry. As the Germans advanced, Kudiak remained in place, climbed into a tank destroyer, and repulsed the German grenadiers. When the gun jammed, he abandoned the tank destroyer and climbed into another one. When that gun jammed, he fired at the German tanks with his M-1 rifle, picking off as many German infantry soldiers as he could.[48] Sgt. Kudiak was awarded the Silver Star for his actions that day.

The 12th Infantry Regiment, 4th Division, replaced the 109th Infantry Regiment, and the 110th Regiment were then used to reoccupy positions in the Vossenack area. A task force consisting of the 3rd Battalion, 109th Infantry Regiment, was sent to extricate the surrounded and beleaguered 112th Infantry and Task Force Ripple at Kommerscheidt. It did not succeed. Some units became lost in the dense forest, some encountered unexpected resistance, and the entirety of the hurriedly organized task force was thoroughly dissipated. The task force finally dug in on the southern slope of a hill south of Vossenack and screened the withdrawal of the 112th Infantry during the night of November 8.[49]

That night, Private Elliott R. Corbett II, Company "B," 109th Infantry, penned a letter to his wife, Sudie: "I might say with little or no compulsion that I miss you hellishly and I've had enough of humping around Europe. I see nothing in Germany to warrant fighting for any of it and being naturally a peaceful character, I look forward to a long life of security and freedom from the elements which are beginning to pall."[50] On November 19, Corbett was captured after being seriously injured. He died of his wounds two days later.

On November 10, the Germans sent a captured American into the 3rd Battalion, 109th Regiment, lines with a demand by the German commander that the unit should surrender. The 3rd Battalion's commander Maj. Howard Topping answered by American artillery batteries, in which artillery battalions of the corps pounded German positions.[51] The 1340th Combat Engineer Battalion's commander Lt. Col. Truman Setliffe was at the site of the demolished Kall bridge on November 10. When he told his engineers of the German ultimatum to surrender or be slaughtered, they said they would "stick it out and fight. That is what they came for."[52]

This evacuation was difficult, and casualties were heavy; the medical evacuation was particularly complicated and dangerous. Vossenack was the hub of three vital roads and key to the Schwammenauel Dam across the Roer River. The area became known as "artillery alley." German self-propelled, railroad, and field guns poured between 2,000 and 3,000 rounds of artillery shells on units of the 1st Battalion, 112th Infantry Regiment, in a twenty-four-hour period. The only road leading into Vossenack was raked with shell fire every hour of the day.

Despite what seemed to be a hopeless situation, soldiers continued to demonstrate their willingness to fight. For example, during the German counterattack spearheaded by three Tiger tanks, twenty-two-year-old Capt. Clifford T. Hackard, commander of Company "C," waited for the tanks to approach. When one came within 50 yards of his observation post, he fired his only rocket, knocking the tank out of action. As the crew attempted to escape, Hackard killed three and wounded two. Later, while checking defensive positions of his men, a German machine gun began firing. Armed with only a rifle, he advanced toward the weapon, leaped into the emplacement, and killed the three crew members. For his actions that day, Capt. Hackard was awarded the DSC.[53]

With such ferocity of battle, it may be hard to imagine that the two sides actually paused for humanitarian purposes. The fighting was so intense and the casualties so great that not once, but three times over the course of five days fighting was paused to evacuate the wounded. So bloody was the fighting in this area that both sides momentarily tempered their enmity so the wounded could have unencumbered transport to medical support in the rear. The first such respite began on November 7 on the Kall Bridge in the town of Schmidt. The second was arranged by 112th Regimental surgeon Maj. Albert Berndt on November 9 and the third occurred two days later.[54]

With the withdrawal of the 112th Infantry Regiment, the attack on Schmidt was temporarily abandoned. On November 10, the 28th Division were instructed by V Corps' headquarters to secure a line along the north and west banks of the Kall River. It was in the fighting for this ground that the 1st Battalion, 110th Infantry Regiment, suffered their heaviest casualties. On November 14, all attacks by the division had ceased. The men were exhausted. Many of the officers stated that they felt no further attacks could have been carried out even had they been ordered.

The men of the 28th Division faced tremendous adversity in several ways during their time in the Hürtgen Forest. During most of the action, rain, fog, and snow in the latter days prevailed. On the days when it did not rain, low-hanging clouds and ground haze prevented effective employment of the considerable air support allocated to the division. The rain turned the narrow firebreak trails inadequate for use as supply routes or armored employment and maneuver. The trails became rutted, slippery quagmires. Even Jeeps and M-24 Weasels—a tracked vehicle designed for operation in snow—became stuck and were unable to extricate themselves. The extreme wetness made it impossible for the under-equipped troops to protect themselves against trench foot.[55]

On average, only 10–15 percent of the men per company were equipped with all-weather boots; the overwhelming majority endured the entire action without them. Foxholes turned into veritable artesian wells during the latter part of the action. The ground became so thoroughly soaked that it was impossible for the men to keep dry. The "28th Division Surgeon's Report of Casualties" shows 750 cases of trench foot.[56] Robert W. Meyer, Company "B," 112th Infantry Regiment, remembered his first night with the company: "Light rain had started to fall and I thought, good grief, what a miserable existence. The Hürtgen Forest was a bloody battlefield of survival. It was a kill-or-be-killed situation. Military trash was everywhere; discarded C-rations, bandoliers, empty ammo crates, unexploded shells, mess gear, helmets, abandoned stretchers, bloody bandages, and corpses were on the ground, stuck to the bushes, and in the trees."[57]

The soldiers of the 28th Division faced daunting terrain throughout. The attack was made into and through the dense Hürtgen pine forest. Visibility, at its optimum, was limited to 150–200 yards. In places, it was less than 25 feet. As the attack progressed, the constant artillery and mortar pounding of the area knocked off tops of trees, knocked down others, and in places so choked the ground with debris that visibility and movement were tremendously hampered. Warm food could not be brought up through the quagmire and woods until hours after it had been prepared, and when it finally arrived, it was cold and sour. In addition, the attack was made into and through terrain dominated by German-held high ground on the north, east, and south. This enabled the Germans to pour observed and, in some cases, direct artillery fire into the heart of the division attack from an arc of 180 degrees. In the opinion of the 28th Division G-3 (operations officer), Lt. Col. Thomas E. Colonial Briggs, this was one of the greatest single causes for the failure of the troops to achieve success.[58] The road network in the area was limited, and it was inadequate for employment of armor. The route from Vossenack through the draw across the Kall River to Kommerscheidt and Schmidt was little more than a trail. As it turned out, this trail caused the breakdown of the movement of supplies and armored support to the Kommerscheidt area.[59]

Communications, always a problem in battle, were never adequate during the 28th Division's operation. The heavy German artillery and mortar fire constantly knocked out wire communications from battalions to companies, and several times for prolonged periods from regiments to battalions. The most exhausting and tireless efforts of the communications personnel to keep communications open, to keep lines repaired, were unable to keep pace with the rate of communications being knocked out. At night, the messengers groped their way through the tangle of shot-down treetops along the frazzled telephone line in order to patch it up again and again. The lack of communication impacted the entire situation. Lack of situational awareness hampered quick, effective decisions on the part of commanders and increased the demoralization of the men. Orders from commanders were slowed or not received at all, delaying vital redeployments and other actions.[60]

Finally, the performance of the 28th Infantry Division's inexperienced personnel significantly hindered the division. Although the division had received replacements during the month of October, bringing it up to full strength after its attempts to penetrate the Siegfried defenses in September, many of the men were not trained infantry soldiers. Rifle company officers and NCOs, in many cases, had been drawn from anti-tank companies, anti-aircraft units, air force ground personnel, and other non-infantry organizations. Even during the period of comparative quiet that the division enjoyed for a brief period at Camp Elsenborn, Belgium, in October, these deficiencies had not been sufficiently remedied according to Col. Theodore A. Seely, 110th Infantry Regiment commander.[61]

As a result of the inexperienced personnel, when the attack began and the casualties mounted, the loss of the few remaining trained men immediately became apparent. Some infantry soldiers broke and ran in Schmidt, in Kommerscheidt, and in Vossenack. Author Ernest Hemingway spent eighteen days on the front in the Hürtgen Forest. He wrote later: "It was a place where it was extremely difficult for a man to stay alive even if all he did was be there."[62]

As the operation continued, the rapid rate of attrition of the companies, the loss of the few experienced officers and NCOs, and the complete lack of trained replacements contributed to the failure of the mission. For the German's part, they conducted a fanatical defense in terrain completely familiar to them. The German troops fought viciously, gave up some ground, but counterattacked frequently. Their losses were also heavy, yet they succeeded in halting and cutting to pieces the attack of the 28th Infantry Division.[63] Many of the American soldiers came to Europe with the idea that the German soldiers were beaten and were therefore complacent. They quickly found the German soldiers to be determined and fearless fighters.

The 28th Infantry Division's soldiers were fatigued from exposure to the cold and rain and the heavy artillery fire pounding for hours on end. Self-care had become all but impossible. Often the dead could not be buried because there were not enough men available and because the ground was either too sodden, solidly frozen, or rocky. Constantly suffering casualties, the strength of the teams manning the positions was increasingly sapped, and yet the men held their positions, went out on patrols, attacked, overcame their fears, and faithfully performed their duty. Some exhibited bravery that earned them battlefield promotions and awards for valor. Their shared experience created a spirit of fellowship among them where each man was prepared to do the utmost to defeat the Nazis.

The Battle of the Hürtgen Forest was characterized by particular rigor, both with regard to the doggedness and determination of the opponents as well as the terrain and weather conditions. There were many instances of close combat. The soldier was dependent only on himself in this forest with interspersed patches of tangled branches and shrubs. He always had to recon with surprise. Most of the time he could use his weapons only at short distances. He had to be fast and positive with his weapons if he wanted to survive. Many times, success depended decisively on a small number of audacious and bold men, who knew how to enthuse young and inexperienced soldiers and helped them to find their way and hold their own in the uncannily dark forest.[64]

The second attack on Schmidt had developed into one of the costliest U.S. divisional actions in the whole of World War II. After the action in the Hürtgen Forest, the 28th Infantry Division was destroyed as an effective fighting force. The division's combat casualties totaled 6,184, including 614 killed, 2,605 wounded, 855 missing, 245 captured, and 1,865 non-battle casualties. More than 750 of the non-battle casualties were from trench foot alone.[65]

Given the difficulties it faced, the 28th Infantry Division fought well against all odds. For fourteen days, its men struggled over steep hills and fought off infantry and tanks while enduring endless artillery barrages. It crossed between the ridges of Vossenack and Schmidt using no more than a narrow, twisting trail. The division briefly captured the towns of Vossenack, Kommerscheidt, Schmidt, and Simonskall. Private soldiers, NCOs, and company-grade officers who fought on those ridges were brave, courageous, and resourceful. The men knew they were fighting for the American way of life and their chaplains and leaders reminded them.

On November 14, 1944, Ivan (Cy) Peterman of the *Philadelphia Inquirer*, who was embedded with the 28th Division, watched the survivors emerge from their struggle with German forces in the Hürtgen Forest and wrote:

> They crouched in their vehicles, staring straight ahead. If there were heroics to recount, someone else had to talk. The men of this unit (28th Infantry) would not. Too many of their companions remained behind, too many were dead or missing. Too many grievously wounded and shattered in nerves and spirit. If they never saw the Hürtgen Forest again it would suit them.... They had enough.[66]

The soldiers of the 28th Division carried with them a potent belief, fueled by wartime propaganda, that painted them as invincible, capable of conquering any obstacle with unwavering success. This perception, while bolstering their confidence, ultimately met its reckoning in the brutal reality of the Hürtgen Forest. Amid the unforgiving terrain and resolute German defenders, they encountered a formidable adversary that could not be easily overpowered. The Hürtgen Forest became a crucible of harsh lessons, where the soldiers' earlier convictions were challenged by the harsh realities of battle on foreign soil. The propaganda's portrayal of their capabilities was tested, and the cost of war became starkly apparent. Despite the trials they faced, these soldiers held firm to their unyielding motivation to fight for the American way of life.

The soldier's unwavering commitment was a testament to their resilience and the values they held dear. Even as the forest's challenges and the tenacity of the enemy wore away the illusions, the soldiers remained steadfast in their determination to uphold the principles and freedoms that defined their nation. The hardships they endured in the Hürtgen Forest served to strengthen their resolve rather than weaken it. Ultimately, this experience encapsulated the complexities of warfare, where idealism met the harshness of reality. The soldiers of the 28th Division emerged from the Hürtgen Forest with a deeper understanding of the sacrifices and struggles that come with defending their homeland. Their unshakable dedication to the American way of life endured, an enduring testament to the human spirit's capacity to endure and prevail in the face of adversity.

In the wake of the intense battles in the Hürtgen Forest, strategic plans were devised to orchestrate the relief of the battle-weary 28th Division by the 8th Infantry Division. From November 16–21, this intricate transition took place. The baton of responsibility was passed, signaling a respite for the 28th Division, which embarked on a journey southward to Luxembourg, where rest and refurbishment awaited. However, fate had its own designs, and their reprieve was short-lived as an unyielding adversary awaited them. As the soldiers of the 28th Division regrouped, they were poised to confront a fresh test of their mettle. Once again, the crucible of combat beckoned, and their resolve was called upon to endure. This time, their steadfastness would be challenged against an enemy equally determined, their unity forged amid the fire of previous battles proving essential yet again.

The ebb and flow of warfare had taken its toll on the bonds that had formed between the soldiers. The comradery and unit cohesion that had been meticulously cultivated prior to combat had faced the crucible of battle, evolving and sometimes dissolving under the relentless pressures of conflict. The composition of the unit had shifted once more as new soldiers with no combat experience joined the ranks. As these green recruits stepped into the shoes of their predecessors, their motivation was singular and unwavering—to safeguard the American way of life, to stand in defense of the values that defined their nation.

This renewed unit faced the complexities of combat with a fresh perspective, informed by the legacy of those who had come before them. The veterans, who had borne witness to the horrors of battle, found themselves once again amid untested soldiers. Yet despite the changes and challenges, their motivation remained unchanged. The conviction to protect their homeland, to defend the principles that had brought them to the battlefield, anchored their resolve. As the 28th Division prepared to face new trials, their resilience and determination would be put to the test once more. The echoes of previous battles resonated within them, an enduring reminder of the sacrifices made and the ideals for which they fought. In the face of adversity, they were united by the common thread that bound them—the unyielding commitment to the American way of life.

The soldiers did not have an opportunity to record their thoughts when they were in the middle of German artillery barrages. Once they got to Luxembourg, they found time to do so. Private Doyle McDaniel, Company "A," 1340th Engineer Battalion, wrote that his platoon had advanced to the crossroads by a church and were pinned down by German sniper fire. McDaniel climbed onto a shed roof to locate the German positions. As he jumped down, he landed beside a German soldier. Before the man could react, McDaniel shot and killed him. He wrote: "I felt bad about killing the German, but knew I had to. I came to Germany to protect my wife and new baby at home."[67]

Private Clarence Skains remembered that he and Private Nathaniel Quentin, both of Company "M," 112th Infantry, were in Kommerscheidt when a general withdrawal was ordered. No one told them of the order, so they remained in town while around them other members of their squad lay dead in their foxholes. Quentin noticed a platoon of enemy soldiers crawling toward him, their uniforms blending with the saturated ground now covered by falling snow. He allowed them to advance within 25 yards and then opened fire with his BAR, killing twenty and forcing the others to retreat. The Germans attacked again, in one- and two-man rushes, running through a turnip patch toward Quentin and Skains. The men held their ground and fired steadily, and the Germans retreated. Skains wrote that there was no way they were going to withdraw, even if they had received the order to. They came to defeat the Germans, and that is what they were going to do.[68]

Russell Arford of Company "G," 110th Infantry, wrote how concern for a job finally brought him to the Hürtgen Forest. "I signed up in February 1941," he said, "figuring I would get my year of service over with and get out. By 1942, I thought jobs would be plentiful. They were, but I didn't get any of them. I sure chose the wrong time to go in, for I was immediately federalized and in the army until the end of the war." In the Kall Valley, he often wondered if he would ever live long enough to work at any of those jobs. His job now was to fight for the people back home to have jobs.[69]

6

Delaying Actions During the Battle of the Bulge

The Hürtgen Forest was a horrible nightmare, but for the men of the division, it was now over. For some, it was over because they were dead, but for the living, the Hürtgen Forest was now just a bitter memory, albeit one that would never really fade. In just two weeks in the forest, the division suffered over 6,000 casualties. Now platoons were the size of squads, companies were the size of platoons, and battalions were the size of companies. The division had been fighting since July in Normandy and badly needed rest and replacements. Veterans needed time to rebuild their shattered nerves, put the misery of the forest behind them, and maybe enjoy life again. New arrivals needed a chance to ease into their new assignments, make friends, feel a part of something, and learn how to survive in combat. The Ardennes, everyone thought, was the ideal place for this rest. However, Adolf Hitler and the German Army had different plans.

The rest period in the Ardennes presented an opportunity to figure out what went wrong and address some of these fundamental issues of teamwork and cohesion. Facing this task, how was the division able to focus its team building efforts during those critical four weeks to make the division a more effective unit? Some might argue that the division's performance did not improve in the Ardennes, or that the terrain and the defensive mission gave it an advantage. However, the evidence suggests that the division did learn from its experiences and focused its reconstitution efforts to become a more effective fighting force. In fact, several units in the division ultimately earned the DUC (forerunner of the Presidential Unit Citation) for their delaying actions.

The Battle of the Hürtgen Forest revealed leadership issues. Events like the disastrous rout of the 110th at Vossenack and the ill-advised commitments of Task Force Ripple to retake Schmidt proved the division was planning poorly, with inaccurate information. For example, the 112th staff reported the fighting effectiveness of the regiment as excellent, despite the obliteration of nearly the entire 3rd Battalion. The division operations section in turn submitted false reports to Maj. Gen. Cota and the VIII Corps regarding the condition of its subordinate units, which encouraged Cota to order impossible tasks. In addition, communication between commanders broke down at times.

Although leadership improvements and focused training helped, morale remained a complex problem, perhaps the most critical one for the division. Improving morale was paramount to cementing the cohesiveness and effectiveness of the division at all levels but required a holistic approach. The problem of morale took two forms. Replacements, who comprised the bulk of the reconstituted infantry companies after the Hürtgen Forest battle, suffered from the rigors of the individual replacement pipeline, while all soldiers yearned for even a brief sense of normalcy during continuous frontline service. By late 1944, the Army had taken significant steps to address the demoralizing aspects of the replacement system but providing any sense of normalcy near the front required a broader national effort and the right conditions. A few years into the war, the Army realized its individual replacement system was destroying morale. One post-war Army study indicated that the experience of replacements *en route* was so great as to destroy their morale and undo the effects of their training. Often separated from friends, these replacements spent many long weeks in rough transit or sitting in replacement depots in substandard conditions. When they reached the front, units often pushed them straight into battle.

By November of 1944, when the 28th Infantry Division was leaving the Hürtgen Forest, the Army's efforts at improving the morale of the individual replacements had reached their high-water mark, but those alone did not overcome the deficiencies of the system. To make matters worse, the replacements to the 28th Division were joining a unit that had just been demoralized in brutal combat. The surgeon general of the Army summarized how the continuous engagement of divisions, constantly refilled with new replacements during the fighting, had created a vicious cycle with respect to battle fatigue, which no system of individual relief could overcome. Multiple supporting elements pitched in to support and raise morale as well. The quartermaster provided clean clothing and a satisfying Thanksgiving dinner for every soldier. Personnel officers stayed busy handling leave, passes, promotions, and awards.

By mid-December 1944, the 28th Infantry Division had been recuperating and replacing its losses in Luxembourg for approximately three weeks. Although it was located in what was believed to be a quiet sector, U.S. VIII Corps had ordered it to hold a defensive line that would have been in more active combat situations untenable. The division was stretched out on a 25-mile front facing the German lines across the Our River. Such a deployment, with large gaps between position, was thought acceptable for a quiet sector even though by the time of the Normandy invasion, it was generally accepted that a division front should be approximately 8 miles.[1] The division's regiments were arrayed with the 112th Infantry Regiment in the north, linking with the 106th Infantry Division's southern flank, the 110th Infantry Regiment in the center, and the 109th Infantry Regiment in the south, tying in with the 9th Armored Division's northern flank.

The men used the time to make sure that everything was ready for battle again. The ranks were filled with new soldiers to fill vacancies. The replacements were green, but the battle-hardened platoon sergeants knew how to manage them. Ammunition was restocked, vehicles lost in the Hürtgen Forest were replaced, and the veterans had a chance to rest. Luxembourg resident and fifteen-year-old distillery worker Adolphe Betzen remembered that he spent his days with preparations in the distillery. The copper boilers were scrubbed, barrels cleaned, the water bath of the boiler filled with water, and wood laid. The Americans also did routine work, such as cleaning weapons, writing letters, and standing guard. In the evenings, everyone went to bed comfortable, though facing the German forces across the Our River in Germany.[2] The men were thinking of Christmas and going home. They were counting their points to see when they could leave.

It was imperative that the Army find a way to send soldiers home in a prompt manner based on objective criteria. Otherwise, it risked provoking widespread protests from restless soldiers who had no enemy to fight. Soldiers more commonly referred to it as the point system. Under this scheme, every U.S. soldier was awarded a number of points based on how long they had been overseas, how many decorations they had received, how many campaigns they had taken part in, and how many children they had. The men of the division soon stopped thinking about how many points they accumulated as the Germans interrupted their rest. They knew that more work had to be done to secure the American way of life. Map 7 shows the disposition of forces in the Ardennes on December 15, 1944.

As the men rested, chaplains attended to their spiritual needs. Chaplains conducted services throughout the European theater attended by many of the men.[3] Military chaplains were essential to sustaining morale in the European theater. Their jobs were a combination of their calling as ministers of faith and keeping up the morale of the soldiers and reminding the soldiers why they were fighting. The original function of a chaplain was clearly to minister to the religious needs of service men, but they were relied on nearly from the start to serve as the conscience of the Army, to maintain troop morale, and to constantly remind the soldiers why they

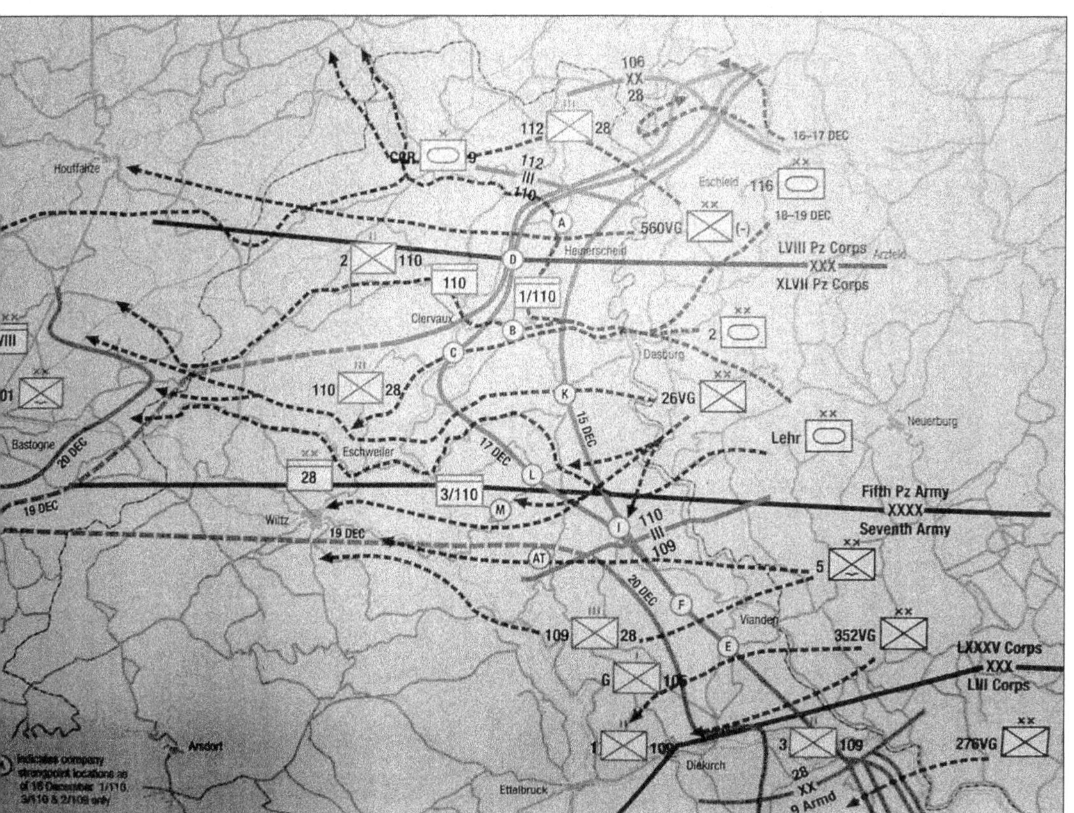

Map 7: The disposition of forces in the Ardennes on December 15, 1944. (*U.S. Army Center of Military History*)

were fighting.[4] Map 8 shows the disposition of American and German forces at the start of the German attack and the position of the Allied front at the battle unfolded.

The positioning of the 28th Infantry Division units allowed for the rotation of soldiers into shelters for rest, minimizing exposure to the tough weather conditions. Soldiers also continued to rotate to divisional and corps' rest centers further to the rear. Some lucky men were able to visit Paris for a few days. "Red Cross clubmobiles and doughnut wagons visited and there was a full schedule of USO (United Service Organization) shows and dances to help raise morale," wrote Geoffrey Perret in *There's a War to be Won.*[5] Despite previous casualties, most soldiers were confident that the end of the war was near—their leaders, from Gen. Dwight D. Eisenhower down, had told them so. A thorough optimism filtered down through command and staff.

Private Robert W. Meyer, Jr., with the 109th, was positioned in Bettendorf. Every three weeks, one battalion would rotate to Diekirch where they could buy sandwiches at the Red Cross Club, get a haircut

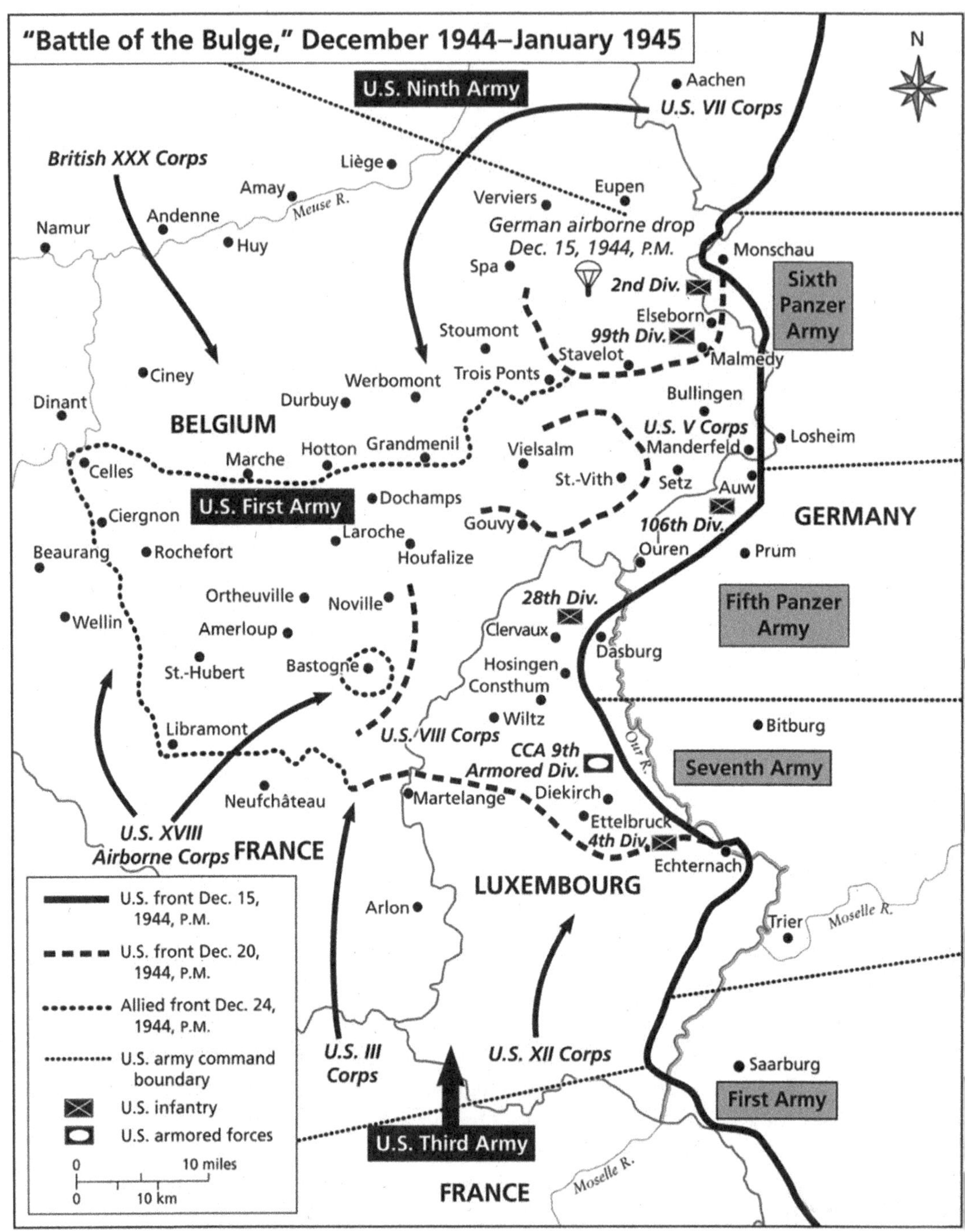

Map 8: 28th Division and German units in the Battle of the Bulge. (*U.S. Defense Mapping Agency*)

from a local barber, attend services at the local churches, or write letters home. While staying in Diekirch, his company had training exercises. Meyer remembered that on one day, they had made a mock attack up a hill. At the completion of the exercise, they were grouped together in a little clearing within a wooded area. An officer, who was not part of their unit, gave the group a peptalk about why they should not be afraid to die. He said as soldiers it was their duty to die if necessary to accomplish a mission. Meyer said: "the lecture was ended with a gung-ho type of question to us troops: What were we to do when encountering enemy troops and what was the best way to avoid being killed by them. The correct answer shouted back, I suspect from a coached GI, was 'Kill the bastards!'" Meyer thought this type of thing was needed by some, but not for him. He knew why he was fighting.[6]

Believing the assurances of their officers that the war would soon end, the soldiers looked forward to a more relaxed Christmas holiday. But even with all the efforts to improve the morale of the soldiers, the weather dampened their spirits. The troops faced freezing rain, thick fog, deep snow drifts, and record-breaking low temperatures. Many people in Luxembourg remember the winter of 1944 as one of the coldest and harshest on memory.[7] Thanksgiving came on November 23 in 1944. For the survivors and replacements alike, there was much to be thankful for. They were secure, warm, and had good food. Some of the men shared their Thanksgiving dinner with the Luxembourgers. The soldiers had established a strong friendship with many of the Luxembourgers. The Americans had liberated Luxembourg, ending four years of German occupation and restoring freedom to a people who yearned for it. The men were proud they had helped free the French people. They had not only fought for American freedom, but also for the freedom of the people of Europe.[8]

The commander of the U.S. Third Army, Gen. George S. Patton, was troubled by the weather. Aircraft were grounded and the conditions on the ground were extremely difficult for the troops. On the morning of December 8, Gen. Patton called the Third Army chaplain, Father James Hugh O'Neill: "This is General Patton; do you have a good prayer for weather? We must do something about those rains if we are to win the war."[9] Chaplain O'Neill looked through the prayer books he had but could not find a prayer for weather, so he wrote one and went to see Gen. Patton with it:

> Almighty and most merciful Father, we humbly beseech Thee, of Thy great goodness, to restrain these immoderate rains with which we have had to contend. Grant us fair weather for battle. Graciously hearken to us as soldiers who call upon Thee that, armed with Thy power, we may advance

> from victory to victory, and crush the oppression and wickedness of our enemies and establish Thy justice among men and nations.[10]

Chaplain O'Neill added a Christmas greeting for the reverse side of the prayer:

> To each officer and soldier in the Third United States Army, I Wish a Merry Christmas. I have full confidence in your courage, devotion to duty, and skill in battle. We march in our might to complete victory. May God's blessings rest upon each of you on this Christmas Day. G.S. Patton, Jr, Lieutenant General, Commanding, Third United States Army.[11]

Gen. Patton approved of the prayer card and instructed Father O'Neill to have it printed and distributed to all soldiers and to put out a training letter on the subject of prayer to all Third Army chaplains to get all the men of the Third Army to pray for the weather to improve. O'Neill typed "Training Letter 5" and the training letter with the prayer cards reached all 486 Third Army chaplains, and every organization commander down to and including the regimental level between December 12 and 14.

"Training Letter 5" not only encouraged the men to pray for the weather to improve, but it also asked them to pray for victory, to pray for the Army, and to pray for "the defeat of our wicked enemy whose banner is injustice and who's good is oppression."[12] Private First Class William Bull, with Company "B" in Marnach, remembered receiving the prayer card and his company commander's instructions to the men to pray for good weather and to pray they would be successful in beating the Nazis. He said it was a reminder of why they were there, not that he needed any reminder.[13]

If the German offensive—code-named *Wacht am Rhein* ("The Watch on the Rhine" is a German patriotic anthem)—was to be successful, it had to accomplish two important objectives. First, German assault companies had to dislodge the American defenders from their positions along the road leading from Ettelbruck/Diekirch in a northern direction towards the Belgian border near Weiswampach. The hard-surface highway (named Skyline Drive by the Americans) gave access to the key towns of Bastogne and St. Vith. The Germans had to reach the far side of the Clerf River before the Americans could react and reinforce the thinly stretched units. Secondly, engineers had to quickly install bridges strong enough to hold armor over the Our River. According to the German plan, all of this had to be accomplished on the first day of the offensive, December 16, 1944. Once they reached the banks of the Clerf River, the Germans had an open shot at the major hub of the area road network, Bastogne. The successful penetration of the 28th Infantry Division lines would place the German elements in the American rear, where few forces existed to counter a determined German thrust.[14]

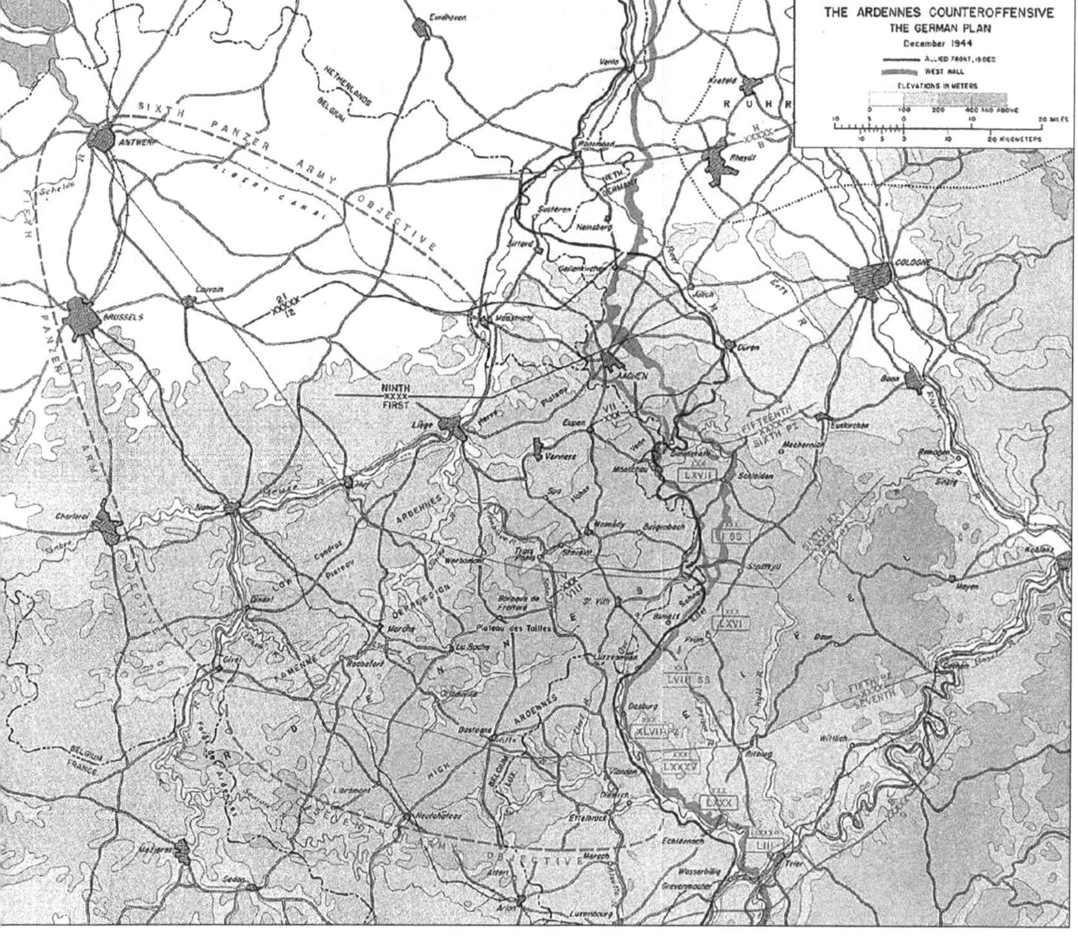

Map 9: The Ardennes counteroffensive, the German plan. (U.S. *Army Center of Military History*)

The German plan of attack was well-developed and had at least some chance of success. The three German armies, the Fifth Panzer, Sixth Panzer, and Seventh Army of the XLVII Panzer Corps, were the maneuver elements for the offensive. Map 9 shows the German plan for their Ardennes counteroffensive, as they termed it.

The German Seventh Army on the southern flank was composed of infantry divisions with no armored support. Its mission was to protect the southern flank of the motorized and armored formations of the other two armies from an expected Allied counterattack from the south.[15] The Fifth and Sixth Panzer Armies were designed to be breakthrough and rapid forces that would race west to the Meuse River and then swing north to capture the deep-water port of Antwerp, Belgium.[16]

On the morning of December 16, 1944, shortly after 5 a.m., the so-called quiet sector in Luxembourg suddenly came to life with a heavy German artillery barrage falling all along the 28th Division's front. The barrage was particularly intense in the Diekirch–Bastendorf area and in the Marnach–Fischbach area. The men of the 28th Division did not realize it at the time, but this was the beginning of the Battle of the Bulge. The victorious optimism of late summer, when "home by Christmas" seemed plausible, had given way to the realization that the Germans were still a tenacious foe—and there was a lot of fighting left to be done.

After the initial artillery barrage, the German assault continued with a massed infantry attack in some sectors and with strong combat patrols probing the line in others. Fighting was particularly heavy in the sectors of the 2nd Battalion, 109th Infantry; the 1st and 3rd Battalion, 110th Infantry; and the 1st Battalion, 112th Infantry. The initial German infantry attacks were repulsed with heavy losses inflicted on the Germans. But, during the day, the German build-up continued, and pressure increased.[17]

On December 16, the 1st Battalion, 112th, was located in the Lutzkampen–Harspelt area, the 2nd Battalion at Leiler, and the 3rd Battalion at Sevenig. At 7:45 a.m., German infantry was observed throughout the regimental sector. The attack came as a surprise. During the period of December 13–15, considerable German truck activity was heard and noticed behind the German lines. This was considered to be the normal traffic necessary for the relief of German troops within the sector. Three weeks previously, the Germans had made such a relief, which created the same sounds.[18]

In the 1st Battalion sector, the Germans attacked with the 1st Battalion, 156th Grenadier Regiment, 116th Panzer Division, and succeeded in penetrating between Company "A" and Company "B." In the 3rd Battalion sector, the attacked was launched by the 1st Battalion, 1130th *Volksgrenadier* Regiment, and 560th *Volksgrenadier* Division, which penetrated the lines between Company "I" and Company "K," overrunning the right flank platoon of Company "L," and reaching the mortar positions, the 3rd Battalion Command Post, and a stone bridge that enabled a line of communications between the 2nd Battalion and the 3rd Battalion.[19]

During the day, the Germans attacked with tanks and infantry in the 1st Battalion area and penetrated into the support positions, to the kitchens, and command post area. Positions were held and the Germans were repulsed, but pockets existed throughout the battalion area. Frank Olsen, Company "A," 1st Battalion, remembered thinking, "Oh no, you don't, you're not going through here. We carried out the order they told us—stay to the end—and that is what we did."[20]

Company "C," 103rd Engineers, and a composite company from the regimental training area counterattacked to force back the German pockets, temporarily restoring the situation. A counterattack was launched by the 2nd Battalion, less one company, in the 3rd Battalion's sector, and their situation was restored. The battalions were again attacked by the German 156th *Panzergrenadier* Regiment of the 116th *Panzer* Division supported by seven tanks in the vicinity of Lutzkampen and by one battalion of infantry in the vicinity of Sevenig. Both attacks were repulsed with heavy German losses.[21]

Late in the afternoon, the Germans employed seven tanks against the 1st Battalion area to overwhelm their defensive positions. The assault was unsuccessful, and one tank was knocked out by a mine. Just before dark, a few German tanks, with flamethrowing devices, attacked the 112th's troops in the vicinity of Lutzkampen. It was estimated that during the day more than 400 German troops were killed and eighty-nine captured.[22]

Private First Class Charles Haug wrote in 1949 about his experiences that winter. Haug recalled that the evening of December 15 came just as all the other evenings had come. Their usual patrol went out in front of their lines and reported back that they had heard or seen nothing.[23] Of the 190 men defending the town of Lutzkampen on December 16, he was one of the twenty-five who survived the Battle of the Bulge without being killed, wounded, or captured.[24]

The next morning, Haug was on guard duty from 4–6 a.m. and remembered wishing that it would soon be 6 a.m. so he could go back and sleep a little bit longer. Little did he know that the little sleep he got that night was the last real sleep he would get for the next ten days. At 5:10 a.m., the sky was illuminated by flares attached to white parachutes with an artillery barrage that followed. Haug was a messenger for his platoon. From 7 a.m. to about 7:30 a.m., there was complete silence in front of Haug's position. It was still semi-dark, except for the light beams coming from the German lines which were aimed into the sky.[25]

A few minutes after 7:30 a.m., Haug experienced what he called perhaps the biggest hair-raising scare of his Army career. Out of the still darkness, he remembered, came the "awfullest screaming and yelling one would ever want to hear." The Germans were advancing and screaming "like a bunch of wild Indians."[26] They came to within 50 feet of Haug's position when the 112th men started firing. The Germans took cover in the ditch of the road they were advancing on. As dawn started to break, Haug and his fellow soldiers could see where the Germans were located. During the first half hour of the battle, the Germans were easy to spot, and many were killed. The men of the 112th had beaten back the first wave of the German attack, but the Germans continued putting on pressure, which began to crumble the American lines. Haug recalled that they still had some faith in the American Army, though, and they prayed that other outfits in the rear would be able to stop the Germans and push them back.[27]

Early on the morning of December 17, after a heavy artillery barrage, the German 60th *Panzer* Regiment of the 116th *Panzer* Division attacked with eighteen tanks along the Lutzkampen–Harspelt ridge in the direction of Ouren. Bitter fighting ensued during the day, and finally, after dark, the Germans infiltrated into Ouren. Fifteen German tanks were disabled and 186 prisoners were taken during the fight. The regiment received orders to withdraw west of the Our River, and during the night of December 17, assumed positions in the Beiler–Leiler–Lansdorn area with the Regimental Command Post in Weiswampach. During the day on December 18, a company of German infantry supported by two tanks attacked between Leiler and Lansdorn. The attack was repulsed with fifteen prisoners taken. The next day, the regiment was pulled back to the vicinity of Huldange where it was attached to the 106th Infantry Division protecting its left flank.[28]

As a result of action during the withdrawal, Lt. Col. William F. Train, executive officer of the 112th Infantry, was awarded the Silver Star for gallantry. Train was in command of a rearguard task force covering the movement of trucks, jeeps, and tank destroyers. Suddenly, a German tank force churned over the rolling hills. The tank destroyers halted and swung their guns to meet the on-rushing Germans. In the ensuing battle, the American convoy was stalled. Vehicles tried desperately to dart out of the line of fire as the tank destroyers and *Panzers* hurled shells at each other. Dashing past the firing guns and exploding shells, Train gathered up scattered elements of the convoy, reorganized the vehicles, and directed the flow of traffic over another route.[29]

The Germans threw more tanks into the fray. While the tank destroyers were engaging, one attacking tank unit from another *Panzer* force attempted to outflank Train's convoy from the front. The convoy swung off the road and bounced over plowed fields, but a half-frozen marsh lay ahead. The leading vehicle plunged into the axle-deep mire, helplessly trapped by the soft mud. Realizing that the marshland would be converted into a death trap for the men and vehicles if discovered by the roving *Panzers*, Lt. Col. Train gathered together a few vehicles and led them back over an open road in plain view of the Germans. Train's gamble was to divert the Germans' attention long enough for the bogged down vehicles to be rescued and permit the main body of the convoy to pick a different route of withdrawal and enable the 112th men and vehicles to reach the safety of Huldange.[30]

Train's decoy convoy raced boldly down an open road and was quickly spotted by prowling German tanks. Believing them to be the initial convoy, they closed in for the kill. Train stopped the smaller convoy, and the men took cover. The armor-piercing shells of the German tanks disintegrated the decoy vehicles; Train's plan had worked. While the Germans were busy raking the decoy convoy, the main convoy was rapidly withdrawing toward friendly lines. Train led the men from the decoy convoy across the German terrain on foot and reached friendly territory without a casualty.[31]

Sacrifice came from not only infantry soldiers and leaders, but also from communications personnel; Private First Class Darius E. Berkey, who was acting message chief for the 1st Battalion, operated a SCR 300 backpack-mounted radio from a house under German fire from 10 a.m. on December 16 to 10 a.m. on December 18. After being shelled out of one house, he entered an adjacent one, which subsequently received eighteen hits from a German tank at point blank range.[32] Before they withdrew, the 112th Infantry Regiment inflicted estimated casualties on the Germans of 1,600, including over 200 prisoners taken and successfully evacuated.[33]

At the beginning of the German attack, the 109th Infantry Regiment headquarters was located at Ettelbruck. Its 2nd Battalion headquarters was located at Bastendorf, with Company "E" in the vicinity of Fouhren; Company "F" in the vicinity of Walsdorf; and Company "G" at Brandenburg. The 3rd Battalion headquarters was located at Bettendorf, with Company "I" in the vicinity of Reisdorf; Company "K" in the vicinity of Hosdorf; and Company "L" in Bettendorf. The 1st Battalion was in reserve located in Diekirch.[34]

Shortly after 5 a.m. on December 16, a heavy artillery barrage started, falling on the entire 109th's regimental front, then held by the 2nd and 3rd Battalions. At 8:20 a.m., both battalions reported strong German patrols operating on the west bank of the Our River in the vicinity of Vianden and Bettendorf. Company "E," 2nd Battalion, reported strong German infiltrations around its right flank in the vicinity of Longsdorf. Company "G" was ordered to move from its position in Brandenburg to the right flank of Company "F," which held the high ground northeast of Brandenburg. This was accomplished and several strong German attacks were repulsed.[35]

During the initial stages of fighting in the 109th's sector, Lt. Col. James C. Rosborough, 107th Field Artillery Battalion commander, organized and led a task force to relieve the pressure on one of his surrounded batteries. The artillery commander personally led a platoon of infantry and two tanks, charged the German positions while firing his submachine gun, and at the same time directed the fire of the two tanks. In the counterattack, the Germans lost 150 killed and 40 captured. Lt. Col. James C. Rosborough was awarded the DSC for his actions.[36]

In another action, Capt. Paul F. Gaynor was directing his anti-tank company into defensive positions when the Germans struck. In the ensuing battle, the 109th's units became scattered, surrounded, and disorganized. Holding a house by himself, Capt. Gaynor killed eight Germans who were supporting a tank with his carbine rifle. When the tank opened fire, blasting the house into rubble in an attempt to trap the lone American officer, Gaynor darted across an open field while German shells tore the ground around him. Reaching the high ground just outside of Diekirch, he discovered only a battered, disorganized force holding the ground. Fearing that the Germans might suspect the strength of his unit, he ran along the hill side firing his pistol in the air to convince the Germans that a powerful force opposed them. For his extraordinary gallantry, Capt. Gaynor was awarded the DSC.[37]

First Lieutenant Moe Katz won the Bronze Star for heroism. Acting as a forward artillery observer for the 108th Field Artillery Battalion, Katz was attached to the 3rd Battalion, 109th Infantry, in the Ettelbruck sector. Moving forward to the Company "L" forward positions, Katz spotted a large German column of regimental strength moving along a road. He radioed the information back to his battalion and to the 109th Infantry's regimental commander. A huge trap was formed and sprung on the unsuspecting Germans, who were moving in as if in a parade formation. At a given signal, all American artillery in the sector fired at the same time, killing an estimated 2,000 Germans. Shortly after, 1Lt. Moe Katz had achieved enough points to be sent home but volunteered for Pacific duty. He said: "I'd feel sort of silly going back to civilian life before this thing blows over."[38]

At 2:25 p.m., the 1st Battalion lost contact with Company "E," which was isolated in Fouhren and under attack by a battalion of German infantry. Company "A" from the 1st Battalion and one platoon of medium tanks was sent north to Longsdorf in an attempt to establish contact with Company "E." They ran into a strong German position supported by three Tiger tanks south of Longsdorf and were held up. At 7 p.m., Company "C" was moved from Diekirch to positions at Brandenburg. During the day, the 3rd Battalion held firm and repulsed several heavy German attacks in its sector.[39] In conjunction with Company "D"'s 1st and 2nd Platoons of heavy machine guns, the 81-mm mortar platoon leaders helped to consolidate and reorganize the unit to resist the Germans.[40]

The second day of the German counteroffensive, December 17, opened with a terrific barrage of artillery in the 109th Infantry sector that started at 5:30 a.m. and lasted until 6:30 a.m. At that time, the 3rd Battalion reported a German attack of approximately two companies in strength. Stiff fighting ensued and the Germans were repulsed. The 2nd Battalion was attacked at the same time in the area of Vianden–Fouhren by a company of infantry and three Tiger tanks. This attack was repulsed with heavy casualties and two battalion tanks were knocked out. Company "A" with a platoon of tanks was still unable to contact Company "E," meeting strong formations of German tanks and infantry south of Longsdorf. The battalion's anti-tank company, which had taken up positions along the road running south from Tandel at the Diekirch–Bettendorf junction, became heavily engaged with approximately two companies of German infantry and three tanks. The attack was repulsed, with 150 Germans killed and twenty-five captured.[41]

A large force of German infantry infiltrated into the gun position area of Battery "A," 107th Field Artillery, and Battery "C," 108th Field Artillery, which brought the attack under direct fire of their howitzers. With the aid of a platoon of infantry and two tanks, the attack was repulsed with heavy German losses. Radio communications was reestablished with Company "E," still isolated in Fuhren, between the hours of 1 a.m. and 4 p.m. Company "B," with four tanks, attempted to link up with Company "E," but by 11 p.m., they had not accomplished their mission. The Germans continued heavy interdictory artillery fire on all positions during the night and extensive patrols and infiltration continued. But as the third day dawned, the lines remained unchanged.[42]

On December 18, Company "K," 2nd Battalion, linked up with Company "A," 1st Battalion, and organized a defense on the high ground south of Longsdorf. At daylight, the Germans heavily engaged the 3rd Battalion, and one platoon of its Company "K" was overrun. Company "C," 1st Battalion, holding positions around Brandenburg, was heavily attacked but repulsed the Germans with no loss of ground. By 12 p.m., Company "B," 1st Battalion, had not been successful in reaching Company "E," 2nd Battalion, meeting heavy resistance south of Fuhren. Some members of Company "B"'s Intelligence and Reconnaissance Platoons made their way to within 200 yards of Fuhren and reported no friendly troops alive in the town. Company E was presumed lost.[43]

The 9th Armored Division, on the 109th Infantry's right flank, withdrew to positions in the vicinity of Ermsdorf at 5 p.m. This left both of the 109th Infantry Regiment flanks wide open, so a withdrawal to positions on the high ground north and east of Diekirch was executed during the evening of December 18. The withdrawal placed the 109th Regiment on commanding terrain in a defensive position. German infantry and armor remained inactive during the withdraw. However, a heavy attack was made in the 3rd Battalion's sector during the morning resulting in 300 Germans dead and eighty prisoners captured. As overwhelming German pressure mounted, the 109th Regiment received orders during the afternoon to pull back to new positions in order to cover the 9th Armored Division's left flank. The 109th Infantry Regiment was then attached to the 9th Armored Division for future operations.[44]

By the aggressive defense of the 109th in successive delaying positions during the beginning of the German attacks, the left flank of the German drive at its base was exposed. The men of the 109th Infantry almost destroyed the entire German 915th and 916th *Volksgrenadier* Regiments and a major part of the 914th *Volksgrenadier* Regiment of the 352nd *Volksgrenadier* Division. Had the 109th not held its ground as long as it did, elements of the 352nd *Volksgrenadier* Division would have more than likely reached the strategic high ground in the vicinity of Heinerscheid–Grosbous–Merzig–Berg, from which it could have launched an attack into the assembly areas of the 80th and 26th U.S. Divisions. By the 109th securing and holding its positions, the U.S. III Corps was able to launch a successful counterattack against the south flank of the German offensive at its base.[45]

Of the frontline positions held by the 28th Infantry Division, the 110th Infantry Regiment occupied the longest and therefore the most tenuous line. The size of the assigned defensive sector precluded the establishment of a cohesive defensive line. Forward elements of the 110th Regiment consisted of only two battalions of the three, because the 2nd Battalion was retained by the division as its only reserve. Thus, two battalions were stretched over a 10-mile front, a length normally occupied by an entire division, and were placed precisely in the middle of the German Fifth *Panzer* Army's line of march. In practice, this meant that various companies were located in strong points and patrols that were regularly sent out to provide a screen in the large gaps between the towns held by the 110th units.[46]

Despite its small numbers, the 110th Regimental Combat Team was assigned a significant task. Its main defensive line ran along Skyline Drive. The road was only a couple of miles west of the Our River. The defensive positions were designed to cover four main east–west roads which ran from the Our River to Skyline Drive and then proceeded west into the heart of Belgium.[47] The inability of armored units to move cross country due to the Ardennes Forest necessitated the Fifth *Panzer* Army to capture and exploit this road network in order to advance.[48]

The three divisions of the German XLVII *Panzer* Corps, two of which were armored, had what seemed to be a fairly easy task to dislodge the two 28th Division battalions stretched over an area too large to hold. The 110th Infantry control of this road network and the German desire to capture it, and to move on to Bastogne, would thrust the men of the 110th Regiment into a major role during the first few days of the Battle of the Bulge. Orders from the division were in effect that every unit and installation was to hold and fight it out at all costs. With that spirit the first day was one of fanatic resistance.[49]

At the beginning of the German attack, the 110th Infantry Regiment headquarters was located at Clervaux. The service company was located at Weicherdange, the cannon company was located at Munshausen, and the anti-tank company was located at Hoscheid. The 1st Battalion Headquarters was located in Urspelt, with its Company A in Heinerscheid, Company B in Marnach, Company C in Munshausen, and Company D in Grindhausen. The 2nd Battalion Headquarters was located in Donnange, with its Company E in Boxhorn, Company F in Eselborn, Company G in Lullange, and Company H in Boevange. The 3rd Battalion Headquarters was located in Consthum, with Company I in Weiler, Companies K and B and 103rd Engineers in Hosingen, and Company L in Holzthum.[50]

By this time, the 110th Infantry Regiment had been upgraded to a regimental combat team, which meant that it was supplied with additional support troops, including armor. After replacing the losses from the Hürtgen Forest battle and adding additional personnel, the regiment reached a strength of about 5,000 men. The standard for a U.S. Army regiment at the time was slightly more than 3,000.[51]

The mission of dislodging the 28th Division defenders from Skyline Drive was given to the German 26th *Volksgrenadier* Division and the 2nd *Panzer* Division. The 26th *Volksgrenadier* Division was to quickly cross the Our River, and while engineers were bridging the river for the 2nd *Panzer* Division to follow, the 26th *Volksgrenadier* was to overrun the positions held by the 110th and advance to the Cleft River. Once this ground had been secured, the 2nd *Panzer* was to race westward and secure Bastogne. According to *Generalmajor* Heinz Kokott, commander of the 26th *Volksgrenadier* Division:

> Success or failure of the entire operation depends on an incessant and stubborn drive westward and northwest. The forward waves of the attack must not be delayed or tied down by any force of resistance. Bastogne should fall on the second day of the offensive or at least be encircled by then.[52]

On the morning of December 16 at 5 a.m., the entire 110th Infantry Regiment front was subjected to a heavy artillery barrage for approximately thirty minutes. From 6 a.m. to 6:30 a.m., it diminished slightly. From 6:30 a.m. to 7:30 a.m., it increased in intensity. At 7:30 a.m., an attack was made by German infantry along the entire regimental front. Enemy armor and more infantry rapidly followed this. As the day progressed, the German build-up in infantry, armor, and artillery was rapid. Communications gradually diminished between the American units as most wire lines were cut early in the day and radio was depended upon for communications.[53]

In the small village of Weiler, Company I, less one platoon in Wahlhausen, was in defensive positions when the German offensive started on December 16 early in the morning. In the early light, the patrol sighted a German force of about 200 men stealthily approaching Weiler through a draw running between the positions of two platoons. Carbine and M-1 rifle fire from the patrol ripped into the German infantry column. The Germans threw themselves behind any cover they could find and laid down such a heavy volume of return fire that the patrol was forced to withdraw to a nearby anti-tank position and seek cover there. At 7:10 a.m., Company I in Weiler observed another German force of about 200 men moving west along the draw between Weiler and Company I's 2nd Platoon. The Germans were riddled with small arms and machine-gun fire and plastered with 81-mm mortar fire. They suffered heavy casualties and hurriedly withdrew. As the day wore on, the attacking Germans exerted continual pressure.[54]

Sgt. Thomas Meller's observation post was behind the enemy lines now. He and a companion had captured two Germans who need medical attention. Meller moved the group to an abandoned farmhouse were a medic bandaged the German's wounds. One of the Germans thanked him for not shooting him and also for dispensing medical care. "I wish to repay your kindness by saving your life and the lives of your men," he said in English. "You have done a commendable job here. There are three hundred companies of three hundred men each, coming down this road. They will take this position. Surrender now and save your life and the lives of your men." Sgt. Meller politely declined, as he thought that the reason he was here was not to surrender, but to defeat the Nazis. Meller and his men were eventually captured by the approaching Germans.[55]

The ammunition situation of the 1st Platoon at the 3rd Battalion observation post became so critical that a call for resupply and tank support was put through to 3rd Battalion Headquarters at about 3 p.m. By nightfall, there was still no sign of the tank platoon which was supposed to bring the ammunition. By then, the men at the observation post and in the 1st Platoon positions were down to their last few rounds of ammunition. Lt. Carl A. Fisher, platoon leader of the 1st Platoon, took the only course left. He called for artillery fire directly on the 1st Platoon and the observation post. Lt. Fisher was awarded the Bronze Star for his actions. Despite the requested artillery fire, the 1st Platoon's positions and the battalion's observation post were overrun. A few of the men from the 1st Platoon managed to work their way back to other American positions. Only one man from the observation post escaped.[56]

Second Lieutenant Jacob P. Welc was awarded the Bronze Star for his action in Weiler. Welc (then an anti-tank squad leader) and his gun squad were attached to Company I, which was located in a forward position along the battalion front. Although superior German forces encircled the town, Welc personally took control of an anti-tank gun and sent round after round of high explosive ammunition into the midst of the onrushing

German infantry. When the supply of high explosive ammunition was exhausted, he started firing armor-piercing shells, and he is credited with killing or wounding four Germans. When his position was overrun, he withdrew his men and conducted a house-to-house battle until they reached the rest of Company I, defending the center of town.[57]

At 8 a.m., Company B, 1st Battalion, reported it was being attacked by a German force estimated at seventy men. All of the Company B men were in prepared positions and still holding. At 8:50 a.m., Company B reported seeing 300 German troops northwest and southwest of Marnach. After contact was lost with Company B, Company A was ordered to send a patrol to Fischbach to link up with Company B. At 10 a.m., Company C was ordered to attack the Germans in Company B's area, as the patrol from Company A was pinned down by German fire in Fischbach and had to withdraw, reporting that 150 Germans were coming up the road to their position. Company C was not able to attack in the Company B area as they became engaged in a considerable fight short of Marnach.[58]

At 11:20 a.m., the battalion ordered two platoons of tanks to proceed from Munshausen to Marnach to link up with Company C and clear resistance. One platoon of tanks went to Marnach and contacted Company C at 4 p.m. The other tank platoon returned to Munshausen. At 4:30 p.m., Company D was ordered to move from Grindhausen to Reuler, just east of Clervaux. The last communication with Company B was made at 6:15 p.m. The company was presumed lost. At 6:30 p.m. Company A reported Germans to its south and north, proceeding west.[59]

Private Ralph Obuchowski, 103rd Engineer Battalion, thought going to Hosingen was like going to Heaven. The town had not yet suffered the ravages of war. It was intact, peaceful, and quiet. There were hot baths, warm beds, and indoor plumbing. Except for pulling guard duty occasionally, there was plenty of time to read, relax, and catch up on letter writing in comfort. The war seemed hundreds of kilometers away. But Hosingen was on the front line.

Private Obuchowski recalled: "Out of Heaven it turned into Hell on Saturday morning, December 16." He and another private were assigned to guard duty. Their station was at a point near the church. Shortly after getting off guard duty, an artillery barrage opened up. Obuchowski and some others decided to take shelter in a cellar. Forty-five minutes later, when the barrage let up, they returned to their quarters to find them completely destroyed. A large piece of shrapnel had penetrated the mattress on Obuchowski's bed.[60]

Later in the morning, Obuchowski's squad was assigned to keep the Germans from attacking across an open field. Armed with their M-1 rifles, they took cover in a barn and fired on the advancing Germans. They were able to repel the attack but started receiving fire from German mortars.

After dark, they made their way back to the center of the town looking for others from their squad and platoon. By daylight on December 17, it was obvious that things had worsened. They could hear German small arms fire. Still left to their own devices, they decided to stay in the building where they had slept to repel any German attempts to take over the building. Just before dark, the Germans attacked, but Obuchowski's squad pinned them down. When it got dark, they retreated.[61]

Early in the next morning, they heard machine-gun fire just down the street. They were told that Capt. William Jarrett, the company commander, after consulting with other officers, decided to surrender. The water was gone, ammunition was low, and the Germans had taken up positions around the town, with infantry and tanks. The men were ordered to destroy everything that might be of value to the Germans, including their weapons. After being searched and relieved of their watches, money, and, in some cases, shoes, the men were marched out of Hosingen toward the Our River and Germany. While the defenders of Hosingen did surrender, they held off the Germans for fifty-two hours.[62]

Holding at all costs meant that by the end of the day the situation for many units was costly. Some elements experienced heavy losses and could not continue to fight as a combat unit. The order to hold at all costs had a chilling effect on the soldiers but did not dampen their resolve. As darkness approached on December 16, many units were running low on ammunition, and all were surrounded. Still, with their staunch defense, they were stalling, creating the time necessary for reinforcements to arrive. Furthermore, they were depriving the German mobile units of the speed they needed and, most important, time they could not afford to lose. Gen. Hasso von Manteuffel, commander of the Fifth *Panzer* Army, described the action of the first day:

> The Clerf River was not reached at any point. The enemy was unquestionably surprised by the attack: he offered, however, in many places tenacious and brave resistance in delaying by skillfully fought combat tactics. His counterattacks, which started at once, partly supported by small, armored groups, resulted in many points in critical situations. The tenacious resistance of the enemy together with the roadblocks placed were the most essential reasons for the slowing up of the attack whose timing was not going according to plan.[63]

The continued presence of the 110th Infantry Regiment strong points on the vital road networks completely upset the German timetable for the first day. Gen. Kokott's division needed to cross the Clerf River by nightfall, and its failure to do so was directly attributed to the stand of the men of the 110th Infantry. The 2nd *Panzer* needed to clear Clervaux and Marnach of American strong points to open the good hard-surfaced road westward.[64] By the end of the first day, the 2nd *Panzer* controlled neither.

The combative spirit of the 110th's men was, in some respects, equally bad for the Germans, who struggled to gain control of the roads.
That combative spirit tempted many German units to diverge from the tactics they were ordered to use in the Ardennes. As noted by Charles MacDonald in *Time for Trumpets*, according to instructions from Gen. Manteuffel and Gen. Kokott, the men of the 26th *Volksgrenadier* were to use the "Hutier" or infiltration tactics and bypass strong points of resistance, pressing on to their objectives.[65] However, the Germans were all too often unable to avoid a fight. "As they moved toward their objectives, they were like a man who tries to sneak past a hornet's nest, only to find the hornets swarming him so furiously that he has to stop and try to destroy them," wrote MacDonald.[66]

Early in the afternoon of December 16, when it became apparent that the command post would have to be evacuated, the regimental commander, Col. Hurley T. Fuller, called for volunteers to remain with the wounded as they could not be moved. Maj. L. S. Frogner, regimental surgeon, was the first to volunteer along with other medical personnel, and two chaplains with their assistant Cpl. Carl Montgomery.[67]

At 2 a.m. on December 17, Battery A, 109th Field Artillery, located at Hupperdange, reported German troops overrunning its position. The 1st Battalion lost contact with the battery at 2:45 a.m. At 8:30 a.m., four light tanks of the 707th Tank Battalion reported to the battalion headquarters, having made the run from Heinerscheid to Fischbach to Urspelt. The 707th lost fourteen tanks along the road. At 1 p.m. Company A reported being attacked by seven German tanks at Heinerscheid. The battalion lost contact with Company A at 1:30 p.m. Company D reported a German company between its position at Reuler and Clervaux at 1:35 p.m. At 3:30 p.m., Company D reported it was abandoning Reuler. Contact was lost with Company D at 3:30 p.m. At 4:50 p.m., four German tanks supported by infantry opened fire on the battalion headquarters. At 5:30 p.m., all contact was lost with the 1st Battalion, and it ceased to operate as a unit.[68]

Col. von Lauchert, commander of the 2nd *Panzer* Division, was concerned about the division's slow rate of advance. Clervaux was a main objective of the tank drive on Bastogne because of its strategic location on the main highway leading to Bastogne. Clervaux should have fallen before noon on the 16th according to the original German timetable. Instead, the Americans continued to hold this key position on the morning of the 17th. A single 57-mm anti-tank gun guarded the bridge near the railroad station where the road coming down from the north entered the town. It was at this anti-tank gun position that 1Lt. Kenneth G. Maddox of HQ Company, 2nd Battalion, 110th Infantry, directed the gun crew in a last desperate attempt to keep the Germans out of Clervaux.[69]

The crew members of the anti-tank gun were so busy firing at the oncoming tanks that they did not notice an infiltrating German soldier moving up on the flank of the gun position. Maddox saw that the German soldier was about to fire at the gun crew and realized after he shouted a warning to them that his men could not hear him above the noise of the battle. There seemed only one other course of action to him. He leaped in front of his men, firing at the German grenadier. As he did so, Maddox received the full burst from the German's machine pistol in his chest. Maddox's sacrifice was in vain as a tank-infantry team from the 2nd *Panzer*'s 2nd *Grenadier* Regiment obliterated the anti-tank gun and breached the defenses of Clervaux.[70]

Maddox, severely wounded, was evacuated by the Germans to one of their field hospitals, where he died of his wounds on Christmas Day. He was posthumously awarded the Silver Star for his actions that day in Clervaux.[71] Private First Class William Bull remembered watching the tanks coming down the road along the narrow ravine that led into Clervaux. "I was scared. I wanted to get out of there, but I knew we had to stay and fight. We couldn't let the Germans beat us, so we prayed."[72]

At 6 p.m., German tanks and infantry had penetrated to within 50 yards of the regimental command post and were firing into the Hotel Claravallis, which was being used as the command post. At 7:30 p.m., the German infantry moved in and occupied the first floor of the hotel. The regimental headquarters' personnel escaped through a second-floor window and regrouped in Allerborn on the morning of December 18.[73]

At 9 a.m., the 2nd Battalion, 110th Infantry, minus Company G, was alerted for movement. At 1 a.m. on December 17, the battalion was ordered to assemble in an area just south of Donnange. It received orders to secure a road junction a quarter of a mile north of Clervaux and to attack and capture Marnach. At 7:30 a.m., the battalion crossed its line of departure, the Clervaux–Bastogne Road just north of Clervaux with Company F on the left and Company E on the right. Almost immediately, both companies were heavily engaged by German infantry and tanks. The battalion, plus supporting tanks and tank destroyers, inflicted heavy losses on the Germans and advanced, retaking Reuler. At 4 p.m., German infantry (supported by an estimated twenty tanks) attacked, forcing both companies back approximately 500 yards, where they dug in about 200 yards west of Reuler.[74]

Ralph Johnson of the 110th Infantry recalled how his faith was tested during the Battle of the Bulge: "The peaceful village of Clervaux, Luxembourg took a look of a nightmare. Communications were impossible. The enemy quickly attacked our strongpoints and smashed its way into our center. The men rolled with the punch, fighting, falling back, defending each crossroad and strongpoint with everything they had. I had faith we would prevail though. We were fighting for the right reasons and God was on our side."[75]

The German attack of tanks and infantry that destroyed Maddox's gun position continued its advance, capturing the regimental command post. At 11:59 p.m., Col. Hurley E. Fuller, the regimental commander, issued orders for the companies to break up into groups of squad size and withdraw west to Donnage, to assemble and await orders. There were a few men remaining in Clervaux by the evening of the 17th. In the castle across town, which dates back to the twelfth century, the officers and men from the regimental headquarters company and a scattering of other units were still holding out. On the morning of December 18, the defending force had run out of ammunition and parts of the castle were set ablaze by German artillery and tank fire. The group decided to surrender at 1 p.m.

By 7 a.m. on December 18, approximately seven officers and sixty men had arrived at the assembly area, in addition to the whole of Company G. Defensive positions were prepared in the vicinity of Donnage. At 8 a.m., the German infantry attacked from the northeast. The defending force was driven from their positions to near Hamiville. At 7 p.m., German tanks and infantry attacked through Hamiville southwest on the main highway, isolating the regiment. Another attack followed, overrunning the position. This was the last action of the 2nd Battalion as an organized force.[76]

In the 3rd Battalion, 110th Infantry sector, Company I observed approximately 200 Germans infantry troops approaching Weiler from the woods east of their position at 6:15 a.m. on December 16. The German column was fired on and dispersed. At 7:30 a.m., Company K reported that a few German infantry troops had infiltrated into Hosingen but were killed. At 10:30 a.m., Company L observed a German force south of Holzthum moving west to attack Consthum. Company L alerted Consthum and opened fire on them.[77]

After five attacks had been repulsed by using direct fire from 105-mm howitzers from Battery C, 109th Field Artillery Battalion, and multiple .50-caliber machine guns from an attached anti-aircraft unit, the Germans withdrew at 1:30 p.m. At 6:30 p.m., the battalion observation post and the 1st Platoon of Company I were overrun by German tanks and infantry at Wahlhausen-strasse. In Weiler, Company I had repulsed six attacks on the town, until the Germans completely surrounded the town. Company I split into two groups and attempted to fight its way north to Consthum to join the 3rd Battalion. At 10:30 p.m., twenty men from Company I made their way into Consthum.

On December 17 at 2:30 a.m., two German tanks accompanied by infantry attacked Company L in Holzthum. Fighting continued in the town throughout the night and the German tanks and infantry were driven out of the town. At 3:30 p.m., Company L was ordered to withdraw from Holzthum and establish defensive positions around Consthum. German tanks clanked into the village. The tanks roared down the village street, methodically blasting gaping holes into houses, while supporting infantry sprayed the area with small arms fire. Company L's radio came on the air, "Town completely surrounded with enemy tanks and infantry. Running low on ammunition. Waiting further orders. Over." Maj. Harold F. Milton, 3rd Battalion commander, who had been trying to reach the company, ordered the company commander to withdraw his men if possible. A reply came back on the radio, "We can't get out, but the Germans are going to pay if they try to get in." Early in the morning, a young lieutenant came on the radio to report that his men were fighting from house to house with no ammunition except grenades. He said: "We've blown everything there is to blow except the radio, it goes next." And then over the headset came the sound of a man sobbing. "I don't mind dying. I don't mind taking a beating," said the lieutenant. "But I'll be damned if we'll give up to these bastards." The radio clicked off, and shortly before 12 p.m. went dead.[78]

At 1 a.m., Company K in Hosingen reported it was encircled and running low on ammunition. The battalion commander ordered Company K to attempt to withdraw to Consthum. Company K replied that it was impossible and that it would hold the position as long as possible. The last contact with Company K was at 10:07 a.m. The company was presumed lost.

At 5 a.m. on December 18, a heavy artillery barrage fell on Consthum, now defended by the battalion's HQ Company, Company M (reduced), and Company L. Three German infantry attacks were repulsed during the morning. SSgt. Edger E. Ridenour, Company L, volunteered to locate and destroy German tanks menacing his company's position. While repairing a damaged bazooka he had located in a nearby field, Ridenour was conspicuously outlined in the bright glow of flares fired by the Germans. During the brightness of the flares, he noticed German tanks maneuvering into position on his right and a long column of German troops advancing toward the town. Lacking protective cover and armed with only a carbine rifle, he crawled back a few yards after the flares burned out and secured a 60-mm mortar from an abandoned reconnaissance car.[79] Plainly in the view of the Germans, SSgt. Ridenour held the mortar between his legs aiming only by the burst of his own weapons and fired at the advancing German unit until his ammunition supply was exhausted. By his courageous stand, Ridenour inflicted enormous casualties on the Germans and delayed the capture of Consthum. He was awarded the Silver Star for his actions.[80]

At 1 p.m., German tanks and infantry overran the defenses north and south of Consthum. At 1:30 p.m., the battalion commander ordered a withdraw to Kauthenbach. The battalion then withdrew to Nocher and established a perimeter defense of the town.[81]

Before the withdrawal, First Sergeant Sam J. Pizzo's actions earned him the Silver Star; Pizzo was part of HQ Company of the 3rd Battalion, 110th Infantry.

When a strong German force led by Tiger tanks surged toward the town, Sergeant Pizzo, without orders and acting on his own initiative, maneuvered to the forward edge of town with a bazooka in an attempt to delay the Germans armored advance. He was successful in halting the advancing tanks long enough for friendly artillery to demolish one of the tanks and force the others to retreat. Later when the security of the battalion's HQ became threatened by the Germans, Pizzo bravely remained to destroy all secret documents despite the fact orders were given to evacuate. He escaped to the outer edge of town and while under fire erected a roadblock that delayed German vehicles sufficiently for friendly troops to escape entrapment.[82]

Even though the German assault was devastating, the American leaders did what they could to protect their men. For example, on December 18, when a concentrated German attack overran his forward positions, Capt. Anthony J. Nastasi (HQ Company, 3rd Battalion) disregarded heavy German artillery fire and advancing German tanks, cleared his men from houses and installations in the area, and directed them to the far edge of Consthum.[83]

In view of the wide area occupied, the resultant gaps between units, lack of depth to the positions, and absence of reserves, the 110th Regiment was able to mount local independent delaying actions against an overwhelmingly superior German force advancing through them. Small, isolated units and detachments of clerical, communications, and service personnel effected considerable disruption to the German plan of attack. In many instances, the men held at all costs, to the point that there were no survivors. In his request for the Presidential Unit Citation for the 110th Infantry Regiment, 28th Infantry Division Commander Brig. Gen. Basil H. Perry wrote:

> The conspicuous gallantry, heroism, and determination of the 110th Infantry to hold at all costs for nearly 96 hours without sleep, without food, without reinforcements and under the most adverse climatic conditions, upset the timetable of Rundstedt to reach Bastogne on the 16th of December as substantiated by maps and orders captured and forwarded to the VIII U. S. Corps, and contributed materially to the

> successful defense of Bastogne and to the defeat of the enemy in the Ardennes; and reflect the highest traditions of the Armed Forces.[84]

Stationed with the 28th Infantry was the 630th Tank Destroyer Battalion with 3-inch towed guns. Company A and the 1st Reconnaissance Platoon supported the 109th Infantry Regiment in the area of Ermsdorf, Gilsdorf, Bettendorf, Reisdorf, Beaufort, and Sauelborn. Company B and the 2nd Reconnaissance Platoon supported the 110th Infantry Regiment along the Heinerscheid–Marnach–Hosingen line. Company C had guns on both sides of the Our River supporting the 112th Infantry Regiment, its positions extending from Weiswampach to the vicinity of Lutzkampen. As the German offensive began, the men of the 630th Tank Destroyer Battalion contributed greatly to delay the Germans long enough for reinforcements to be brought up on the shoulders of the bulge. The 1st Reconnaissance Platoon in Marnach was encircled by the Germans but continued to hold a vital road network until the Germans employed tanks and infantry on the night of December 18. The battalion lost twenty-four of thirty-six towed guns, but destroyed twenty-eight German tanks, two 88-mm guns, thirteen other vehicles, and numerous other equipment, as well as killing several hundred Germans.[85]

Many of the 28th Infantry defenders recognized that they were surrounded and that there was no relief or escape, save as prisoners. Yet despite this sober conclusion, they continued to resist until there was simply no other means to resist. The stand of the men of the 28th Infantry Division had indeed been stubborn. In the first three days of fighting, heavy casualties had been inflicted on the German forces. The exact toll they extracted from the Germans is difficult to determine. In 1979, the Army officially recognized that the 28th Infantry Division cost the Germans over 12,000 casualties in the Ardennes campaign.[86] The 112th Infantry Regiment was awarded the DUC for its performance during the Battle of the Bulge. The citation reads:

> The 112th Infantry Regimental Combat Team consisting of the 112th Infantry Regiment with the 229th Field Artillery Battalion, Company C, 103rd Engineering Battalion, Battery C 447th Antiaircraft Battalion and Company C, 640th Tank Destroyer Battalion attached is cited for extraordinary heroism, efficiency and achievement in action against the enemy from 16 to 24 December 1944. On 16 December 1944 the 112th Infantry Regimental Combat Team from Lutz Kampen, Germany to Lieler, Luxembourg, was holding 6-1/2 miles of the front line sector assigned to the 28th Infantry Division. During the period 16 to 18 December 1944, despite repeated infantry and tank attacks involving the elements of nine enemy divisions, the 112th Infantry Regimental Combat Team held its

> ground. In this period, it inflicted estimated casualties on the enemy of 1,600, including over 200 prisoners taken and successfully evacuated. All elements of the 112th Infantry Regimental Combat Team were involved in this action. The 229th Field Artillery Battalion was engaged in direct fire on the enemy at a range of 150 yards. The Cannon Company of the 112th Regiment and Company C 630th Tank Destroyer Battalion, by direct fire, succeeded in disabling 18 enemy tanks. Company C 103rd Engineering Battalion together with the 2nd Battalion 112th Infantry Regiment, repeatedly counterattacked enemy penetrations. The Headquarters, Headquarters Company and Service Company manned the lines and drove off by fire a number of groups of the enemy which had infiltrated into the rear areas. The Kitchens, being overrun on night of 16–17 December 1944, the kitchen personnel fought with rifles to recover the positions. All this was done under withering small-arms and artillery fire from enemy positions throughout the entire front.
>
> On the night of 17–18 December 1944, under orders from higher headquarters, the 112th Infantry Regimental Combat Team was withdrawn to the high ground west of the Our River. This withdrawal was accomplished successfully in spite of strong enemy infiltrations throughout the entire sector. From 18 until 23 December 1944 the 112th Infantry Regimental Combat Team was continually engaged in rear guard action covering the withdrawal of the right flank of the First American Army. On the night of 23–24 December 1944, the action of the 112th Infantry Regimental Combat Team was especially notable. Being ordered by higher headquarters to act as a covering force for units withdrawing to the American lines, it held its position under furious enemy infantry and tank attacks until the Regimental Headquarters and 1st Battalion 112th Infantry were surrounded. The 1st Battalion then fought its way clear to friendly lines, bringing with it a number of vehicles and personnel of other units. The gallantry under extremely hazardous and physically trying conditions, the stubborn defense of the sectors assigned to them, and the heroic conduct of all personnel of the 112th Regimental Combat Team, in nine days of continuous fighting, exemplify the highest traditions of the armed forces of the United States.[87]

Supporting the 28th Division was the 103rd Medical Battalion. Three collecting companies were in operation, each supporting its respective regiments. Company A was located at Petitvoir, Belgium; Company B was one mile west of Straimont, Belgium; and Company C was located at Bomal, Belgium. The division clearing station had one platoon in operation at Epioux, Belgium. The other platoon was in reserve at Chiney, Belgium. The location of adjacent medical units and supporting elements were:

1. Right flank: Collecting-Clearing Company of Combat Command "A," 9th Armored Division, Longlier, Belgium.
2. Left flank: Division Clearing Station, 87th Infantry Division, Bouillon, Belgium.[88]

Supporting the evacuation of the division clearing station were:

1. Ambulances of the 595th Ambulance Company, 170th Medical Battalion, 64th Medical Group, Gerouville, Belgium.
2. Casualties were being evacuated to the 107th Evacuation Hospital at Sedan, France and 635th Clearing Station at Villers, France.
3. During December, the following units also services this battalion: 580th Ambulance Company, 32nd, 102nd, 103rd, 106th and 110th Evacuation Hospitals, the 42nd Field Hospital, the 130th General Hospital, and the 618th Clearing Station.

The medical battalion continued to carry out its normal function of supporting the 28th Division by evacuating, treating, and disposing of the casualties of the division. During the first half of the month, the division carried out defense operations on a wide front. The width of the front and concurrent wide separation of the medical units necessitated the split of the clearing company, with sections so located as to best support the collecting stations.

During the first half of the month, with a very low division casualty rate, a training and re-equipping program was continued, and efforts were made to correct any deficiencies previously noted. All of the units were comfortably billeted in available buildings, and all stations were likewise set up in comfortable surroundings.

In the latter half of the month, the Germans on the front became most active and aggressive. The medical units were constantly subjected to shell fire and sometimes small arms fire. They were forced out of their positions by the tactical situation which became very fluid. The units were kept on the move continuously endeavoring to best continue the support of the tactical units and avoid capture by the Germans. Companies A and C with their regiments, were attached temporarily to other Divisions as the tactical situation caused the release from control by the Division. The clearing station supporting Company A remained with that other division combat team until the 109th Regiment rejoined the Division. Company B continued to evacuate casualties to the clearing station, and when conditions allowed, established medical department straggler points for the division. Company B also examined all stragglers for medical disabilities, as in a most critical period, it was necessary for the Division to use all available personnel and stragglers for the defense of the front. Medical service in these rapidly changing situations, was maintained by the formation of provisional medical detachments to serve the hastily organized defense units, utilizing medical personal and equipment from available medical detachments, the collecting company and medical department stragglers. The results of operations were:

1. Company A: 573 patients
2. Company B: 418 patients
3. Company C: 515 patients
4. Clearing Company: 1,958 patients (including 151 Germans and thirty-five civilians)

In a war, heroes and heroic actions are important, and it is important to publicize them as the epitome of American valor and thus strengthen both units and the war effort. Bastogne is a superb example of the American soldier, standing his ground and holding his position against all odds and winning. Conversely, it is recognized that valorous stands do not always result in holding one's position and emerging intact from the fray. Sometimes valorous actions result in the destruction of a command rather than its survival, but the valorous act still produces an advantage for their country. In such a case, their valor is no less deserving of recognition and study. Such was the case of the men of the 28th Infantry Division. They came to Europe to fight for freedom and the American way of life and did the best they could.

The historical record clearly shows that for the first three days of the Battle of the Bulge, the men stood in their assigned positions denying the German Army clear access to the road networks that it so desperately needed. For the perspective of Col. Meinrad von Lauchert, the commander of the 2nd German *Panzer* Division during the battle, see Appendix VIII.

Without the desperate stand by the division, which had been so recently mauled in the Hürtgen Forest, the Germans would have, in all likelihood, been able to follow their schedule and would have achieved far more of their Ardennes Offensive objectives. In fact, without the determined resistance of the 28th Infantry Division, there may never have been a defense of Bastogne by the 101st Airborne Division. As the months and years passed many of the veterans reflected on why they fought so heroically against the Nazis.

7

Motivating Factors in the Words of the Veterans

Many Americans viewed the issues at stake during World War II in terms of clearcut right and wrong: democracy against fascism, defense against aggression, good against evil. The country showed remarkable unity in support of a conflict that seemed good and just. Dissenters were few and silent. Stephen Ambrose captured their feelings, "At the core, the American citizen soldiers knew the difference between right and wrong, and they didn't want to live in a world in which wrong prevailed."[1]

The press corps that was stationed in Europe did their best to keep the American population informed of what their boys were doing overseas. Larry Newman, with the International News Service, who covered Patton's Third Army and was embedded with the American troops in Belgium, wrote the article published in newspapers across America "A Saga of Gallant Men; How Heroic 28th Halted Nazis And Saved Our Armies," on January 6, 1945. Two Pennsylvania war correspondents, Morley Cassidy with the *Philadelphia Sunday Evening Bulletin* and Ivan H. (Cy) Peterman from the *Philadelphia Inquirer*, both who were embedded with the 28th Division, told heroic stories of the men of the division.[2] One such article written by Morley Cassidy ended up in the *Kansas City Star* newspaper. In his dramatic style, he wrote: "They battled all day into the next. Then, late Sunday, encircled, their ammunition gone, they radioed their battalion that the situation was critical. They were ordered to withdraw if possible. Two company commanders radioed back. We can't get out but will make them pay. They fought to the last man..."[3] Cy Peterman wrote an article on November 16, 1944 about the 28th Division in the Hürtgen Forest, titled "Great Unsung Battle of the 28th Division": "In the Hurtgen Forest, that gloomy expanse below Aachen, where trees, terrain, and weather, even without entrenched Germans, make formidable opposition, and mud-sluiced roads and clinging snow penetrate like a plague in the bones, American troops fought a great but unsung battle for freedom."[4]

Stephen Ambrose hypothesized:

> Cause and country were as critical to the GIs as to the Civil War soldiers. The differences between them were not of feeling, but of expression. Civil War soldiers were accustomed to using words like duty, honor, cause, and country. The GIs did not like to talk about country or flag and were embarrassed by patriotic bombast. While they may not have said that they were fighting for the American way of life, they were all proud Americans and believed in their cause. They knew they were fighting for decency and democracy and they were proud of it and motivated by it.[5]

While few 28th Infantry Division veterans talked or wrote about the ideology of America's involvement in the war or their specific religious beliefs, some did keep a diary of their experiences during the war. Others, participated in interviews and after-action reports shortly after their battle experience. Others reflected on the reasons for fighting in interviews conducted by the U.S. Army European theater Historical Section in September 1944 and January 1945. Other veterans participated in interviews conducted by the 28th Division Historical Section in December 1988. Many soldiers commented about their reason for fighting in wartime logs, journals, after-action reports, and diaries kept during the war. During the war, the YMCA distributed logbooks to prisoners through the International Red Cross. They served as sketch books, journals, autograph books, cookbooks, song books, scrapbooks, and photo albums.

The men of the 28th Division were reminded of why they were fighting by the actions of the German SS troops. Some German units, in particular the SS units, refused to take prisoners during the Battle of the Bulge.[6] The most famous incident occurred near Malmédy, a Belgian village just a few miles above Luxembourg and west of the German border. Early on the afternoon of December 17, the Germans overran Battery B of the 285th Field Artillery Observation Battalion, all of whom promptly surrendered. After briefly interrogating the men, including medics wearing red crosses, they were lined up and gunned down with machine guns, rifles, and pistols.[7] Word of the massacre spread like wildfire in unit newsletters, even to the soldiers in the middle of their own fight, causing Americans to stiffen their defenses, eliminate surrender (if possible), and become more determined to destroy Hitler's army.[8, 9]

American chaplains in Europe after D-Day did more than stay with their units during heavy combat. They worked alongside medics to care for the wounded and became litter bearers. After the massacre at Malmédy, many chaplains discovered they could not turn the other cheek. Chaplain Leo Weigel told the men he was with that the SS was "a menace that should be exterminated now because it will not be checked any other way."[10] Jesuit historian Donald F. Crosby discovered that the troops no longer viewed SS troops as well-trained elite fighting men. They now saw the storm troopers as evil animals deserving extermination.

Jewish chaplains, as well as Christian priests and ministers and the troops who battled their way across France, Belgium, Luxembourg, and the Low Countries and onto the German fatherland, increasingly saw that they were fighting for much more than the liberation of German-occupied countries and the silencing of German guns. They were fighting to stop a well-planned and organized program of genocide designed to eliminate all Jewish people from the earth. Rumors of Nazi atrocities against Jews, as well as eyewitness accounts of mass executions, had been circulating since the late 1930s.

Faith was an important factor for the soldiers during World War II. In a 2004 article for *The Spokesman-Review*, writer Katharine Goodloe captured some reflections by war veterans on faith in God. These reflections were indicative of most of the men of the 28th Division. "When you're in combat, you pray for safety, you pray for deliverance, you pray to stay alive. It's not always apparent how it's going to happen. It's a leap of faith," commented Norman Ford.[11] Jonnie Henderson said: "When I wasn't actually in combat, I was thanking the Lord for getting me through the day or asking his help to get through the next. When I stepped out of that foxhole and wasn't killed, I knew that the Lord was right there with me." Robert Brooks commented, "I think we all had faith.... We all had faith and knew that everything would work out. We had faith in our fellow man and in our military. We knew that we would overcome. And we had faith in God. We knew he was on our side."[12] Henry Greenbaum recalled: "I always prayed every day, quietly, to myself, for God to help me make it another day. I never gave up my faith."[13]

Robert E. Merriam was the chief of the Ardennes section of the U.S. Army Historical Division, and he had the opportunity to interview leaders, talk with German officers, and examine battle records on both sides. He recalled that "to the highly disciplined Germans, American normal unmilitary bearing, and apparent lack of discipline seemed completely contrary to their conception of a good soldier. The Germans felt that the American soldier was inexperienced, not completely interested in the war, and somewhat slipshod in his methods."[14] These same Germans were unable to comprehend the sudden stiffening of the backbone, the complete change of attitude which occurred when the 28th Division seemed trapped. When the first hours of the Battle of the Bulge seemed like chaos, the Germans wrung their hands with glee and said, "Did we not tell you that the Americans were cowards; did we not say they would wilt if surprised and overwhelmed?"[15]

The Germans failed to understand the psychology of the American soldier. As the initial shock wore off, and the terror and dismal uncertainty of those first hours diminished, a perceptible change swept through the 28th Division's ranks. The grim truth suddenly dawned on the dazed troops and leaders. The war was far from over. Americans buckled down to the grim business of killing Germans in large numbers. The soldiers forgot for the moment their desire to get home and remembered why they were fighting.[16] The following vignettes are examples of how soldiers felt about why they were fighting. In each case, they reflect the concept of fighting for the American way of life. Their comments answer the question of why the 28th Division soldiers fought so fiercely against the Germans during the first days of the Battle of the Bulge.

Cedric Foster Broadcast, January 19, 1945

Cedric W. Foster was the top news analyst for the Mutual Broadcasting System. He was best known for his 'News Out of Europe Tonight' broadcasts during World War II.

> This is Cedric Foster speaking from the studios of WNAC in Boston, the key station of the Yankee Network in New England.... Morley Cassidy of North American Newspaper Alliance, who is accredited to the United States 28th Infantry Division, has told today, for the first time, the story of the 28th Division's heroic stand in the German breakthrough of last December. He said that it is the "merest justice to declare that the Keystone 28th Division, under the command of Major General Norman D. Cota, deserves equal credit with the gallant 101st Airborne for stemming the German drive." Three days before the 101st began its stand, the men of the 28th Division were taking the full brunt of von Rundstedt's mightiest offensive in Luxembourg, they were fighting desperately in hundreds of scattered battles.
>
> Cassidy revealed that on the 15th of December the 28th Division was stretched as tight as a fiddle string along a twenty-five mile front of the Our River. This front extended from the northeastern tip of Luxembourg to the area of Wellendorf at the mouth of the Sure River. It was the widest front held by any division in Europe, five times the length of a normal division front and bigger that the front of some army corps. It was recorded as a rest area. The front was quiet and the 28th Division was recovering from its bitter battle in the Hürtgen Forest in the north. The Germans struck the rest camp of the 28th at Clervaux, twenty-four miles east and slightly north of Bastogne early on December 16.

Doughboys were thrown out of bed by the shell fire. Three hours later, swarms of Germen Infantrymen struck the 28th Division lines in full power. By nightfall the whole central sector of the front was a fluid mass of penetrations and encirclements. It was a day and a night of incredible heroism as the thinly scattered troops of the 28th fought to hold a paper-thin line. The Germans threw a total of eight divisions at the reeling men of the 28th Division. Then came another panzer division. Fighting desperately on the American flanks, the 109th and 112th Regiments gave ground slowly but they blocked every German attempt to widen the breakthrough. On the third day of fighting the 110th Regiment of the 28th Division fought as few men are ever called upon to fight. Cooks and clerks and chairborne officers at headquarters turned into infantrymen to hold off the attack. "The 28th Division performed one of the greatest feats," Cassidy revealed, "in the history of the American Army, Against nine German divisions they had held so firmly that the German timetable had been thrown completely off." Bastogne was supposed to have been captured, according to German documents, the first day. It took days to surround it. The 101st Airborne was planted in Bastogne and the flanks had been held by the 28th Division in an immortal stand.[17]

Russell Hark

Russell Hark was like many young men at the outset of war. He was standing on the corner of Delevan and Main Streets in Buffalo, New York, on the afternoon of December 7, 1941, when a gas station attendant suddenly came running out shouting, "The Japanese have bombed Pearl Harbor in Hawaii."[18] The news led Hark to situations that he never thought he would find himself in. After the shock of the news went away, he became aware of the situation that the United States was in. America had to fight to defend the way of life that Hark and others had become accustomed to. A few days later, Hark went to the draft board and asked when he would be called for active duty. They told him that his draft number would not be called until the following August. He asked if he could leave sooner, and a week later he received his notice. He was to report to the main post office in Buffalo for his physical. He was sworn into the Army after he passed the exam. He left the next morning for basic training at Fort Bragg, North Carolina.[19]

He was sent to A.P. Hill Military Reservation, Virginia, after eight weeks of training to the 626th Tank Destroyer Battalion. After training, he was assigned to the 630th Tank Destroyer Battalion. The battalion set sail for Wales, and five weeks later, it landed on Omaha Beach in

Propaganda poster for the fight for liberty. (*U.S. National Archives and Records Administration*)

Members of Company "K," 110th Infantry, at Fort Indiantown Gap, 1943. (*28th Division Archives*)

Paris citizens greet the 28th Division's soldiers. (*28th Division Archives*)

Above and below: Paris liberation parade. (*28th Division Archives*)

28th Division soldiers sharing franks with French citizens. (*28th Division Archives*)

Hürtgen Forest after German shelling. (*28th Division Archives*)

28th Division soldiers line up for food in Clervaux, Luxembourg. (*28th Division Archives*)

28th Division soldiers celebrate an early Christmas with Luxembourg children on December 5, 1944. (*28th Division Archives*)

28th Division soldiers in front of a Red Cross donut wagon. (*28th Division Archives*)

Rifle Squad 2, Company "C," 109th Infantry, 28th Division, in the Ardennes, December 1944. (*28th Division Archives*)

Soldiers in the chow line with a Red Cross nurse, Luxembourg, 1944. (*28th Division Archives*)

Drawing of the start of the Battle of the Bulge. (*U.S. National Archives and Records Administration*)

Above left: American soldiers in a snow trench. (*U.S. National Archives and Records Administration*)

Above right: Soldiers in line for a hot meal. (*U.S. National Archives and Records Administration*)

A U.S. soldier on bedrolls after the first night in Battle of the Bulge. (*U.S. National Archives and Records Administration*)

Above left: American engineers emerge from the woods in Luxembourg. (*U.S. National Archives and Records Administration*)

Above right: An American soldier in his foxhole. (*U.S. Army Photo*)

A Company "C," 109th Infantry, 28th Division, soldier establishing a fighting position near Ettelbruck, Luxembourg, December 16, 1944. (*28th Division Archives*)

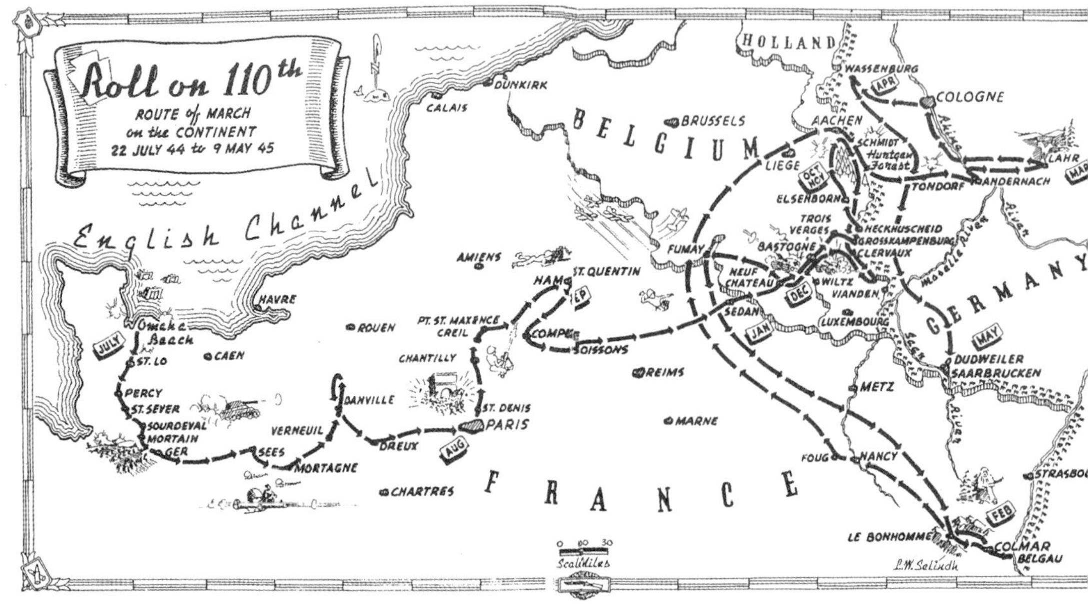

Above: The 110th Infantry, 28th Division, route of march. (*28th Division Archives*)

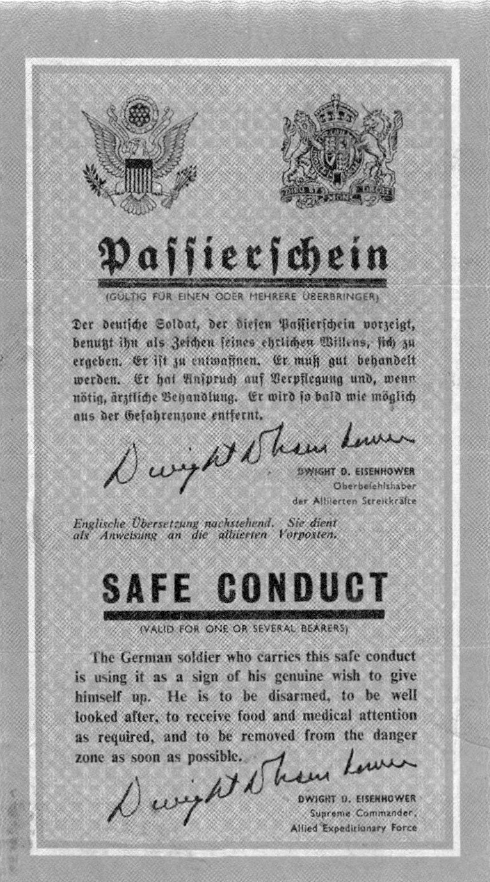

Passierschein

(GÜLTIG FÜR EINEN ODER MEHRERE ÜBERBRINGER)

Der deutsche Soldat, der diesen Passierschein vorzeigt, benutzt ihn als Zeichen seines ehrlichen Willens, sich zu ergeben. Er ist zu entwaffnen. Er muß gut behandelt werden. Er hat Anspruch auf Verpflegung und, wenn nötig, ärztliche Behandlung. Er wird so bald wie möglich aus der Gefahrenzone entfernt.

Dwight D. Eisenhower

DWIGHT D. EISENHOWER
Oberbefehlshaber
der Alliierten Streitkräfte

Englische Übersetzung nachstehend. Sie dient als Anweisung an die alliierten Vorposten.

SAFE CONDUCT

(VALID FOR ONE OR SEVERAL BEARERS)

The German soldier who carries this safe conduct is using it as a sign of his genuine wish to give himself up. He is to be disarmed, to be well looked after, to receive food and medical attention as required, and to be removed from the danger zone as soon as possible.

Dwight D. Eisenhower

DWIGHT D. EISENHOWER
Supreme Commander,
Allied Expeditionary Force

Left: A safe conduct pass signed by General Eisenhower. (*28th Division Archives*)

28th Division soldiers prepare to defend Wiltz, Luxembourg. (*28th Division Archives*)

28th Division soldiers attending a Catholic Mass in the field. (*28th Division Archives*)

Offloading supplies. (*U.S. National Archives and Records Administration*)

Heading out on patrol. (*U.S. National Archives and Records Administration*)

Above left: On guard duty in the Ardennes, December 1944. (*U.S. National Archives and Records Administration*)

Above right: American soldier alone with his mess kit. (*U.S. National Archives and Records Administration*)

Trying to stay warm in the bad weather. (*U.S. National Archives and Records Administration*)

After fighting stubbornly, some men of the 110th Infantry were captured. (*U.S. National Archives and Records Administration*)

Luxembourg citizens greeting American soldiers. (*U.S. National Archives and Records Administration*)

Above left: In a foxhole, ready for the Germans. (*U.S. National Archives and Records Administration*)

Above right: A GI with an M1918 Browning Automatic Rifle peering across a snowy field in the Ardennes during the Battle of the Bulge, in December 1944. (*U.S. National Archives and Records Administration*)

Thanksgiving in the Ardennes, 1944. (*U.S. National Archives and Records Administration*)

Americans setting up a .50-caliber machine gun. (*U.S. National Archives and Records Administration*)

28th Infantry Division soldiers dig into the snow in Luxembourg. (*28th Infantry Division Archives*)

Normandy on July 22, 1944. When the battalion arrived at an assembly area near Colombeires, France, it was attached to the 28th Division. Hark traveled with the 110th Infantry Regiment across France, supporting the regiment.[20] After the attacks and withdrawal from the Siegfried Line, the 630th was moved to Elsenborn with the rest of the division. Soon he and his unit were in the Hürtgen Forest. After this, the division was pulled out and sent to the Luxembourg, to the tiny hamlet of Enscherange. Hark stayed in a schoolhouse and did not bother to set up the guns since they were told they were in a quiet sector. On December 16, they were awakened by artillery and the start of the German onslaught.[21]

After firing at the Germans, they were eventually overcome and pulled back to Morhet, about 8 km from Bastogne. They had five of their thirty-six guns left and were attached to the 17th Airborne Division. It was very cold, and all Hark had to wear was his leather combat boots. One day he received rubber shoes with leather tops. When he removed his combat boots, his feet were blue. The medics took him to an aid station. After his frozen feet healed, he went to a replacement center and then returned to his unit and found out that he had enough points to go home. In the replacement center, Gen. George Patton visited and gave the men a speech about the necessity of winning the war. Here is an excerpt from his speech as Hark remembered it:

> Men, all this stuff you hear about America not wanting to fight, wanting to stay out of the war, is a lot of bullshit. Americans love to fight. All real Americans love the sting and clash of battle. When you were kids, you all admired the champion marble shooter, the fastest runner, the big-league ball players and the toughest boxers. Americans love a winner and will not tolerate a loser. Americans play to win all the time. That's why Americans have never lost and will never lose a war. The very thought of losing is hateful to Americans.[22]

It appears that Patton repeated some of his "Blood and Guts" speech that he delivered to his troops in England. Hark said that the men who listened to it loved every word of it. Russell Hark returned home, having done his duty, and became a supervisor of heavy equipment for Niagara Mohawk Power Company in Buffalo, New York.[23]

Louis Jurosek

Private First Class Louis Jurosek, Company A, 1st Battalion, 110th Infantry Regiment, kept a diary during the war. He wrote about being at an outpost just east of Heinerscheid, about a mile from the German border. Having no real rank, he was an old timer looking after the new replacements. At 5:30 a.m., the Germans opened up with a heavy artillery barrage from Echternach in the south to Monschau in the north. Jurosek and his new replacements responded as best as they could against the overwhelming German attack. Jurosek said he would constantly have to remind his scared replacement of why they were fighting. When it became obvious that their position was going to be overwhelmed, Jurosek gathered his group of replacements around him and started a fighting retreat toward St. Vith.[24]

They were constantly engaged in skirmishes with the Germans as they made their way through the woods. During one of the skirmishes outside of St. Vith, Jurosek was wounded by some shrapnel from a German 88-mm round. The shrapnel penetrated his upper right leg. He would not leave his replacements until they were safely in the hands of a sergeant at the mess facility.[25] After medical attention, he returned to service and continued on with the 110th Regiment. Except for recuperating for fourteen days from his leg wound, Louis Jurosek was in action with the 110th Regiment from July 22, 1944 to May 9, 1945. He wrote in his diary that he was determined to beat the Nazis; they could not win. He made it back home to Detroit, Michigan, on August 2, 1945.[26]

Richard F. Leech

Richard F. Leech was the company commander of Company D, 109th Infantry. Capt. Leech started keeping a journal of sorts up until the end of the war. After many battles across France and in the Siegfried Line, his unit became stymied for approximately two weeks. They were pulled out of the line and after a brief rest they were sent northward to the Hürtgen Forest to relieve the 9th Division who had been held up in the vicinity of Vossenack, Germeter, and Schmidt. After several days of fighting and crawling in and out of the basements of houses in Vossenack and Germeter, the 109th Regiment was ordered to launch an attack to the northeast to the town of Hürtgen.[27]

The attack was through heavy forest. Leech went along with Lt. Col. Dan Strickler, regiment commander, and his headquarters group, which was following Company C, commanded by Capt. John Ritter, so that Leech could call a mortar fire ahead of the battalions as it advanced. Leech had a radio operator and several runners with him. About a mile after they left to go into the forest, they came across Capt. Ritter who had just been shot through the mouth. He was on his feet and gargling with Cognac and spitting blood and broken teeth, but still leading his men and directing the company. Lt. Col. Strickler ordered him to immediately turn over his command of the company to someone else and go to the rear. Leech found out later that Ritter did not go and kept on fighting.[28] Leech and the others knew why they were there.

Leech's group advanced another mile within sight of the town of Hürtgen. The remaining Germans that they had not killed were flushed out of the forest and across the fields. Leech's group held up at the edge of the forest to regroup and reorganize. Many of the men were completely lost and separated from their units, and they flushed the Germans out through the fallen trees. They were then hit with a heavy German artillery barrage. Leech hit the ground as did everyone else until the barrage was over.[29]

When the barrage lifted, Leech started to get up and found that his left elbow would not work. He looked down and saw a hole in his jacket where a piece of shrapnel had pierced through. Leech made his way back to the company command post and found his bed roll had been riddled with a mortar burst right where he had slept the night before. He turned over command of Company D and his driver drove him to the aid station. Richard Leech made it home to Colorado Springs, Colorado, and became the president of the Colorado Association of Real Estate Brokers.[30]

Ruth Puryear

The fighting men of the 28th Division were not the only ones there to defeat the Germans. Ruth Puryear was a nurse with the 107th Evacuation Hospital that supported the 28th Division. She kept a journal during the war and wrote about her experiences. In September 1944, the 107th had a long drive through France, Belgium, and Luxembourg. In October, it opened its hospital in Clervaux. Its staff consisted of forty doctors, forty nurses, and 205 soldiers with tents for 400 beds. In October and November, the unit suffered through terrible rain and mud, and in December, there was snow.[31] On the night of December 15, Ruth and another nurse went to the latrine tent in the forest. They thought they heard German voices. Her friend was so upset that she let her flashlight fall into the latrine hole. A few weeks later, a military policeman came into the hospital and said he had passed through an area that must have been used by a special unit because they had an illuminated latrine.[32]

On December 16, the hospital staff were woken in the middle of the night and were ordered to put warm clothes on as the Germans were attacking. They heard German tanks in the distance. No one wanted to leave as they were there to support the troops to beat the Nazis. Finally, they decided to leave, abandoning everything but their patients. It was very cold that night as they traveled to an old castle in Libramont,

Belgium. Other units helped them with supplies until they were able to get resupplied. The ballroom of the castle was used as a surgery room. In one room there were all kinds of animal heads on the wall. It was in this room that the nurses attached the plasma bottles for the wounded to the antlers and heads of animals. They worked around the clock conducting surgical operations. Ruth remembered that it was hard, but they had to do it.

Ralph Johnson

Chief Warrant Officer Ralph Johnson, a staff officer with the 110th Infantry Regiment, kept a diary of his experiences during the war. In 1976, he wrote his memoirs from the notes in his diary. He was in the Pennsylvania National Guard 28th Infantry Division training in North Carolina on December 7, 1941. He was asleep in a corn field near Halifax, Virginia, his blanket covered with snow, when a loud, noisy radio was blasting in the early dawn. He remembered cursing the radio operator as he tried to go back to sleep, but the blast persisted, so he uncovered his head and tried to listen. He could hear that Pearl Harbor, Hawaii, had been bombed. It was a matter of hours before the shock took effect. All he had on his mind was visiting his family at Christmas. "The true meaning of Pearl Harbor did not sink in for days afterwards. I don't think anyone ate breakfast that morning. Periods of hushed silence mingled with harsh accusing oaths accompanied the remaining one hundred miles to our base at Indiantown Gap Military Reservation, near Harrisburg, Pennsylvania," wrote Johnson.[33]

The 28th Division was originally scheduled to land at Omaha Beach on D-Day, June 6, but instead landed on July 22, 1944. Johnson recalled seeing a sign on the beach placed by the U.S. 1st Division that read: "Welcome to Normandy-Courtesy of the First Division." Johnson and his fellow soldiers hung their heads as they safely walked ashore and bivouacked in a Normandy apple orchard. Johnson read from the pocket Bible he had received before he left the United States.[34] The men were disappointed that they had not come ashore on June 6. It was the topic of conversation for everyone as they awaited orders. They wanted to get a crack at the Nazis. They came to Europe to fight for freedom, and they wanted to get at it. Soon Johnson and his regiment would get their chance. After chasing the Germans across France and into Germany, the 110th Infantry Regiment was in Luxembourg on December 16, 1944.[35]

Johnson wrote in his diary, "I had faith we would prevail though. We were fighting for the right reasons and God was on our side."[36] Ralph Johnson thought "the men who fought in the Battle of the Bulge were like the Minutemen who stood at Concord Bridge in 1776. We were in the business of destroying the enemy and returning home to a full and productive life." Ralph Johnson returned home on October 1, 1945, and stayed in the Army for another six months to help with paperwork.[37]

Charlie Waldrup

Charlie Waldrup, Company K, 110th Infantry Regiment, had his first combat experience of the war in Percy, France. In his 1989 memoir, he recalled: "We were all green. It was something different from what we'd ever experienced. Of course, we'd seen a lot of beat-up troops back on the beach, Omaha Beach, and into Saint-Lô, but this was altogether different because they were shooting at us."[38] They had taken Percy after a pretty fierce fight, lost some troops but they were going out of Percy and one of his buddies said, "Look at that. There is a dead German." Waldrup replied, "Yes, and if you don't mind, these Germans will kill you too."[39] About the same time, a German burp gun opened fire on them. After a few minutes, the Germans left. Waldrup remembers thinking that the Germans had to be defeated or they would kill everyone. They would come to America and kill everyone. After the Siegfried Line, they went into the Hürtgen Forest. To him, it was one of the roughest battles. The Germans were killing Americans by the hundreds. They had to dig a hole, put brush on it, and put dirt on top. That was the only way they could survive the shrapnel from the artillery barrages.[40]

The 3rd Platoon of Company K were captured east of Hosingen during the Battle of the Bulge. Waldrup escaped capture. He commented: "People say the Bulge was the worst in Europe. It was bad, all of it was bad. The ones who talk about the Bulge didn't serve in the holes in the Hürtgen Forest. There the weather was against us, the trees were against us, and the Germans were against us. When you get three against you, I'll tell you, you can't win. But we knew that we had to win. I prayed every night."[41] Charlie Waldrup was thankful that God showed him a way to get through it and he believed that God saved him for a purpose.

Harold M. Snedden

Harold M. Snedden, Service Company, 110th Infantry Regiment, was captured by the Germans at Clervaux on December 18, 1944. In 1989, he wrote: "After interrogation, we were marched back behind the lines. The question they asked was where was Patton's tanks? We were not about to tell the Germans anything. Patton's tanks were going to beat them. They had to beat them. Patton knew why we were fighting."[42] After marching for several days and sleeping on the hard, frozen ground, they came to a railhead and about 100 prisoners were herded into boxcars that had previously been used to transport horses for their artillery. No sanitary facilities were available, and water was scarce. Snedden and his fellow prisoners were taken to the *Stalag* 9B prison camp at Bad Orb, Germany.[43]

Their menu consisted of a cup of colored water, which was supposed to be coffee, for breakfast. They might get some beans or bread or a piece of horse meat soup for lunch or dinner. There were no sanitary facilities. Their toilet was an open trench. They were housed in an old, dirty, wooden barracks. There were no blankets unless they had one when they were captured. The men were soon infected with body lice. Snedden had a copy of the New Testament which the Germans let him keep, along with pictures of his wife. He read the Bible often and prayed for the Germans to be defeated. He remembered the prayer from Patton that he received before he was captured. He remembered the Germans coming through the camp rounding up American Jews. They were marched away from camp and never returned.[44]

On April 2, 1945, Easter Monday, a tank column from Patton's Third Army knocked down the main gate and they were liberated. The lieutenant in the head tank was from Snedden's hometown, Ogleby, Illinois. Snedden said: "I never gave up hope the entire time I was a prisoner. I knew that someday General Patton would beat the Germans. He had to."[45]

Richard G. Gooley

During the 28th Division's second day of action on the Western Front, Capt. Gooley, Company C, 112th Infantry, was part of a force committed to take Hill 210 near Percy, south of Saint-Lô. Heavily outnumbered, the company hit a solid wall of German infantry men, 88-mm guns, tanks, and many automatic weapons. After organizing two platoons for the assault, Gooley went back to bring forward a third. As he was leading back to the platoon to the front, a German three-man patrol armed with hand grenades ambushed him, throwing their grenades at his feet, and faded away. Although he was seriously wounded in several places, he continued to reorganize his troops for a half-hour, gave first aid to a soldier wounded in the stomach, and returned to the aid station only when his condition became such that he could no longer move about.

Prior to this action, Capt. Gooley had wiped out an entire tank crew plus five Germans guarding the tank. After locating the tank, he leaped a hedge and landed in the midst of the five-man guard. He killed four of the guard with his Tommy gun before it ran out of ammunition, then killed the fifth with his trench knife. The commander of the tank, which was within arm's reach of Capt. Gooley, opened the turret hatch when he heard the firing outside and started to fire at Gooley. However, Gooley had been able to reload and killed the tank commander. Then he threw a grenade into the turret of the tank and killed the rest of the crew. Gooley later commented: "It was a pretty busy morning. When the Jerries finished throwing grenades at me the seat of my pants was blown off, and when they carried me back on the stretcher my first sergeant had to go along to shoot it out with snipers taking pot-shots at me. It was all worth it though because I came here to win."[46]

Elliot Johnson

Elliot Johnson remembers vividly the day of December 7, 1941. He was eating with some friends at a Chinese restaurant when one of the workers emerged from the kitchen with a portable radio in hand. It was then that they learned of the Japanese attack on Pearl Harbor. Furious that their homeland had come under attack, all four of the men immediately went to the recruiting headquarters to enlist. Even though he was fighting for the American way of life, for Johnson, the code of honor was a fundamental component of his service. As a forward observer, he would scout out the location of the Germans and call for firepower from the division behind him. While observing in the Hürtgen Forest from a forester's tower, he spotted someone in a nearby tower, "There was a German lieutenant looking right at me. We waved at each other. I marked him on the map. I got my guns zeroed in on him, and I know in my heart he did the same thing to me. He was also an artillery observer. Along my ridge was a road. German tanks rolled along there. The German artillery observer would watch my shooting."[47]

The German observer had a close eye on Johnson, indeed. One day, several German vehicles approached on the nearby road, among them ambulances. Recognizing that ambulances were hands off, Johnson merely watched as they rolled by. However, another American began shooting at them, and the German observer assumed that Johnson had ordered the fire on the convoy of ambulances. Though he tried to signal to the German lieutenant that he had not called for that fire, it was too late. The German called a hit upon Johnson and his crew, and they were barely able to escape the shells that were lobbed their way. When the fire had ceased, Johnson once more climbed the tower and signaled to the German observer: "I had my hands up and I was waving and shaking my head: not me. He looked at me. Then he took off his helmet. I guess that was his apology to me."[48]

Eddie Pfannenstiel

Private Eddie Pfannenstiel kept a wartime log, which was provided to many prisoners of war by the YMCA, of his experiences during war. Eddie's experience as a driver and cook took a back seat to the need for combat infantry riflemen. He was transferred to a replacement battalion while still in the United States. As part of the 112th Infantry Regiment, he was among replacements for the casualties they were suffering. With the 112th in the Hürtgen Forest, he wrote about the tree bursts, shells that exploded above the trees to illuminate their positions. "We felt like sitting ducks. When not fighting, we fought the cold and rain in our foxholes, and prayed to God that he would save us."[49] Eddie felt that the replacements during the battle were poorly trained but enthusiastic about fighting the Germans. After some rest, Eddie found himself facing the German attack on December 16. He was part of the rearguard assigned to cover the withdrawal of his unit.[50]

On December 18, he was taken prisoner after spending eighteen hours with four other men in the second story of a house in Ouren, Belgium, hoping their forces could return to rescue them. They had taken refuge in the house because they had used up all their ammunition and grenades fighting towards the rear. The Germans first searched the house and did not discover them. Thinking they were in the clear, they continued to hide while the Germans occupied the main floor. Finally, a German came upstairs, lit a cigarette, and found them. They had no choice but to surrender. Their captors were German SS troops, who guarded them on the way to their prison camp. A German lieutenant learned that Eddie could speak German, so he put him in charge of the first small group of prisoners. They were taken to *Stalag* IXB in Bad Orb, Germany.

Each nationality was kept in separate compounds. The Geneva Convention rules provided that prisoners be allowed to select a representative among them. Since Eddie spoke German, he was selected as "Chief Man of Confidence." In that position, he was responsible for keeping detailed records of what was happening in the camp. He entered details of his stay in his wartime log and hid many of the documents from the German guards. Regular Catholic and Protestant services were held in the camp. Eddie recalled that everyone believed God would save them from the ordeal. Church services were attended by most of the men. Eddie tried to attend services no matter what was happening.

The Germans segregated the known American Jews and transferred them from the camp. Eddie never saw them again. In his position, he was able to write to the Red Cross and request supplies for the prisoners. He was keenly aware that the religious needs of the prisoners included supplies. He was successful in obtaining supplies for the Protestant chaplains that included Bibles, Testaments, Communion wine, and wafers and religious music. For the Catholic chaplains, he obtained 1,000 Sunday Missals, 500 Rosaries, and twelve Kyrials (a collection of Gregorian chant settings for Mass).[51]

Eddie was attending church on Easter Sunday when he was called out. A man had come up from Bad Orb to report that shells had hit the town. Eddie was sent into Bad Ord to accompany unarmed German officers to surrender the town. After liberation, Eddie received a letter that he was to be flown to the Pentagon in Washington, D.C., to turn over his records from the prison camp. After five days in Washington, Eddie was given six days of leave and scheduled to report for officer training in Texas. He turned down the officer training and returned home to Kansas. Schools and organizations asked him to give talks. He said that he hated to do it and did not like talking about his time in Europe. He just wanted to be left alone. He believed that, in his own way, he contributed to the war effort.[52]

Robert W. Pocklington

Private First Class Robert W. Pocklington, HQ Company, 2nd Battalion, 110th Infantry, recalled the week before December 16, 1944 during an interview in December 1988. Pocklington had kept a journal during the war and referred to it during his interview. He remembered the floodlights and music from the German side, not only in German but in English. It was kind of a morale booster for the men on the frontlines. The weather was cold, overcast, foggy, and very damp. They had plenty to eat and were well-equipped with ammunition and hand grenades. It felt like the war would be over soon. They had beat the Nazis and would soon go back to normal living at home. Originally in the 106th Infantry Division, he was transferred to the 28th Division four days before leaving the harbor in Boston.[53]

Pocklington said that when they came into the area in Luxembourg, they knew it was a rest area. But their main objective was to protect the main roads that came from Germany. He commented: "If they [the Germans] got by this point, and they got by that point, we were surrounded and we would have had it. Bastogne would have been next. We couldn't let that happen. We could not let the Germans win and screw-up our way of life. No, we won't let that happen."[54]

Pocklington's job was in the Pioneer Platoon, specializing in demolition with the use of TNT, explosives, booby traps, and land mines. He was set up in one of the foxholes overlooking Skyline Drive. It was cold, dark and he heard the sound of a tank coming down through a gully. He did not know if it was an American or German tank. He thought it might be an

American tank from the 707th Tank Battalion or from the 9th Armored Division needing repairs. He was just lying in his foxhole, having his last cigarette and loosening his boots, when he heard the clanking sound of tank treads coming close to where he lay. The next thing Robert heard was the sound of a .50-caliber machine gun firing at the tank. He got up from his foxhole and saw two Germans getting off the tank and running down the hill. German infantry soon showed up and the fighting started.[55]

Pocklington and the others who were in foxholes made their way up a stream and found an American convoy. There were a lot of men in Pocklington's unit that were not killed or captured but gave their best in the fight. He commented: "Well you know in the military we are always to fight and to hold. You are taught to shoot first and ask questions later, because that son of a bitch ain't going to testify against you. So, in war time that was the first thing I thought of. We came here to fight for freedom and to keep these bastards from winning. That is why there were so many heroes there."[56]

Morris Katz

First Lieutenant Morris Katz was in the 108th Field Artillery Battalion as a forward observer at an observation post in Hoesdorf. Katz kept a journal and wrote that on December 15 there had been some activity reported in the area around Vianden. He was ordered to go to the Vianden Castle, observe what he could and fire some registration checkpoints, and get some corrections so that they could bring fire on any portions of the terrain across the Our River. He had no reason to believe that there was anything going on—anything other than a routine registration mission. In fact, Katz had a date to go to a party that night in Ettelbruck.[57]

He finished his job around 3 p.m. and started back in his jeep with his radio operator and driver, hoping to drop them off in Diekirch and to continue on to attend the party. Before they got to Fouhren, the party drew some machine-gun fire and drove off the road. Another jeep was behind them. The firing ceased and Katz told the driver of the other jeep to get back and report what happened and give a note to Marion Conny, who was with the Red Cross in Ettelbruck, his date for the party. With no more machine-gun fire, Katz proceed to the party. Little did he know that that would be the last party he would attend for a while. The 108th Field Artillery fired in support of the 109th Infantry until they could no longer continue. When asked if he thought his unit made a difference in the war, Katz responded: "I think they made a tremendous difference. The preservation of peace and freedom was on the line. I keep thinking that we did the best we could do. We delayed the Germans and they didn't win."[58]

Robert H. Henschen

Capt. Robert H. Henschen, 3rd Battalion, 110th Infantry Regiment, kept a journal during the war. A few years after the war, he started to write his experiences from his journal notes. He recalled that his driver and he were feeling the freedom of the day as the slow tail end of the divisional movement was on the road to the long-promised rest period in Luxembourg. Henschen had finished his part of clearing the last 28th Division troops from the Hürtgen Forest.[59] It was a typical early December day, gray overcast sky and patches of snow here and there on the rolling hills. As open trucks filled with men moved along, the chilling wind caused the soldiers to huddle together under blankets for warmth. Despite their discomfort, the men were beginning to relax from the tenseness of the previous week.[60]

There were jokes passing around and a little horseplay was going on. Everyone had the sense that the war was about to be over. They were still wearing the same uniforms, wearing the same beards, and had most of the same dirt on them that went with them into the Hürtgen Forest many weeks before. "The real grit, stamina, fearlessness, and dogged courage of the American boys were still to be more severely tested and proven in a way they least expected. The men proved themselves once again. They knew in order to make it home that had to keep the Nazis from winning, and they did," recalled Henschen.[61]

Frank Kusnir

SSgt. Frank Kusnir joined Company B, 110th Infantry Regiment, in 1936 and was with the same regiment across France, Germany, and Luxembourg after the Hürtgen Forest battle. On the night of December 15, Frank and another soldier were sent out to reconnoiter downtown Clervaux. He was with the intelligence reconnaissance section and suspected that there were some German sympathizers in town. He thought that by having a conversation with some of the villagers, they might be able to find out if anything was going to develop in the area. They no sooner got into the town when three German artillery shells dropped in. Frank thought: "hey, our artillery goofed up again. They are shelling us again." There was a period of ten minutes or so with no shelling. The next thing he knew, two more shells dropped in and he thought, "the damn fools made another mistake."[62] There was no more shelling that night. Years later, Frank thought: "the Germans must have been registering their artillery and we did not realize it."[63]

Early the next morning, there was an artillery barrage landing on the hill above town. When the artillery firing stopped, he looked up at the hill and a whole line of German tanks were parked on the hillside facing the Americans. The tanks were firing at the medieval castle that Frank was stationed in. The walls were very thick so they were well protected.[64] They could not answer the fire from the German tanks as the men were only armed with carbines and rifles. The German tanks and artillery kept firing at the castle for three days, but Frank and the men held their ground. They would occasionally shoot at any careless tank crewmen who ventured out of their tanks. The Americans who occupied the castle had one order. They were to hold the castle at all costs.[65]

On the third day, the Germans sent infantry to capture the castle. Frank recalled: "They came right up to the castle courtyard. They were foolhardy because they had no chance. We killed quite a few of them. Then they would withdraw. Then they wanted to know if we would surrender."[66] The company commander said no; they would fight to the last man. The Germans assaulted again, and the Americans would kill more of their enemy and the Germans would withdraw again. Finally on the afternoon of December 18, Frank's group was out of ammunition and the castle was on fire, so they made the decision to surrender.[67]

The Americans had captured three Germans earlier and walked out of the castle with them in tow. A German colonel told the Americans to stand against a wall. "He said line them up and we'll shoot them over there."[68] The colonel asked one of the Germans who had been captured how they had been treated. He told the colonel they had been treated well, fed well, and their wounded taken care of. Frank recalled the colonel stated in perfect English, "You men are lucky. My intention was to shoot all of you for my dead comrades laying strewn through the courtyard. You are now prisoners of the German Army." Frank and the other 110th Infantry men were sent to the prison camp at Bottorf, Germany.[69]

During his interview, Frank was asked if he thought it was important that people remember what happened during the Battle of the Bulge. Frank replied: "They should. There were a lot of people who did a lot of things. I believe every man who was there was a hero. Sometimes when you felt like a guy was a laggard, you pepped him up a little, but there were no cowards. I was scared, we were all scared, but it didn't keep us from fighting for freedom. That is why were there."[70]

David T. Hurwitz

Lt. Col. David Y. Hurwitz, G-2 (intelligence officer) of the 28th Division and former sporting goods dealer from Laramie, Wyoming, could not have joined the division at a more difficult time. When he arrived at the division command post in Wiltz, the troops were enjoying what was supposed to be a rest and reorganization period in a so-called quiet sector. Almost simultaneously with Hurwitz's arrival at the headquarters, he hardly had time to orient himself in the division staff before the Germans launched their attack. As the division fought delaying actions toward Bastogne, Sibret, and Vaux-lez-Rosières, Hurwitz not only assisted in the intelligence work, but he became a regular frontline foxhole soldier when the division's forward and rear headquarters put down their pencils, their band instruments, and their typewriters to participate in the last-ditch stands before the German onslaught.

Hurwitz later commented: "You can have Germany, Belgium, France, Luxembourg and anyplace else you want, if you'll just reserve Laramie for me. I've thought of a lot of swell ideas for my store, and it's tough waiting to get back to see how they'll work." He would later be awarded the Bronze Star for his actions to defeat the Germans.[71]

John R. Chernitsky

Sgt. John R. Chernitsky was with the 110th Regiment Anti-tank Company. Chernitsky also kept a diary while he was with the division. He came from a small mining town in Pennsylvania. In 1939, the Pennsylvania National Guard was recruiting by telling young men that they could get a year in service before being called up for the draft. John joined the National Guard shortly after graduating from high school. He attended weekend drills with his unit until they were called up to federal service on February 17, 1941. His unit had just pulled into a bivouac area at A.P. Hill, Virginia, on the night of December 7, 1941. Someone had a portable radio and heard that the Japanese had bombed Pearl Harbor, Hawaii. John recalled: "While making our trip through the south, we Yankees were not treated too politely. The southerners didn't appreciate Yankee soldiers floating around the south, but on December 8, all that changed."[72]

In the morning, they got up early and all of the Catholics went to Mass. John's faith was important to him and he always tried to attend services, even throughout Europe. If there was not a Catholic chaplain, then many of the Catholics would attend Protestant services. After Mass on December 8, the men returned to the company area and prepared to convoy to Indiantown Gap in Pennsylvania. One of the first things that John and the men noticed was that the attitude of the southerners had changed overnight. Men were dropped off at road junctions with signs to direct the convoy. The local people would come out and talk with them, wishing them the best. At every stop, local people would bring them hot coffee, cakes, and doughnuts. John figured, "the southerners treated them better because they knew we soldiers would be protecting them from the Nazis and the Japs."[73]

After being sent to Luxembourg, John was with the 3rd Platoon in Hosingen. The division headquarters in Wiltz started an NCO refresher school, which was necessary because there had been so many casualties that so many men were promoted to ranks of corporal and sergeants in the field without having any understanding of what the duties of leadership were. Sgt. Chernitsky was one of the sergeants picked as an instructor in the school. He got to Wiltz on December 15 and was shown to his quarters in a portion of a leather warehouse and told he and the other instructors could go to the theater where movies were being shown that night. They got out of the movies, went back to the warehouse, and were greeted by an officer who told them to get their barracks bags together as they would be taken back to their units. On the way out of Wiltz early the next morning, they ran into German troops, leading them to return to Wiltz and assign a rifle platoon to defend the town. Sgt. Chernitsky was with band members, clerical staff, cooks, bakers, and anyone who was caught between Wiltz and Clervaux trying to get back to their units.[74]

The men defended Wiltz as long as they could and eventually broke up into small groups to make their way west toward Bastogne. While trying to go to Bastogne, Chernitsky was captured and became a POW; he was sent to *Stalag* 2B at Hammerstein, Germany, and moved to various prison camps. He eventually made it back to the United States on May 11, 1945, returning home to Uniontown, Pennsylvania. In his interview, John said: "Although my wife had asked me repeatedly to write my army and war remembrances, I wouldn't do it. Even though I can't remember what happened at each prison camp, there are some things I'll never forget, like how degrading it was being a prisoner of war. They stripped me of my freedom. I kept thinking that they [the Germans] had to lose. They can't be allowed to strip anyone else of their freedom."[75]

James E. Rudder

Lt. Col. James E. Rudder, commander of the 109th Infantry Regiment, was interviewed by the 3rd Information and Historical Services, HQ U.S. III Corps on January 6, 1945 at Buzancy, France. Discussing the events of December 16 and after, he commented that when the first reports started to come in on December 16, all the 109th Infantry Regiment units were alerted, and the division headquarters was notified. All of the battalions reported that the company-strength attacks by German infantry did not include tanks. Rudder said: "Everyone was holding and I saw no cause for alarm. We were in a good position and had a distinct advantage of terrain. As the attack progressed, it became apparent that it was in great strength. Still, we did not even consider giving up any ground and the division order was to hold as long as the positions were tenable. After all, we were there to beat the Nazis. We were not going to let them win."[76]

During the night of December 17, the German attack continued in force, but the American artillery was breaking up much of the German infantry and the attack was being stopped in many places. The situation began to deteriorate on all fronts and the 109th Infantry reserve battalion from Diekirch was committed. On December 18, the decision was made to withdraw the regiment in the direction of Bastogne. That night the battalions were pulled back to the northwest of Ettelbruck to cover the 9th Armored Division. Lt. Col. James E. Rudder believed they did the best they could under the circumstances and commended his men for their sacrifices.[77]

John F. Marshall

John F. Marshall was with Company B, 707th Tank Battalion. His battalion had landed with the 28th Division and supported the division across France, the Siegfried Line, the Hürtgen Forest, and to Luxembourg. John would write to his wife Daisy and tell her what he could about his experiences. In a January 5, 1945 letter, he wrote: "Daisy, you asked me several times who stands out as a good soldier. They were all good. We were cooperative and fought with any unit we were attached to and there were many. It probably sounds like an old cliché, but I am proud of my conduct and performance in combat, nothing heroic, just did what had to be done to stop the Germans and was blessed to live through it. For this guidance and intelligence, I thank Almighty God."[78]

Joseph L. Macsalka

Lt. Col. Joseph L. Macsalka, the commander of the 2nd Battalion, 112th Infantry Regiment, was interviewed by the 3rd Information and Historical Services, HQ U.S. III Corps on January 22, 1945 in the mountains south of Kaysersberg, France. Macsalka explained that on the morning of December 16, Companies E and F were on line with Company G at Weiswampach where it had been sent two days previously for training. At

6 a.m., the battalion S-2 was informed by the regimental S-2 that strong German patrol groups of fifty to sixty infantrymen were putting pressure on the 1st and 3rd Battalions. At 8:30 a.m., the regimental S-2 informed the battalion S-2 that the Germans were launching a full-scale attack. Macsalka said that he was not worried at that point since five different plans had been set up to engage the Germans.[79]

At 11:30 a.m., the regiment called for Plan B to be put into effect. All the plans involved an attack against any enemy penetration into the 2nd Battalion main assembly area. From this assembly area, Plan A called for the battalion to move through the right flank of the 3rd Battalion area; Plan B through the center of the 3rd Battalion; Plan C between the 1st Battalion and 3rd Battalions; Plan D through the center of the 1st Battalion; and Plan E through the left flank of the 1st Battalion. Plan B was called for because the Germans were known to be near a footbridge that the Americans had built.[80]

As the regiment was overrun, they fell back to Burtonsville and mined the road behind them and eventually were reassigned. Macsalka was confident that one of the plans that had been formulated would have stopped the German advance. He commented: "We knew that we had to beat these Germans. They were bringing no good to the people of Europe. If left unchecked, they would bring no good to us too."[81]

William H. Allen

Lt. Col. William H. Allen, commander of the 1st Battalion, 112th Infantry Regiment, was interviewed by the 3rd Information and Historical Services, HQ U.S. III Corps on January 16, 1945 at Montfaucon, France. In the interview, he stated: "The principal reason for the success of the enemy penetration of December 16–17, 1944 was that there just wasn't enough troops available at the time to offset the German attack in force." Early in the morning on December 16, Allen received a report from the regiment S-2 that approximately fifty German infantry soldiers were attacking the Company H mortar position, which was set up within the 3rd Battalion. A kitchen truck returning to the rear from Company A was ambushed by an unknown number of Germans. Late in the afternoon, seven tanks approached Allen's position. Allen manned a .50-caliber machine gun and fired 150 rounds at the advancing Germans. After the last burst, forty Germans surrendered. "After enormous pressure from the Germans we had to withdrew to fight another day," commented Allen. "We were not going to give up on beating the Nazis. That is what we traveled across Europe to do. To beat them back and end their reign of terror."[82]

Daniel B. Strickler

On December 10, Col. Strickler was assigned as executive officer of the 110th Regiment and reported in at the regimental command post at Consthum, Luxembourg. He found that the regiment was holding a defensive line of about 15 miles along the Our River facing the Siegfried Line. It was supposed to be a quiet sector as no aggressive fighting by either side had taken place in that area since the initial push to the German border in September. Most of the officers of the regiment were replacements, and likewise the majority of the men were reinforcements, having been sent to the regiment after the grueling battle in the Hürtgen Forest during November. The regimental command post was moved to Clervaux on December 13 and set up in the Claravallis Hotel. The front was quiet as usual on the night of December 15, with nothing coming in but routine reports.

At about 5:30 a.m. on the morning of December 16, Strickler was awakened by the noise of large-caliber artillery shells that were falling in the town. Soon the entire front seemed to be subjected to extremely heavy artillery fire. At first, he thought the Germans were having some artillery practice or probably were preparing to stage a local raid. The regimental commander, Col. Fuller, sent him to the division headquarters in Wiltz to find out what was happening. To the division, it looked like a large-scale attack was being made against the 110th but the extent of the enemy objective could not yet be determined. The division commander issued an order to hold at all costs though.

Strickler left Wiltz and proceeded to Consthum, the command post of the 3rd Battalion about 6 miles from Wiltz. He determined the situation and sent a message to Col. Fuller in Clervaux. The Germans were coming right up to the American front lines and unloading from trucks. American artillery was slaughtering the Germans, but still they came. On the morning of the 17th, individual companies were still holding out, but everyone was engaged in their front yards. During the day, they ordered the civilians to leave town. Consthum was the only strong point left between the German front and Wiltz, where the division headquarters was already being threatened by infiltrating Germans. During the night, German artillery pounded Strickler and the 3rd Battalion troops incessantly. Col. Fuller reported that the 1st Battalion had been overrun in his front and that the 2nd Battalion had been released to him, from the division reserve, but it was too late to help the 1st Battalion.

To his amazement, on the night of the second day, a friendly cook put a plate of hot food into his hands and some hot coffee too. That kept him going and he kept alert all night. Strickler ordered two friendly tanks that were on the street near their command post to move up to the ridge in front of them. They started to move out, firing on the tank and on the command post. In a few minutes, just 200 yards up the street, they saw this tank in flames. It burned all night, lighting up the command post in grand style; the ammunition going off in the tank gave the men in the command post plenty of disturbance in their own vicinity all night long.

On the morning of the 18th, the Germans made an attack on the command post. This was preceded by heavy artillery and tank and mortar fire from all directions. Attack after attack was repulsed but the Germans kept coming. The troops were running low on ammunition, so Strickler ordered Maj. Milton, 3rd Battalion commander, to hold his position while Strickler went back to Wiltz for a situation report and more ammunition. He got as much information as he could, a small amount of ammunition, and returned to the 3rd Battalion. The troops had held out and established a defensive position around Nocher. The men were tired, battle weary, and hungry. Food was out of the question. Strickler set up a command post in Nocher and waited for action. The night was fairly quiet. The next morning, he returned to Wiltz for orders and found the situation had become so bad that the division headquarters had decided to move about 12–15 miles to the rear to Sibret, just south of Bastogne.

General Cota ordered Strickler to take command of the defense of Wiltz, giving him a small task force and remnants of the 110th Infantry that Strickler had brought back with him. By mid-afternoon on December 19, the situation at Wiltz looked serious. The decision was made to withdraw to the west. They destroyed all maps and command post equipment and headed for Bastogne.

Col. Strickler wrote in his after-action report: "Hundreds of similar stories can be told about the fighting of the 110th Infantry in the bulge. The men of the 28th Division had taken the full brunt of Von Rundstedt's mighty offensive in Luxembourg. They fought gallantly and desperately in hundreds of scattered battles. There were days and nights of incredible heroism. The 110th Infantry was in the center of the division, direct in the path of the enemy in its advance to Wiltz and Bastogne."[83]

Jack Colbaugh

First Lieutenant Jack Colbaugh, 108th Field Artillery Battalion, was the forward observer who directed the first artillery shell fired into Germany during the Siegfried Line campaign. During a 1985 interview with Gus Hickock, 28th Division Association Historian, Colbaugh recalled a story about the British Royal West Kent Regiment fighting in Burma who were surrounded by a Japanese division. The regiment had killed over 4,000 Japanese soldiers before they were finally relieved. Someone from the British regiment left behind an inscription from World War I. It read: "When you go home, tell them of us and say, for their tomorrow we gave ours today."[84] Colbaugh went on to say: "Well, that's what our buddies did. We were men at that moment and we held at all cost in the Bulge. The Luxembourgers will never forget. They were in love with the men of the 28th Division."[85]

When asked why he thought the 28th Division was there, Colbaugh replied: "We went to war to defeat a monstrous animal, a Nazi Dictator, enslaving the people of Europe, who had his eyes on enslaving us. Roosevelt sent us with a message for him. It was victory at all cost, those were our orders."[86] In Colbaugh's judgement, the action of the 28th had become known as the greatest single achievement in the history of the United States Army. The German attack failed to crash through to the Meuse and Antwerp. "It may have been the crucial moment of the war."[87]

Francis Y. Slanger

Second Lieutenant Francis Slanger was a nurse in a U.S. Army Field Hospital. She wrote an editorial to *Stars and Stripes* and mailed it on October 21, 1944. That evening, she was killed by a German shell. When the shelling began, Slanger and her friends put their helmets on and huddled together, waiting for a chance to run for shelter. The third shell fell in the middle of the hospital area and fragments ripped through the tent, hitting the girls as they kneeled with their arms round each other. Francis was the first nurse to land in France, wading ashore with the hospital platoon four days after D-Day. In her editorial she wrote:

> It is 0200 and I have been lying awake for one hour, listening to the steady even breathing of the other three nurses in the tent. Thinking about some of the things we had discussed during the day. The rain is beating down on the tent with a torrential force. The wind is on a mad rampage and its main objective seems to be to lift the tent off its poles and fling it about our heads.
>
> The fire is burning low and just a few live coals are on the bottom. With the slow feeding of wood, and finally coal, a roaring fire is started. I couldn't help thinking how similar to a human being a fire is; if is allowed to run down too low and if there is a spark of life left in it, it can be nursed back. So can a human being. It is slow, It is gradual, it is done all the time in these Field Hospitals and other hospitals in the ETO [European theater of operations].

> We have read several articles in different magazines and papers sent in by grateful GIs, praising the work of the nurses around the combat areas. Praising us for what? I climbed back Into my cot. Lt. Bowler was the only one I had awakened. I whispered to her. Lt. Cox and Lt. Powers slept on. Fine nurses and great girls to live with ... of course, like in all families, an occasional quarrel, but these were quickly forgotten.
>
> I'm writing this by flashlight. In this light it looks something like a "dive." In the center of the tent are two poles, one part chimney, the other plain tent pole. Kindling wood lies in disorderly confusion on the damp ground. We don't have a tarp on the ground. A French wine pitcher, filled with water, stands by. The GIs say we rough it. We in our little tent can't see it. True, we are set up in tents, sleep on cots and are subject to the temperament of the weather. We are ancle deep in mud. Sure we rough it, but in comparison to the way you men are taking it, we can't complain, nor do we feel that bouquets are due us. But you men behind the guns, the men driving our tanks, flying our planes, sailing our ships, building bridges and to the men who pave the way and to the men who are left behind, it is you we doff our helmets. To every GI wearing the American uniform, for you we have the greatest admiration and respect.[88]

The men of the 28th Division were proud of what they accomplished. They felt that they were strong in the face of overwhelming odds and honored their dead. Perhaps a poem written by Private First Class Russell G. Ogborn, Company E, 112th Infantry Regiment, in August 1945 exemplifies the attitude of the soldiers of the division. They knew what they came to Europe to do and were proud of what they had done. It was published in the division newsletter, distributed to the troops, and reads:

They were formed in Pennsylvania,
Joined by men from every state,
With the keystone for their emblem
They were called the twenty-eight!
They hit the beach at Omaha,
Crossed the hedges row by row,
Where the Jerry learned to hate and fear
The keystone's ruddy glow.
Fire and movement were their watchwords
As they climbed up Hill 210,
Wrote a bloody page for history
In the woods of Compiègne.
A victory march in Paris,
Ever forward with the dawn,

Through Belgium, France and Luxembourg
The twenty-eighth "rolled on."
The Siegfried Line has seen them
All along its mighty wall,
From Aachen, South to Alsace,
Where they fought at Colmar's fall.
There are towns they'll long remember—
Vossenack, Schmidt and Kommerscheidt,
And the break-through in December
When they slowed the German tide.
With blood and sweet they carved a niche,
In history's hall of fame.
With deeds of valor shining bright
And victory was their aim.
In Valhalla's halls their heroes live,
Who fell along the way,
They're resting now, awaiting call
To march on judgement day.
When my last recall is sounded
May I go there to dwell,
And march again with the legions
Of the Gentlemen from Hell![89]

Epilogue

As the last major German offensive of the war, and the United States' largest land battle of World War II, the Battle of the Bulge is frequently examined in literature. Despite this, historians continue to focus primarily on physical aspects, unit cohesion and fighting for one's buddy, and suggesting that physical forces were the single influence on the final result. The research for this book employed primary and secondary sources to conduct the historical analysis and provide an interpretation of the motivating factors that caused the soldiers of the U.S. Army 28th Infantry Division to delay the Germans. By analyzing the various interpretations presented in the literature and personal accounts, this research produced a reinterpretation of the first days of the Battle of the Bulge through the perspective of combat motivating factors.

The specific actions that were taken by the 28th Division soldiers to slow the German advance were examined. This study has shown that the actions of the division soldiers delayed the German plan to capture Antwerp, Belgium, long enough for the Allies to re-enforce the Bastogne, Belgium, area and halt the German advance. While organized in strongpoints along the Luxembourg–German border, the 28th Division troops were able to establish fields of fire at key road intersections, avenues of approach to towns, and hilltops to interdict the German attacks. In some cases, the men fought to the last man and in a few cases surrendered only when all ammunition was expended, and they no longer had the means to resist.

Despite intense artillery, mortar, small arms, and tank fire and a scarcity of ammunition, the men continued to fight. Taking the brunt of the German assault were the three regiments of the 28th Infantry Division—the 109th, 110th and 112th. Facing overwhelming German forces, without any sleep, often without food, the soldiers of the division fought nonstop, often until the last bullet and last man, to stop the German drive. Overall, the 28th

Division would identify elements of nine German divisions in its sector before the battle was over.

The spectrum of religious beliefs and practices soldiers brought with them and experienced during war and how much they influenced them to fight were examined. The study found that the soldiers brought with them to Europe their religious beliefs and continued to practice their faith even in adverse circumstances. Religion and faith were tremendously important to American soldiers in World War II. Religious beliefs and practices and ideas of freedom of religion are basic elements in American culture and this ethos naturally extended to the U.S. military. Many soldiers attended religious services when they were available. Soldiers read from the pocket Bibles chaplains handed out. Some men felt that God protected them as they faced their enemy. The freedom to practice their religion was an integral part of why they fought so bravely.

American soldiers found comfort and motivation through prayer on the front lines of World War II. Despite witnessing horrific acts, most soldiers remained steadfast in their religious beliefs. Some even performed heroic acts believing that God would not permit them to be killed. General Patton's prayer was distributed to every man prior to the German attack on December 16, as a reminder that prayer was not only important, but encouraged by their leadership. The soldiers were constantly reminded that freedom of religion was part of the American way of life.

This study followed the division from their training in the U.S. and England, their landing on the beach in Normandy, and their fight and pursuit of the Germans through the hedgerow country at Percy, Hill 210, Gathemo, and Hill 288, across France, as it faced the pillboxes in the Siegfried Line in Germany and the nightmare of the Hürtgen Forest. All the way the personal commitment of the soldiers of the need to fight for the American way of life never wavered. The 28th Infantry Division went to rest in Luxembourg, thinking that the war would soon be over. They had sustained some 6,184 casualties in eighteen days of fighting in some of the worst conditions imaginable in the Hürtgen Forest. They relaxed and thought about Christmas and going home. When the Germans attacked on December 16, the thoughts of going home soon evaporated and the men realized their fight was not over. They summoned their strength and confronted the overwhelming German onslaught. Many asked God to protect them as they frustrated the Germans by whatever means they had.

In the Ardennes, the division was in the process of absorbing replacements for their casualties and rebuilding the three infantry regiments that had been decimated. Tribute is due to the men who were together for only a couple of weeks, who had not trained together, almost total strangers, and yet were soldiers all and fought until killed, wounded, or overrun.

Research identified stories about the men who had taken the brunt of the German offensive in Luxembourg. They fought gallantly and desperately in hundreds of scattered battles. There were days and nights of incredible heroism. Stories of some who were awarded the Silver Star, Bronze Star, and Distinguished Service Cross for their actions serve as a testament to the commitment of the Americans. Some of them received awards posthumously. These stories offer us insight into sacrifice on the battlefield and demonstrate the honor and courage with which they and so many other soldiers fought. A review of the literature about the Battle of the Bulge yielded significant gaps in the understanding of what motivated the 28th Infantry Division soldiers during the first few days of the Battle of the Bulge. Some literature argues that soldiers fight because of unit cohesion or fighting for one's buddy, while others suggest that ideology plays a role, albeit a secondary one.

The soldiers had read and seen films about life in Nazi Germany in theaters before going to war and posters appeared that emphasized the need to defeat the Nazis. They had heard speeches by political leaders and were constantly reminded of the reason they were fighting the Germans. The government had a concerted effort to gain support for the war. Citizens were encouraged to support the war effort and were encouraged to enter the military to fight. Along with instilling teamwork, and learning the basics of survival, drill sergeants stressed the importance of winning to preserve the American way of life. The *Why We Fight* films along with other orientation films and materials were shown to American soldiers during basic training, and chaplains not only tended to the soldiers' religious needs, but they also continued to underscore why it was necessary to defeat the Germans.

The war was fought by a largely united people, whose shared purpose not only led them to make sacrifices for the common good but also enabled them to transcend ethnic divisions and religious differences. Some historians have called World War II a "good war." The reason why the war seemed to be good had less to do with what happened than what did not happen. The war did not lead to the harsh curtailment of civil liberties that many had feared. Freedom of speech, press, and assembly were widely protected. There were few prosecutions for sedition. There was no public hysteria or mob violence, and critics of the war were, in general, treated leniently. The soldiers fighting on the continent of Europe and in Asia knew that the situation at home was stable and they aimed to keep it that way.

William Henderson argues that cohesion is the primary motivational factor that must be considered in any study of combat motivation. He equates cohesion with terms such as *esprit de corps*, group morale, and elan. While Henderson's conclusions are plausible when groups of soldiers train together and fight together over time, due to the losses the division encountered during its fighting across Europe, the division units were filled with replacement soldiers. Many companies experienced dips in effective strength of 50 percent or greater, even as they attempted to assimilate new replacements. For example, the men of the 28th Division were only in Luxembourg after their Hürtgen Forest experience for three weeks before the Germans attacked, and it is unlikely that the men could have developed a sense of unit cohesion. As a result of the significant turnover of personnel, the bonds that had been developed between the veterans who had been with the division since its initial training did not exist. In many cases, leaders did not know the names of their replacements and the veterans found it difficult to bond with the new replacements.

Unit cohesion and camaraderie undoubtedly were strong motivators when soldiers were together and had a chance to get to know each other and learn to rely on each other. As the 28th Division confronted the Germans from one battle to the next, the number of casualties grew. The men who left training in Wales were not the ones who fought the next major battle. The attrition of war since the division landed in Normandy steadily thinned out the ranks. Lone replacements found themselves among groups of strangers with little chance to get acquainted before being flung into battle, so there had to be other factors that motivated the men to fight as they did. Challenging the conventional ideas about why soldiers fight and the contribution of the 28th Infantry Division during the Battle of the Bulge, this study concluded overwhelmingly that the soldiers of the 28th Division believed they were fighting to preserve the American way of life, which included freedom to worship, freedom from oppression, and freedom of movement.

As many of the soldiers of the 28th Infantry Division found themselves ensnared within the theater of conflict, a somber realization began to take hold—they were encircled, with no avenues of relief or escape except through surrender as captives of war. Despite this grim assessment, their spirit of defiance endured, and they persisted in their resistance until no further recourse remained. This steadfast determination marked the essence of their character, encapsulating the unyielding spirit that defined the men of the 28th Division. Facing an almost insurmountable situation, the defenders recognized the bleak reality before them. Surrounded by enemy forces, they comprehended the limited options that lay ahead. Yet, even in the face of this stark truth, they forged ahead with a tenacity that refused to waver. The soldiers knew that their stance was not just about victory or survival, but about upholding the ideals they fought for—the very essence of the American way of life.

Their resolute stand was nothing short of remarkable. From the inception of the battle, their ferocity took its toll on the opposing German forces. In those initial three days of intense combat, the defenders of the 28th Infantry Division inflicted significant casualties upon the enemy. The exact extent of their impact remains elusive, as the fog of war can obscure the toll of battle. However, in 1979, the U.S. Army officially acknowledged the profound contribution of the 28th Infantry Division, revealing that their actions had exacted a formidable cost from the Germans—over 12,000 casualties throughout the Ardennes campaign. The soldiers' indomitable spirit and resolute resistance illuminated the battlefield, serving as an example of courage and fortitude. Theirs was a stand that went beyond the strategic implications of victory or defeat. It embodied the unwavering commitment to principles, the unshakable faith in their mission, and the valor that comes with putting oneself in harm's way for the greater good. In the annals of history, the legacy of the 28th Infantry Division endures as a testament to the human capacity to rise above adversity. Their stand was not just stubborn; it was a manifestation of the very essence of what it means to fight for freedom, honor, and the enduring values that define a nation.

Despite the near destruction of its infantry regiments, the division retained significant resilient structure with an experienced headquarters that continued to function proficiently, supporting elements survived generally intact, and most companies retained small veteran cores. The core of veterans continued to support the idea of fighting for the American way of life with the new replacements. It is clear from interviews and personal accounts that the overriding reason why the men of the 28th Infantry Division fought so fiercely to delay the Germans during the first days of the Battle of the Bulge was to insure the American way of life. Personal narratives, interviews, unit historical summaries, journals, and after-action reports constituted a substantial portion of the research for this book. The comments made by veterans were substantiated by comparing their statements with after-action reviews, unit reports and interviews conducted shortly after the battles.

Throughout the soldiers' personal interviews, and writings, we see the soldiers return to the idea that the Nazis had to be defeated so that freedoms in America would not be affected. This sense of duty and willingness to fight is reflected in letters the soldiers wrote home and in diaries and journals they kept during the war.

This book adds to the historiography of the Battle of the Bulge by discovering previously unpublished details about the specific actions taken by the three regiments of the 28th Infantry Division and placing them in the larger context of the battle. Historians and writers have virtually skipped over the heroic efforts of the 28th Division units who had been badly battered by their engagements attempting to breach the German Siegfried Line and in the fierce battles in the Hürtgen Forest. Future researchers can now have a more thorough understanding of why the Germans were not able to execute their plans, and what caused the soldiers on the front line to fight so determinedly.

Many veterans of World War II were reluctant to talk about their experiences, their religious beliefs, and what motivated them to fight. Most say they did their duty and came home. Interviews of veterans many years after the war may be skewed with sentimental memories and jaded with time. In future studies, the circumstances described by veterans in these interviews should be corroborated with reports and interviews conducted as close to the events as possible.

This book lays the groundwork for future research on the role that such motivations have on the soldiers' willingness to fight and the role leaders and government efforts play in motivating soldiers.

Appendix I

28th Infantry Division Combat Statistics (Source: U. S. Army Center of Military History)

Chronology	
Inducted into Federal Service	17 February 1941
Arrived European theater of operations	18 October 1943
Arrived Continent on European Continent	24 July 1944

Entered Combat	
First Elements	22 July 1944
Entire Division	27 July 1944

Days in Combat:	196

Casualties	
Killed	1,901
Wounded	9,157
Missing	2,599
Captured	2,247
Battle Casualties	15,904
Non-Battle Casualties	8,936
Total Casualties	24,840
As a Percent of Authorized Strength	176.3

Campaigns

Normandy

Northern France

Ardennes

Rhineland

Central Europe

INDIVIDUAL AWARDS

Medal of Honor	1
Distinguished Service Cross	16
Legion of Merit	4
Silver Star	258
Soldiers Medal	16
Bronze Star	2,029
Air Medal	92

Prisoners of War Taken:	8,661

Appendix II

28th Division Composition
(Source U. S. Army Center of Military History)

Organic Units
109th Infantry
110th Infantry
112th Infantry
28th Reconnaissance Troop (Mechanized)
103d Engineer Combat Battalion
103d Medical Battalion
28th Division Artillery
107th Field Artillery Battalion (105 Howitzer)
109th Field Artillery Battalion (105 Howitzer)
229th Field Artillery Battalion (105 Howitzer)
108th Field Artillery Battalion (155 Howitzer)
Special Troops
728th Ordnance Light Maintenance Company
28th Quartermaster Company
28th Signal Company
Military Police Platoon
Headquarters Company
Band

Attachments
Antiaircraft Artillery

447th AAA AW Battalion (Mobile)*	July 27, 1944–July 30, 1944
18th AAA Group	July 28, 1944–August 25, 1944
447th AAA AW Battalion (Mobile)	August 26, 1944–September 30, 1944

*AAA AW is Antiaircraft Artillery (Automatic Weapons)

Armored

Unit	Dates
744th Tank Battalion	July 30, 1944–August 27, 1944
707th Tank Battalion	October 6, 1944–January 8, 1945

Cavalry

Unit	Dates
113th Cavalry Group	July 29, 1944–August 2, 1944
113th Cavalry Group	August 2, 1944–August 4, 1944
85th Cavalry Recon. Sqdrn, (5th Armor Division)	September 7, 1944–September 9, 1944
32nd Cavalry Recon. Squadron	November 19, 1944–December 10, 1944

Chemical

Unit	Dates
Coy. D	
87th Chemical Battalion Coy. C	October 26, 1944–November 4, 1944
86th Chemical Mortar Battalion	October 28, 1944–November 15, 1944
86th Chemical Mortar Battalion (Coy. C)	October 28, 1944–November 19, 1944

Engineer

Unit	Dates
20th & 1340th Engineer Combat Battalions	
1171st Engineer Combat Group	October 24, 1944–November 19, 1944
146th Engineer Combat Group (Coy. B)	October 30, 1944–November 19, 1944
44th Engineer Combat Battalion	December 17, 1944–December 22, 1944

Field Artillery

Unit	Dates
18th Field Artillery Battalion (105 Howitzer)	August 1, 1944–August 6, 1944
187th Field Artillery Battalion (155 Howitzer)	August 30, 1944–September 3, 1944
Battery A, 987th Field Artillery Battalion (155 Gun)	October 7, 1944–November 9, 1944
76th Field Artillery Battalion (105 Howitzer)	October 28, 1944–November 19, 1944
687th Field Artillery Battalion (105 Howitzer)	November 19, 1944–January 1, 1945
58th Armored Field Artillery Battalion	December 17, 1944–December 23, 1944
770th Field Artillery Battalion (4.5" Gun)	December 24, 1944–December 29, 1944
73rd Armored Field Artillery Battalion	December 24, 1944–December 29, 1944

Tank Destroyer

630th Tank Destroyer Battalion (Towed)	July 20, 1944–September 30, 1944
803rd Tank Destroyer Battalion (Self-Propelled)	August 2, 1944–August 4, 1944
629th Tank Destroyer Battalion (Self-Propelled)	September 16, 1944–September 30, 1944
741st Tank Destroyer Battalion (Self-Propelled)	September 19, 1944–September 30, 1944
893rd Tank Destroyer Battalion (Self-Propelled) (Coy. A)	October 29, 1944–November 19, 1944
602nd Tank Destroyer Battalion (Self-Propelled) (-)	December 24, 1944–December 31, 1944
7th Tank Destroyer Group (-)	December 27, 1944–December 30, 1944

Appendix III

Command Post Locations through December 1944 (Source: U. S. Army Center of Military History)

DATE	TOWN	REGION	COUNTRY
1943			
19 October	Tenby (Hotel Belgrave)	Pembs	England
1944			
15 April	Chiseldon	Wiltshire	England
24 July	Omaha Beach	Manche	France
24 July	Treveries (3 miles SW)	Manche	France
29 July	Agneau (½ mile W)	Manche	France
31 July	La Denisiere (1½ miles NE)	Manche	France
2 August	La Tilandiere (¼ mile NW)	Manche	France
3 August	Margueray (½ mile NE)	Manche	France
4 August	Courson (1½ miles NE)	Calvados	France
6 August	St-Sever Calvados (3 miles SE)	Calvados	France
10 August	Champ du Boult (1 mile E)	Calvados	France
12 August	Gathemo (1 mile N)	Manche	France
14 August	Sourdeval (1½ miles S)	Manche	France
15 August	Ger (1 mile SE)	Manche	France
21 August	Barre (¼ mile NW)	Manche	France
22 August	Beauche	Eure-et-Loire	France
23 August	Damville	Eure	France
24 August	Quittebeuf	Eure	France
27 August	Houdan	Seine-et-Oise	France
28 August	Versailles	Seine-et-Oise	France
29 August	Paris	Seine	France
29 August	St-Denis	Seine	France
30 August	Chatenay-en-France	Seine-et-Oise	France
31 August	Raray (1 mile W)	Oise	France
3 September	Marest	Oise	France

4 September	Nizy-le-Compte	Aisne	France
5 September	Wagnon (1 mile SW)	Ardennes	France
6 September	Boulzicourt (1 mile E)	Ardennes	France
7 September	Douzy (1 mile E)	Ardennes	France
8 September	Florenville	Luxembourg	Belgium
10 September	Habay La Neuve (3 miles NE)	Luxembourg	Belgium
11 September	Trois Vierges (2 miles NE)	Luxembourg	Belgium
4 October	Elsenborn (1 mile NW)	Liege	Belgium
25 October	Rott	Rhineland	Germany
19 November	Wiltz	Rhineland	Luxembourg
19 December	Sibret	Liege	Belgium
21 December	Vaux Les Rosieres	Luxembourg	Belgium
22 December	Neufchateau	Luxembourg	Belgium

Appendix IV

Opposing Units on December 16, 1944 (Source: 28th Infantry Division Archives)

German Troop Strength in the First Line Ahead of Operation on December 16, 1944

Unit	Troop Strength
1st SS *Panzer* Division	21,292
12th SS *Panzer* Division	20,700
3rd *Fallschirmjager* Division	12,474
12th *Volksgrenadier* Division	9,517
277th *Volksgrenadier* Division	7,249
SS *Panzer* Brigade 150 (Greif)	2,955
Kampfgruppe von der Heydte	1,200
Total for 6th SS *Panzerarmee*	75,387
2nd *Panzer* Division	4,457
116th *Panzer* Division	15,468
Panzer Lehr Division	14,892
18th *Volksgrenadier* Division	12,117
26th *Volksgrenadier* Division	10,580
62nd *Volksgrenadier* Division	11,050
560th *Volksgrenadier* Division	11,197
Total for 5th SS *Panzerarmee*	89,761
5th *Fallschirmjager* Division	16,342
352nd *Volksgrenadier* Division	10,595
212th *Volksgrenadier* Division	11,151
276th *Volksgrenadier* Division	9,320
Total for 7th *Armee*	47,408
Grand Totals	212,556

U.S. Troop Strength in the First Line Ahead of Operation on December 16, 1944

Unit	Troop Strength
VIII Corp:	
106th Infantry Division	18,233
28th Infantry Division	16,996
9th Armored Division	12,025
7th Armored Division*	11,950
V Corp:	
99th Infantry Division	16,480
2nd Infantry Division	17,176
Total for 1st Army	92,860
4th Infantry Division, Third Army	16,843
Grand Total	109,703

* Transferred to VIII Corps on 16 December 1944.

Appendix V

Roosevelt's State of the Union Address to Congress on January 6, 1941 (Source: The American Presidency Project)

January 06, 1941

Mr. President, Mr. Speaker, Members of the Seventy-seventh Congress:

I address you, the Members of the Seventy-seventh Congress, at a moment unprecedented in the history of the Union. I use the word "unprecedented," because at no previous time has American security been as seriously threatened from without as it is today.

Since the permanent formation of our Government under the Constitution, in 1789, most of the periods of crisis in our history have related to our domestic affairs. Fortunately, only one of these—the four-year War Between the States—ever threatened our national unity. Today, thank God, one hundred and thirty million Americans, in forty-eight States, have forgotten points of the compass in our national unity.

It is true that prior to 1914 the United States often had been disturbed by events in other Continents. We had even engaged in two wars with European nations and in a number of undeclared wars in the West Indies, in the Mediterranean and in the Pacific for the maintenance of American rights and for the principles of peaceful commerce. But in no case had a serious threat been raised against our national safety or our continued independence.

What I seek to convey is the historic truth that the United States as a nation has at all times maintained clear, definite opposition, to any attempt to lock us in behind an ancient Chinese wall while the procession of civilization went past. Today, thinking of our children and of their children, we oppose enforced isolation for ourselves or for any other part of the Americas.

That determination of ours, extending over all these years, was proved, for example, during the quarter century of wars following the French Revolution.

While the Napoleonic struggles did threaten interests of the United States because of the French foothold in the West Indies and in Louisiana, and while we engaged in the War of 1812 to vindicate our right to peaceful trade, it is nevertheless clear that neither France nor Great Britain, nor any other nation, was aiming at domination of the whole world.

In like fashion from 1815 to 1914—ninety-nine years—no single war in Europe or in Asia constituted a real threat against our future or against the future of any other American nation.

Except in the Maximilian interlude in Mexico, no foreign power sought to establish itself in this Hemisphere; and the strength of the British fleet in the Atlantic has been a friendly strength. It is still a friendly strength.

Even when the World War broke out in 1914, it seemed to contain only small threat of danger to our own American future. But, as time went on, the American people began to visualize what the downfall of democratic nations might mean to our own democracy.

We need not overemphasize imperfections in the Peace of Versailles. We need not harp on failure of the democracies to deal with problems of world reconstruction. We should remember that the Peace of 1919 was far less unjust than the kind of "pacification" which began even before Munich, and which is being carried on under the new order of tyranny that seeks to spread over every continent today. The American people have unalterably set their faces against that tyranny.

Every realist knows that the democratic way of life is at this moment being' directly assailed in every part of the world—assailed either by arms, or by secret spreading of poisonous propaganda by those who seek to destroy unity and promote discord in nations that are still at peace.

During sixteen long months this assault has blotted out the whole pattern of democratic life in an appalling number of independent nations, great and small. The assailants are still on the march, threatening other nations, great and small.

Therefore, as your President, performing my constitutional duty to "give to the Congress information of the state of the Union," I find it, unhappily, necessary to report that the future and the safety of our country and of our democracy are overwhelmingly involved in events far beyond our borders.

Armed defense of democratic existence is now being gallantly waged in four continents. If that defense fails, all the population and all the resources of Europe, Asia, Africa and Australasia will be dominated by the conquerors. Let us remember that the total of those populations and their resources in those four continents greatly exceeds the sum total of the population and the resources of the whole of the Western Hemisphere-many times over.

In times like these it is immature—and incidentally, untrue—for anybody to brag that an unprepared America, single-handed, and with one hand tied behind its back, can hold off the whole world.

No realistic American can expect from a dictator's peace international generosity, or return of true independence, or world disarmament, or freedom of expression, or freedom of religion—or even good business.

Such a peace would bring no security for us or for our neighbors. Those who would give up essential liberty to purchase a little temporary safety, deserve neither liberty nor safety.

As a nation, we may take pride in the fact that we are softhearted; but we cannot afford to be soft-headed.

We must always be wary of those who with sounding brass and a tinkling cymbal preach the "ism" of appeasement.

We must especially beware of that small group of selfish men who would clip the wings of the American eagle in order to feather their own nests.

I have recently pointed out how quickly the tempo of modern warfare could bring into our very midst the physical attack which we must eventually expect if the dictator nations win this war.

There is much loose talk of our immunity from immediate and direct invasion from across the seas. Obviously, as long as the British Navy retains its power, no such danger exists. Even if there were no British Navy, it is not probable that any enemy would be stupid enough to attack us by landing troops in the United States from across thousands of miles of ocean, until it had acquired strategic bases from which to operate.

But we learn much from the lessons of the past years in Europe—particularly the lesson of Norway, whose essential seaports were captured by treachery and surprise built up over a series of years.

The first phase of the invasion of this Hemisphere would not be the landing of regular troops. The necessary strategic points would be occupied by secret agents and their dupes—and great numbers of them are already here, and in Latin America.

As long as the aggressor nations maintain the offensive, they—not we—will choose the time and the place and the method of their attack.

That is why the future of all the American Republics is today in serious danger.

That is why this Annual Message to the Congress is unique in our history.

That is why every member of the Executive Branch of the Government and every member of the Congress faces great responsibility and great accountability.

The need of the moment is that our actions and our policy should be devoted primarily—almost exclusively—to meeting this foreign peril. For all our domestic problems are now a part of the great emergency.

Just as our national policy in internal affairs has been based upon a decent respect for the rights and the dignity of all our fellow men within our gates, so our national policy in foreign affairs has been based on a decent respect for the rights and dignity of all nations, large and small. And the justice of morality must and will win in the end.

Our national policy is this:

First, by an impressive expression of the public will and without regard to partisanship, we are committed to all-inclusive national defense.

Second, by an impressive expression of the public will and without regard to partisanship, we are committed to full support of all those resolute peoples, everywhere, who are resisting aggression and are thereby keeping war away from our Hemisphere. By this support, we express our determination that the democratic cause shall prevail; and we strengthen the defense and the security of our own nation.

Third, by an impressive expression of the public will and without regard to partisanship, we are committed to the proposition that principles of morality and considerations for our own security will never permit us to acquiesce in a peace dictated by aggressors and sponsored by appeasers. We know that enduring peace cannot be bought at the cost of other people's freedom.

In the recent national election there was no substantial difference between the two great parties in respect to that national policy. No issue was fought out on this line before the American electorate. Today it is abundantly evident that American citizens everywhere are demanding and supporting speedy and complete action in recognition of obvious danger.

Therefore, the immediate need is a swift and driving increase in our armament production.

Leaders of industry and labor have responded to our summons. Goals of speed have been set. In some cases these goals are being reached ahead of time; in some cases we are on schedule; in other cases there are slight but not serious delays; and in some cases—and I am sorry to say very important cases—we are all concerned by the slowness of the accomplishment of our plans.

The Army and Navy, however, have made substantial progress during the past year. Actual experience is improving and speeding up our methods of production with every passing day. And today's best is not good enough for tomorrow.

I am not satisfied with the progress thus far made. The men in charge of the program represent the best in training, in ability, and in patriotism.

They are not satisfied with the progress thus far made. None of us will be satisfied until the job is done.

No matter whether the original goal was set too high or too low, our objective is quicker and better results. To give you two illustrations:

We are behind schedule in turning out finished airplanes; we are working day and night to solve the innumerable problems and to catch up.

We are ahead of schedule in building warships but we are working to get even further ahead of that schedule.

To change a whole nation from a basis of peacetime production of implements of peace to a basis of wartime production of implements of war is no small task. And the greatest difficulty comes at the beginning of the program, when new tools, new plant facilities, new assembly lines, and new ship ways must first be constructed before the actual materiel begins to flow steadily and speedily from them.

The Congress, of course, must rightly keep itself informed at all times of the progress of the program. However, there is certain information, as the Congress itself will readily recognize, which, in the interests of our own security and those of the nations that we are supporting, must of needs be kept in confidence.

New circumstances are constantly begetting new needs for our safety. I shall ask this Congress for greatly increased new appropriations and authorizations to carry on what we have begun.

I also ask this Congress for authority and for funds sufficient to manufacture additional munitions and war supplies of many kinds, to be turned over to those nations which are now in actual war with aggressor nations.

Our most useful and immediate role is to act as an arsenal for them as well as for ourselves. They do not need manpower, but they do need billions of dollars' worth of the weapons of defense.

The time is near when they will not be able to pay for them all in ready cash. We cannot, and we will not, tell them that they must surrender, merely because of present inability to pay for the weapons which we know they must have.

I do not recommend that we make them a loan of dollars with which to pay for these weapons—a loan to be repaid in dollars.

I recommend that we make it possible for those nations to continue to obtain war materials in the United States, fitting their orders into our own program. Nearly all their materiel would, if the time ever came, be useful for our own defense.

Taking counsel of expert military and naval authorities, considering what is best for our own security, we are free to decide how much should be kept here and how much should be sent abroad to our friends who by their determined and heroic resistance are giving us time in which to make ready our own defense.

For what we send abroad, we shall be repaid within a reasonable time following the close of hostilities, in similar materials, or, at our option, in other goods of many kinds, which they can produce and which we need.

Let us say to the democracies: "We Americans are vitally concerned in your defense of freedom. We are putting forth our energies, our resources and our organizing powers to give you the strength to regain and maintain a free world. We shall send you, in ever-increasing numbers, ships, planes, tanks, guns. This is our purpose and our pledge."

In fulfillment of this purpose we will not be intimidated by the threats of dictators that they will regard as a breach of international law or as an act of war our aid to the democracies which dare to resist their aggression. Such aid is not an act of war, even if a dictator should unilaterally proclaim it so to be.

When the dictators, if the dictators, are ready to make war upon us, they will not wait for an act of war on our part. They did not wait for Norway or Belgium or the Netherlands to commit an act of war.

Their only interest is in a new one-way international law, which lacks mutuality in its observance, and, therefore, becomes an instrument of oppression.

The happiness of future generations of Americans may well depend upon how effective and how immediate we can make our aid felt. No one can tell the exact character of the emergency situations that we may be called upon to meet. The Nation's hands must not be tied when the Nation's life is in danger.

We must all prepare to make the sacrifices that the emergency—almost as serious as war itself—demands. Whatever stands in the way of speed and efficiency in defense preparations must give way to the national need.

A free nation has the right to expect full cooperation from all groups. A free nation has the right to look to the leaders of business, of labor, and of agriculture to take the lead in stimulating effort, not among other groups but within their own groups.

The best way of dealing with the few slackers or troublemakers in our midst is, first, to shame them by patriotic example, and, if that fails, to use the sovereignty of Government to save Government.

As men do not live by bread alone, they do not fight by armaments alone. Those who man our defenses, and those behind them who build our defenses, must have the stamina and the courage which come from unshakable belief in the manner of life which they are defending. The mighty action that we are calling for cannot be based on a disregard of all things worth fighting for.

The Nation takes great satisfaction and much strength from the things which have been done to make its people conscious of their individual stake in the preservation of democratic life in America. Those things have toughened the fiber of our people, have renewed their faith and strengthened their devotion to the institutions we make ready to protect.

Certainly this is no time for any of us to stop thinking about the social and economic problems which are the root cause of the social revolution which is today a supreme factor in the world.

For there is nothing mysterious about the foundations of a healthy and strong democracy. The basic things expected by our people of their political and economic systems are simple. They are:

Equality of opportunity for youth and for others.

Jobs for those who can work.

Security for those who need it.

The ending of special privilege for the few.

The preservation of civil liberties for all.

The enjoyment of the fruits of scientific progress in a wider and constantly rising standard of living.

These are the simple, basic things that must never be lost sight of in the turmoil and unbelievable complexity of our modern world. The inner and abiding strength of our economic and political systems is dependent upon the degree to which they fulfill these expectations.

Many subjects connected with our social economy call for immediate improvement. As examples:

We should bring more citizens under the coverage of old-age pensions and unemployment insurance.

We should widen the opportunities for adequate medical care.

We should plan a better system by which persons deserving or needing gainful employment may obtain it.

I have called for personal sacrifice. I am assured of the willingness of almost all Americans to respond to that call.

A part of the sacrifice means the payment of more money in taxes. In my Budget Message I shall recommend that a greater portion of this great defense program be paid for from taxation than we are paying today. No person should try, or be allowed, to get rich out of this program; and the principle of tax payments in accordance with ability to pay should be constantly before our eyes to guide our legislation.

If the Congress maintains these principles, the voters, putting patriotism ahead of pocketbooks, will give you their applause.

In the future days, which we seek to make secure, we look forward to a world founded upon four essential human freedoms.

The first is freedom of speech and expression—everywhere in the world.

The second is freedom of every person to worship God in his own way—everywhere in the world.

The third is freedom from want—which, translated into world terms, means economic understandings which will secure to every nation a healthy peacetime life for its inhabitants-everywhere in the world.

The fourth is freedom from fear—which, translated into world terms, means a world-wide reduction of armaments to such a point and in such a thorough fashion that no nation will be in a position to commit an act of physical aggression against any neighbor—anywhere in the world.

That is no vision of a distant millennium. It is a definite basis for a kind of world attainable in our own time and generation. That kind of world is the very antithesis of the so-called new order of tyranny which the dictators seek to create with the crash of a bomb.

To that new order we oppose the greater conception—the moral order. A good society is able to face schemes of world domination and foreign revolutions alike without fear.

Since the beginning of our American history, we have been engaged in change—in a perpetual peaceful revolution—a revolution which goes on steadily, quietly adjusting itself to changing conditions—without the concentration camp or the quick-lime in the ditch. The world order which we seek is the cooperation of free countries, working together in a friendly, civilized society.

This nation has placed its destiny in the hands and heads and hearts of its millions of free men and women, and its faith in freedom under the guidance of God. Freedom means the supremacy of human rights everywhere. Our support goes to those who struggle to gain those rights or keep them. Our strength is our unity of purpose. To that high concept there can be no end save victory.

Appendix VI

Harold L. Ickles' Speech during "I am an American Day" Gathering in New York (Source: Harold L. Ickes Papers, ID No.: MSS27011, Library of Congress)

May 18, 1941

I want to ask a few simple questions. And then I shall answer them.

What has happened to our vaunted idealism? Why have some of us been behaving like scared chickens? Where is the million-throated, democratic voice of America?

For years it has been dined into us that we are a weak nation; that we are an inefficient people; that we are simple-minded. For years we have been told that we are beaten, decayed, and that no part of the world belongs to us any longer.

Some amongst us have fallen for this carefully pickled tripe. Some amongst us have fallen for this calculated poison. Some amongst us have begun to preach that the "wave of the future" has passed over us and left us a wet, dead fish.

They shout—from public platforms in printed pages, through the microphones—that it is futile to oppose the "wave of the future." They cry that we Americans, we free Americans nourished on Magna Carta and the Declaration of Independence, hold moth-eaten ideas. They exclaim that there is no room for free men in the world anymore and that only the slaves will inherit the earth. America—the America of Washington and Jefferson and Lincoln and Walt Whitman—they say, is waiting for the undertaker and all the hopes and aspirations that have gone into the making of America are dead too.

However, my fellow citizens, this is not the real point of the story. The real point—the shameful point—is that many of us are listening to them and some of us almost believe them.

I say that it is time for the great American people to raise its voice and cry out in mighty triumph what it is to be an American. And why it is that only Americans, with the aid of our brave allies—yes, let's call them allies—the British, can and will build the only future worth having. I mean a future, not of concentration camps, not of physical torture and mental straitjackets, not of sawdust bread or of sawdust Caesars—I mean a future when free men will live free lives in dignity and in security.

This tide of the future, the democratic future, is ours. It is ours if we show ourselves worthy of our culture and of our heritage.

But make no mistake about it; the tide of the democratic future is not like the ocean tide--regular, relentless, and inevitable. Nothing in human affairs is mechanical or inevitable. Nor are Americans mechanical. They are very human indeed.

What constitutes an American? Not color nor race nor religion. Not the pedigree of his family nor the place of his birth. Not the coincidence of his citizenship. Not his social status nor his bank account. Not his trade nor his profession. An American is one who loves justice and believes in the dignity of man. An American is one who will fight for his freedom and that of his neighbor. An American is one who will sacrifice property, ease and security in order that he and his children may retain the rights of free men. An American is one in whose heart is engraved the immortal second sentence of the Declaration of Independence.

Americans have always known how to fight for their rights and their way of life. Americans are not afraid to fight. They fight joyously in a just cause.

We Americans know that freedom, like peace, is indivisible. We cannot retain our liberty if three-fourths of the world is enslaved. Brutality, injustice and slavery, if practiced as dictators would have them, universally and systematically, in the long run would destroy us as surely as a fire raging in our nearby neighbor's house would burn ours if we didn't help to put out his.

If we are to retain our own freedom, we must do everything within our power to aid Britain. We must also do everything to restore to the conquered peoples their freedom. This means the Germans too.

Such a program, if you stop to think, is selfishness on our part. It is the sort of enlightened selfishness that makes the wheels of history go around. It is the sort of enlightened selfishness that wins victories.

Do you know why? Because we cannot live in the world alone, without friends and without allies. If Britain should be defeated, then the totalitarian undertaker will prepare to hang crepe on the door of our own independence.

Perhaps you wonder how this could come about? Perhaps you have heard them—the wavers of the future—cry, with calculated malice, that even if Britain were defeated we could live alone and defend ourselves single handed, even against the whole world.

I tell you that this is a cold blooded lie.

We would be alone in the world, facing an unscrupulous military-economic bloc that would dominate all of Europe, all of Africa, most of Asia, and perhaps even Russia and South America. Even to do that, we would have to spend most of our national income on tanks and guns and planes and ships. Nor would this be all. We would have to live perpetually as an armed camp, maintaining a huge standing army, a gigantic air force, two vast navies. And we could not do this without endangering our freedom, our democracy, our way of life.

Perhaps such is the America they—the wavers of the future—foresee. Perhaps such is the America that a certain aviator, with his contempt for democracy, would prefer. Perhaps such is the America that a certain Senator desires. Perhaps such is the America that a certain mail order executive long for.

But a perpetually militarized, isolated and impoverished America is not the America that our fathers came here to build.

It is not the America that has been the dream and the hope of countless generations in all parts of the world.

It is not the America that one hundred and thirty million of us would care to live in.

The continued security of our country demands that we aid the enslaved millions of Europe—yes, even of Germany—to win back their liberty and independence. I am convinced that if we do not embark upon such a program we will lose our own freedom.

We should be clear on this point. What is convulsing the world today is not merely another old-fashioned war. It is a counter revolution against our ideas and ideals, against our sense of justice and our human values.

Three systems today compete for world domination. Communism, fascism, and democracy are struggling for social-economic-political world control. As the conflict sharpens, it becomes clear that the other two, fascism and communism, are merging into one. They have one common enemy, democracy. They have one common goal, the destruction of democracy.

This is why this war is not an ordinary war. It is not a conflict for markets or territories. It is a desperate struggle for the possession of the souls of men.

This is why the British are not fighting for themselves alone. They are fighting to preserve freedom for mankind. For the moment, the battleground is the British Isles. But they are fighting our war; they are the first soldiers in trenches that are also our front-line trenches.

In this world war of ideas and of loyalties we believers in democracy must do two things. We must unite our forces to form one great democratic international. We must offer a clear program to freedom-loving peoples throughout the world.

Freedom-loving men and women in every land must organize and tighten their ranks. The masses everywhere must be helped to fight their oppressors and conquerors.

We, free, democratic Americans are in a position to help. We know that the spirit of freedom never dies. We know that men have fought and bled for freedom since time immemorial. We realize that the liberty-loving German people are only temporarily enslaved. We do not doubt that the Italian people are looking forward to the appearance of another Garibaldi. We know how the Poles have for centuries maintained a heroic resistance against tyranny. We remember the brave struggle of the Hungarians under Kossuth and other leaders. We recall the heroic figure of Masaryk and the gallant fight for freedom of the Czech people. The story of the Yugoslavs', especially the Serbs' blows for liberty and independence is a saga of extraordinary heroism. The Greeks will stand again at Thermopylae, as they have in the past. The annals of our American sister-republics, too, are glorious with freedom-inspiring exploits. The noble figure of Simon Bolivar, the great South American liberator, has naturally been compared with that of George Washington.

No, liberty never dies. The Genghis Khans come and go. The Attilas come and go. The Hitlers flash and sputter out. But freedom endures.

Destroy a whole generation of those who have known how to walk with heads erect in God's free air, and the next generation will rise against the oppressors and restore freedom. Today in Europe, the Nazi Attila may gloat that he has destroyed democracy. He is wrong. In small farmhouses all over Central Europe, in the shops of Germany and Italy, on the docks of Holland and Belgium, freedom still lives in the hearts of men. It will endure like a hardy tree gone into the wintertime, awaiting the spring.

And, like spring, spreading from the South into Scandinavia, the democratic revolution will come. And men with democratic hearts will experience comradeship across artificial boundaries.

These men and women, hundreds of millions of them, now in bondage or threatened with slavery, are our comrades and our allies. They are only waiting for our leadership and our encouragement, for the spark that we can supply.

These hundreds of millions, of liberty-loving people, now oppressed, constitute the greatest sixth column in history. They have the will to destroy the Nazi gangsters.

We have always helped in struggles for human freedom. And we will help again. But our hundreds of millions of liberty-loving allies would despair if we did not provide aid and encouragement. The quicker we help them the sooner this dreadful revolution will be over. We cannot, we must not, we dare not delay much longer.

The fight for Britain is in its crucial stages. We must give the British everything we have. And by everything, I mean everything needed to beat the life out of our common enemy.

The second step must be to aid and encourage our friends and allies everywhere. And by everywhere I mean Europe and Asia and Africa and America.

And finally, the most important of all, we Americans must gird spiritually for the battle. We must dispel the fog of uncertainty and vacillation. We must greet with raucous laughter the corroding arguments of our appeasers and fascists. They doubt democracy. We affirm it triumphantly so that all the world may hear:

Here in America we have something so worth living for that it is worth dying for! The so-called "wave of the future" is but the slimy backwash of the past. We have not heaved from our necks the tyrant's crushing heel, only to stretch our necks out again for its weight. Not only will we fight for democracy, but we will also make it more worth fighting for. Under our free institutions, we will work for the good of mankind, including Hitler's victims in Germany, so that all may have plenty and security.

We American democrats know that when good will prevails among men there will be a world of plenty and a world of security.

In the words of Winston Churchill, "Are we downhearted," No, we are not! But someone is downhearted! Witness the terrified flight of Hess, Hitler's Number Three Man. And listen to this—listen carefully:

"The British nation can be counted upon to carry through to victory any struggle that it once enters upon no matter how long such a struggle may last or however great the sacrifices that may be necessary or whatever the means that have to be employed; and all this even though the actual military equipment at hand may be utterly inadequate when compared with that of other nations."

Do you know who wrote that? Adolf Hitler in *Mein Kampf*. And do you know who took down that dictation? Rudolf Hess.

We will help to make Hitler's prophecy come true. We will help brave England drive back the hordes from Hell who besiege her and then we will join for the destruction of savage and blood-thirsty dictators everywhere. But we must be firm and decisive. We must know our will and make it felt. And we must hurry.

Appendix VII

General Patton's Address to the Troops on June 5, 1944 (Source: General George Patton Museum of Leadership)

Men, this stuff that some sources sling around about America wanting out of this war, not wanting to fight, is a crock of bullshit. Americans love to fight, traditionally. All real Americans love the sting and clash of battle. You are here today for three reasons. First, because you are here to defend your homes and your loved ones. Second, you are here for your own self-respect because you would not want to be anywhere else. Third, you are here because you are real men and all real men like to fight. When you, here, every one of you, were kids, you all admired the champion marble player, the fastest runner, the toughest boxer, the big league ball players, and the All-American football players. Americans love a winner. Americans will not tolerate a loser. Americans despise cowards. Americans play to win all of the time. I wouldn't give a hoot in hell for a man who lost and laughed. That's why Americans have never lost nor will ever lose a war; for the very idea of losing is hateful to an American.

You are not all going to die. Only two percent of you right here today would die in a major battle. Death must not be feared. Death, in time, comes to all men. Yes, every man is scared in his first battle. If he says he's not, he's a liar. Some men are cowards but they fight the same as the brave men or they get the hell slammed out of them watching men fight who are just as scared as they are. The real hero is the man who fights even though he is scared. Some men get over their fright in a minute under fire. For some, it takes an hour. For some, it takes days. But a real man will never let his fear of death overpower his honor, his sense of duty to his country, and his innate manhood. Battle is the most magnificent competition in which a human being can indulge. It brings out all that is best and it removes all that is base. Americans pride themselves on being He Men and they ARE He Men. Remember that the enemy is just as frightened as you are, and probably more so. They are not supermen.

All through your Army careers, you men have bitched about what you call chicken shit drilling. That, like everything else in this Army, has a definite purpose. That purpose is alertness. Alertness must be bred into every soldier. I don't give a fuck for a man who's not always on his toes. You men are veterans or you wouldn't be here. You are ready for what's to come. A man must be alert at all times if he expects to stay alive. If you're not alert, sometime, a German son-of-an-asshole-bitch is going to sneak up behind you and beat you to death with a sock full of shit!

There are four hundred neatly marked graves somewhere in Sicily. All because one man went to sleep on the job. But they are German graves because we caught the bastard asleep before they did. An Army is a team. It lives, sleeps, eats, and fights as a team. This individual heroic stuff is pure horse shit. The bilious bastards who write that kind of stuff for the Saturday Evening Post don't know any more about real fighting under fire than they know about fucking!

We have the finest food, the finest equipment, the best spirit, and the best men in the world. Why, by God, I actually pity those poor sons-of-bitches we're going up against. By God, I do.

My men don't surrender. I don't want to hear of any soldier under my command being captured unless he has been hit. Even if you are hit, you can still fight back. That's not just bull shit either. The kind of man that I want in my command is just like the lieutenant in Libya, who, with a Luger against his chest, jerked off his helmet, swept the gun aside with one hand, and busted the hell out of the Kraut with his helmet. Then he jumped on the gun and went out and killed another German before they knew what the hell was coming off. And, all of that time, this man had a bullet through a lung. There was a real man!

All of the real heroes are not storybook combat fighters, either. Every single man in this Army plays a vital role. Don't ever let up. Don't ever think that your job is unimportant. Every man has a job to do and he must do it. Every man is a vital link in the great chain. What if every truck driver suddenly decided that he didn't like the whine of those shells overhead, turned yellow, and jumped headlong into a ditch? The cowardly bastard could say, Hell, they won't miss me, just one man in thousands. But, what if every man thought that way? Where in the hell would we be now? What would our country, our loved ones, our homes, even the world, be like? No, Goddamnit, Americans don't think like that. Every man does his job. Every man serves the whole. Every department, every unit, is important in the vast scheme of this war. The ordnance men are needed to supply the guns and machinery of war to keep us rolling. The Quartermaster is needed to bring up food and clothes because where we are going there isn't a hell of a lot to steal. Every last man on K.P. has a job to do, even the one who heats our water to keep us from getting the "G.I. Shits."

Each man must not think only of himself, but also of his buddy fighting beside him. We don't want yellow cowards in this Army. They should be killed off like rats. If not, they will go home after this war and breed more cowards. The brave men will breed more brave men. Kill off the Goddamned cowards and we will have a nation of brave men. One of the bravest men that I ever saw was a fellow on top of a telegraph pole in the midst of a furious fire fight in Tunisia. I stopped and asked what the hell he was doing up there at a time like that. He answered, Fixing the wire, Sir. I asked, Isn't that a little unhealthy right about now? He answered, Yes Sir, but the Goddamned wire has to be fixed. I asked, Don't those planes strafing the road bother you? And he answered, No, Sir, but you sure as hell do! Now, there was a real man. A real soldier.

There was a man who devoted all he had to his duty, no matter how seemingly insignificant his duty might appear at the time, no matter how great the odds. And you should have seen those trucks on the road to Tunisia. Those drivers were magnificent. All day and all night they rolled over those son-of-a-bitching roads, never stopping, never faltering from their course, with shells bursting all around them all of the time. We got through on good old American guts. Many of those men drove for over forty consecutive hours. These men weren't combat men, but they were soldiers with a job to do. They did it, and in one hell of a way they did it. They were part of a team. Without team effort, without them, the fight would have been lost. All of the links in the chain pulled together and the chain became unbreakable.

Don't forget, you men don't know that I'm here. No mention of that fact is to be made in any letters. The world is not supposed to know what the hell happened to me. I'm not supposed to be commanding this Army. I'm not even supposed to be here in England. Let the first bastards to find out be the Goddamned Germans. Someday I want to see them raise up on their piss-soaked hind legs and howl, Jesus Christ, it's the Goddamned Third Army again and that son-of-a-fucking-bitch Patton.

We want to get the hell over there. The quicker we clean up this Goddamned mess, the quicker we can take a little jaunt against the purple pissing Japs and clean out their nest, too. Before the Goddamned Marines get all of the credit.

Sure, we want to go home. We want this war over with. The quickest way to get it over with is to go get the bastards who started it. The quicker they are whipped, the quicker we can go home. The shortest way home is through Berlin and Tokyo. And when we get to Berlin, I am personally going to shoot that paper hanging son-of-a-bitch Hitler. Just like I'd shoot a snake!

When a man is lying in a shell hole, if he just stays there all day, a German will get to him eventually. The hell with that idea. The hell with taking it. My men don't dig foxholes. I don't want them to. Foxholes only slow up an offensive. Keep moving. And don't give the enemy time to dig one either. We'll win this war, but we'll win it only by fighting and by showing the Germans that we've got more guts than they have; or ever will have. We're not going to just shoot the sons-of-bitches, we're going to rip out their living Goddamned guts and use them to grease the treads of our tanks. We're going to murder those lousy Hun cocksuckers by the bushel-fucking-basket. War is a bloody, killing business. You've got to spill their blood, or they will spill yours. Rip them up the belly. Shoot them in the guts. When shells are hitting all around you and you wipe the dirt off your face and realize that instead of dirt it's the blood and guts of what once was your best friend beside you, you'll know what to do!

I don't want to get any messages saying, "I am holding my position." We are not holding a Goddamned thing. Let the Germans do that. We are advancing constantly and we are not interested in holding onto anything, except the enemy's balls. We are going to twist his balls and kick the living shit out of him all of the time. Our basic plan of operation is to advance and to keep on advancing regardless of whether we have to go over, under, or through the enemy. We are going to go through him like crap through a goose, like shit through a tin horn!

From time to time there will be some complaints that we are pushing our people too hard. I don't give a good Goddamn about such complaints. I believe in the old and sound rule that an ounce of sweat will save a gallon of blood. The harder we push, the more Germans we will kill. The more Germans we kill, the fewer of our men will be killed. Pushing means fewer casualties. I want you all to remember that.

There is one great thing that you men will all be able to say after this war is over and you are home once again. You may be thankful that twenty years from now when you are sitting by the fireplace with your grandson on your knee and he asks you what you did in the great World War II, you won't have to cough, shift him to the other knee and say, Well, your Granddaddy shoveled shit in Louisiana. No, Sir, you can look him straight in the eye and say, Son, your Granddaddy rode with the Great Third Army and a Son-of-a-Goddamned-Bitch named Georgie Patton!

Appendix VIII

Extracts from 2nd German Panzer Division Reports (Source: Official World War II German Army Documents, National Archives)

Training Status and Equipment Needs Prior to 1944 Offensive

Due to reinforcements obtained from a multitude of unit remnants returning from the Eastern front, there is no uniformity in required levels of experience and efficiency. Initial emphasis was placed on new weapons training, non-commissioned officer leadership skills, mobile offensive operations and maintenance. Approximately 350 squad leaders are needed. The 3rd Regiment is forth three tank crews short, equating to the fact that half of all combat ready tubes cannot be made operational until fully staffed and trained.

Anti-aircraft guns are fully manned and quite effective. One of the light armored scout vehicle companies has no rolling stock. Of required truck resources only 50 percent remain and only half of these are operational. Of 125 required howitzer tow vehicles, only twenty eight are available. Most heavy weapons are therefore stationary, which includes 213 of the functioning anti-aircraft guns. Replacement parts are very difficult to obtain or non-existent. Another major shortage is in the areas of optical equipment for heavy weapons, binoculars and field compasses. Clothing supplies are marginal, especially for overcoats and winter underwear! The Division is currently not capable to conduct offensive operations.

Advanced Training and Equipment Status Report Prior to 1944 Offensive

Mobile operations at squad and platoon level received highest training emphasis. At present, company and battalion exercises are in motion. Pioneers are lagging behind due to their lengthy training requirements. Missing squad leader backlog was reduced to 150. Heavy weapon mobile operations. Training is hampered by fuel shortages. Twenty nine tank crews are still missing. Special training is being conducted in critical maintenance operations.

Communications training is not yet to standards due to the time requirement of three weeks minimum for high caliber personnel. Manpower shortages are most critical among pioneers. Not one company is functional at this time and vital bridge components are unobtainable.

Boot supplies are critically short. Attempts were made to exchange footwear with logistics troops to the best degree possible. There are no current provisions for any exchange of uniforms.

The Division's mobility has greatly improved due to the recent augmentation of towing vehicles. Massive operations are still not possible due to the great number of inoperable truck type vehicles, especially those of foreign make. A great number and variety of civilian sedans are available, but none of these are useful as communications or command vehicles. There are now 300 types of motorized vehicles under Division control. Ordering spare parts became a logistic nightmare. None of them arrived to-date. Currently, 35 percent of the Division is motorized and mobile. Another 35 percent can be loaded and moved. About 50 percent of Division troops can be logistically sustained during an offensive. We should be able to accomplish limited objectives.

Assessment of 2nd Panzer Division Capabilities during Ardennes Offensive, 3 January 1945

After extensive losses suffered during enemy engagements near Dinant, the following Division components are still functional and combat ready: A partial tank regiment consisting of four light tanks, four anti-tank guns and two heavy tanks, supported by 100 grenadiers, one howitzer, two mortar rocket launchers and several light anti-aircraft guns. With the exception of supply and support troops, the balance of the Division is no longer fit for action.

Due to heavy casualties, there is a dangerous void of leadership at all levels which hinders successful attempts at reorganizing the Division.

Internally organized leadership training is not feasible under these conditions.

Remnant unit mobility is extremely low, primarily due to the high number of lost vehicles and the unusual proportion of foreign makes still in the operational stage for which spare parts, tires and batteries cannot be obtained. Only 42 percent of vehicles currently under Division control are operational. Only 32 percent of the still operational heavy weapons can be towed at this time. Any contemplated heavy weapon augmentation must be complete with towed vehicles. The current lack of spare parts severely handicaps operation ability of remaining tanks. There are further no specialized tools available to facilitate needed repairs. Because of this fact, only 20 percent of the available light tanks were still operational after the first day of the assault. We further lost eight tanks due to muzzle explosions caused by faulty projectiles. Replacement of lost heavy weapons and anti-aircraft guns is desperately needed.

Uniform supplies are ample, except for socks and underwear, heavy overcoats, canteens and mess kits are needed. The morale of our troops has been negatively influenced by the total lack of promised friendly air cover during the assault.

Appendix IX

VIII Corps After-Action Report for December 1–31, 1944 (Source: Headquarters VIII Corps (April 1945)

The VIII Corps After Action Reports for December 1944 provides an understanding of the overall situation and positioning of forces prior to and as the German Ardennes Offense unfolded.

During October and November 1944, the First and Third United States Armies regrouped and launched attacks against the Siegfried Line in an effort to penetrate the German defenses and reach the Rhine River. The Third Army shaped up its attack in the Metz area; the First Army made its main effort in the Aachen sector and the area immediately to the south where an attempt was made to secure dams controlling flood waters of the Roer River. Between these two major efforts an extensive line of defense was maintained by the First Army, the southern and major part of which was manned by the VIII Corps.

The sector occupied by VIII Corps extended from Losheim, Germany, on the north to a point where the Moselle River crosses the Franco-German boundary at the southeast corner of the Duchy of Luxembourg. It generally paralleled the German frontier along eastern Belgium and Luxembourg and comprised a front of eighty-eight miles. This section of the country is known as the Ardennes and its rugged terrain is characterized by high plateaus, deeply incised valleys and a restricted road net. Facing the sector in the north was the still more rugged Eifel Massif, while south of the junction of the Moselle and the Our Rivers the Hunsruck region stretched from the upper Moselle eastward to the Rhine. The mission assigned to VIII Corps was to defend this sector in place.

In the northern part of the sector the 2nd Infantry Division held a salient in the Siegfried Line along a high wooded ridge known as the Schnee Eifel. To the right of the 2nd Division, the 28th Infantry Division defended a front along the Our River, and the 83rd Infantry Division held the southern part of the sector along the Our River to its confluence with the Moselle and thence up the Moselle to the boundary between the VIII and XX Corps of the Third Army. The 9th Armored Division, a unit without battle experience, was supporting the 83rd Division with its artillery and from Corps Reserve positions was rotating infantry units in infantry division front lines. Combat Command "B" of the 9th Armored and most of the Corps artillery were located in the 2nd Division zone in order to counter any effort the Germans might make to regain positions in the Siegfried Line. A combat command was a combined-arms military organization of comparable size to a brigade or regiment employed by armored forces. The structure of combat commands was task-organized and so the forces assigned to a combat command often varied from mission to mission.

The 28th Division was new to VIII Corps, having replaced the 8th Infantry Division during the middle of November. Before that time it had participated in the First Army attack to secure the Roer River dams. The seizure of these dams was essential to the success of the main attack farther north, for the dams controlled waters with which the Germans could inundate flood plains in front of Duren and spoil the attack. The division sustained severe infantry losses in the attack, and on arrival in the VIII Corps sector it needed some 3,400 reinforcements. As a whole, the division was worn out but it was expected that necessary rest and rehabilitation could be gained while occupying a defensive sector in the VIII Corps. During the latter part of November, division strength was brought within 300 of that authorized, and the division zone was slightly narrowed down from the area which was held by the 8th Division. The smaller sector was accomplished by extending the 83rd Division over a wider area in the south.

The 4th Infantry Division, under VII Corps, had also fought a tiring and costly battle through the Hurtgen Forest below Duren in the November attack by the First Army. Because it was in much need of rest and rehabilitation, the division was exchanged for the rested 83rd Division which was holding the southern sector of the VIII Corps zone. The exchange was initiated on 1 December, transfer of responsibility for the division sector was accomplished on 7 December, and troop movements were completed on 12 December.

The 106th Infantry Division, newly arrived on the Continent, was assigned to VIII Corps and closed in an assembly area in the 2nd Division sector near St. Vith on 8–10 December. It was intended that the 106th should relieve the 2nd Division so that the 2nd could take part in the V Corps attack planned for the middle of December. The 106th was to be given an opportunity to gain combat experience while occupying defenses in the relatively quiet VIII Corps sector. The regiments of the 2nd Division moved out as relieved. The 106th took over responsibility for the sector at 7:00 p.m. on 11 December, and the last elements of the 2nd Division cleared on 12 December. In addition, Combat Command "B" of the 9th Armored Division was attached to V Corps and moved out under direction of the 2nd Di vision on 13 December. Combat Command "R" of the 9th was moved to the vicinity of Trois Vierges to replace Combat Command "B" as an armored reserve in the rear of the 106th Division.

North of the positions in the Schnee Eifel a ten-kilometer front had been occupied by Task Force "X" under the 2nd Division. When the 106th took over in sector, the 18th and 32nd Squadrons, 14th Cavalry Group, were attached to the division to occupy this sector and maintain contact between the 106th Division and the 99th Division of V Corps on the north.

The 9th Armored was given a four-kilometer front from the right flank of the 28th Division zone on 10 December, which they occupied with the 60th Armored Infantry Battalion. Although this change cut the zone of the 28th Division slightly, the 28th still held a 40-kilometer front. The majority of this front lay along the Our River and was held by two battalions each of the 109th and 110th Regiments, thereby giving each battalion a front of six to eight thousand yards. Defensive organization consisted of a series of strong points with patrols operating in between. The left flank of the 28th Division extended into Germany away from the river and was more strongly held by the 112th Infantry which occupied defensive positions built by Corps Engineers the previous month.

The Germans had been quiet on the Corps front for two months, and as December opened it was estimated that four German divisions faced VIII Corps. From north to south, these infantry divisions were the 18th, 26th, 352nd and 212th. On 2 December the 112th Infantry, 28th Division in a raid destroyed two German pillboxes and captured two prisoners from the 26th Volks Grenadier Division, thus re-identifying this division. On 4 December the 28th took a prisoner from the 352nd Division, confirming reports that the 352nd had replaced the 353rd Division the latter part of November. There had been persistent reports of one or more panzer units in rear of infantry divisions on the Corps front, but this was never confirmed by capture or prisoners from such units and the weather was so bad that very little information was available from tactical air reconnaissance. On 9 December the 2nd Division reported that the Germans on its front appeared new to the area, since observed actions indicated unfamiliarity with the sector. On the nights of 12–13 and 14–15 December vehicular movement was heard all along the front.

On the morning of 16 December the VIII Corps front flared up suddenly without warning. The sector which had been comparatively quiet since the latter part of September became the scene of von Rundstedt's desperate thrust to upset the Allied offensive. German action commenced at about 5:00 a.m. when heavy artillery preparatory fires were laid down along the entire VIII Corps front. The fires were quickly followed by tank and infantry attacks with the greatest pressure initially in the north near the boundary between V and VIII Corps. As the morning advanced, pressure developed along the entire front and became indicative of a strong coordinated offensive. The German pressure intensified during the afternoon, bit it was still strongest in the north where thrusts were being made against the 99th Division of V Corps, the 14th Cavalry Group and the 106th Division. By nightfall elements of three Volks Grenadier, two Panzer and one Parachute Division had been identified on the Corps front, all in addition to the four Volks Grenadier divisions already known in the line.

In the zone of the 106th Division, the enemy opened the attack at 5:30 a.m. by shelling Afst, Roth, and the division command post at St. Vith. The shelling was followed by an infantry attack at approximately 8:00 a.m., reinforced with about fifteen tanks. Two battalions from the 18th Volks Grenadier Division struck the 14th Cavalry Group near Krewinkle. By 11:00 a.m. Auw had been captured and Roth and Kobscheid were surrounded. The 14th Cavalry had been forced back about 1.5 miles, and the 32nd Cavalry Squadron was moved from the vicinity of Vielsalm to meet the penetration. The 2nd Battalion, 523rd Infantry was moved from its reserve position north of St. Vith to a position north of Schonberg to protect the left rear of the 422nd and 423rd Infantry Regiments, which were in position along the Schnee Eifel. German pressure in the north sector continued to build up, and by midnight the Cavalry had been forced back a total distance of eight kilometers. Concurrent with this attack in the north, the 62nd Volks Grenadier Division attacked in the direction of Winterspelt against the left flank of the 424th Infantry. The 1st Battalion, 424th was committed at 11:15 a.m., but by late evening German forces and American troops jointly occupied Winterspelt. Although German infantry exerted heavy pressure in the Heckusheid area against the center of the 424th Infantry, they were unable to effect any penetration.

The immediate objective of the German attacks seemed to be St. Vith and the good road network which converged on the city. German documents captured the first day of the attack substantiated this belief and also indicated that the Germans expected to capture St. Vith the first day.

In the center of the VIII Corps sector the enemy attacked the 28th Division along its entire front with infantry and tanks preceded by an artillery preparation. The immediate objective appeared to be to cut the "Ridge Road" running north and south just west of the Our River. From north to south, identifications were made of the German 116th Panzer

Division, the 560th Infantry Division, the 2nd Panzer Division, the 26th Infantry Division, the 352nd Infantry Division, and the 5th Parachute Division. Heavy pressure was placed against the 112th Infantry on the division north flank, but prepared defensive positions held the enemy. Lutkempen's capture was the only gain of more than minor proportions. In the center of the 28th Division sector, Engineers of the 2nd Panzer Division launched an attack against the 1st Bn, 110th Infantry.

Artillery fire caused severe losses to the German engineers, particularly their officers who were nearly all casualties, but enemy strength enabled the attack to continue. Marnach and Bockholz were captured during the night of 16–17. The 26th Volks Grenadier Division attacked the southern flank of the 3rd Bn, 110th Infantry with tank support and drove through to the north–south highway, a distance of about 4 kilometers. The 352nd Division hit the northern flank of the 2nd Bn, 109th Infantry just below the drive of the 26th Division, cutting the road north of Hoscheid. The 5th Parachute Division attacked the southern flank of the 109th in a drive toward Diekirch but made little progress. German tactics along the 28th Division front were to infiltrate the positions, pin down the American troops by all-around attack, and then flow through the gaps between the encircled strong points.

In the narrow zone held by the 9th Armored three boatloads of Germans crossed the Our River to the right flank of the 60th Armored Infantry Battalion. By 10:30 a.m. the enemy was attempting bridging operations near Wallendorf, but the operations were broken up by our artillery fire. The Germans, however, infiltrated our defensive positions in small groups, some units of the 276th Volks Grenadier Division being identified.

In the southern part of the VIII Corps sector, the German 112th Infantry Division launched an attack against the 4th Division. Company E, 12th Infantry was isolated in Echternach, and the garrisons in Dickweiler and Osweiler were engaged. By evening the Germans had advanced to Lauterborn and Berdorf and had surrounded the American troops in Osweiler and Dickweiler. Generally, however, the attacks against the 4th Division were in its northern sector and were not as heavy as those farther north in the Corps zone.

At the start of the German attack reserves available to VIII Corps consisted of the Reserve Command of the 9th Armored and four battalions of combat engineers. During the morning of the 16th the engineers were called from their normal. duties and assembled as a mobile reserve. In the afternoon the 168th Engineer Combat Battalion was attached to the 106th Division to a assist in the defense of St. Vith. Combat Command "R" of the 9th Armored was held at Trois Vierges awaiting development of the German attack.

As the seriousness of the enemy thrust became apparent during 16 December, additional troops were made available to VIII Corps. Combat Command "B" of the 9th Armored Division was released from attachment to V Corps at 11:20 a.m. It was attached to the 106th Division and upon arrival in that zone the next morning it was committed to action. The 7th Armored Division was also ordered to join the Corps, and it was given a concentration area east of Vielsalm. Reconnaissance elements arrived in St. Vith by 3:00 p.m. of the 17th, and by 10:00 p.m. the Reconnaissance Squadron, Combat Command "A," Combat Command "B," Combat Command "C," and the division headquarters tactical command post had closed into their assigned areas. Combat Command "B" was committed around St. Vith as it arrived, and before midnight the defense of St. Vith was established. In the south the 10th Armored Division was assigned an assembly area near Luxembourg, and Combat Command "A" moved into an area behind the 12th Infantry Regiment, 4th Division. The 10th Armored command post opened at Hollerich at 2:30 p.m. on the 17th and the division closed on its assigned areas before midnight.

Orders were issued to move the 101st and 82nd Airborne Divisions to the threatened area. These two divisions were resting and refitting in the Rheims area after recent participation in Holland in the British attack. Plans were made to concentrate the 101st in the vicinity of Bastogne and the 82nd in the Houffalize area.

During the evening of 16 December instructions issued to all divisions established a line in the rear of front lines which was to be held at all costs. This line followed the west side of the Our, Clerf and Sure Rivers and took advantage of the gorges cut by these streams. Units were to retire to this line only if forced back and any breaches of the line were to be restored by counterattack.

German documents captured on the first day of the attack disclosed that the Germans would conduct Operation Grief in conjunction with the attack. The plan was to employ in the American rear areas English-speaking German soldiers dressed in American uniforms and using American jeeps, tanks, half-tracks and weapons. Their mission was sabotage and creation of confusion and panic among the troops. Recognition signals such as wearing bandages about the head and removing the helmet were employed during daylight hours, while at night colored light signals protected them from fire of their own troops

Few instances of this operation were reported on the first day, but as the German attack progressed and the penetration became deeper, reports of such activities grew more frequent. Some measure of success was obtained through the ruse. Prompt introduction of control posts, extensive use of the password, and the alertness of all personnel to the danger of inadequate identification, however, did much to discourage these activities in spite of the fact that inability to distinguish friend or foe caused much apprehension.

The 106th Division held a salient in the Schnee Eifel which penetrated the defenses of the Siegfried Line. Before the German offensive it was felt that the Germans might attack in this area to recover lost fortifications and restore their original line. Possession of the Schnee Eifel, moreover, would be of material assistance to VIII Corps should it desire to launch an offensive in the direction of Bonn. For these two reasons the defensive position in the salient was thickly organized and comparatively well-manned. During occupancy by the 106th Division, the salient was defended by the 422nd and the 423rd Regiments. The 14th Cavalry Group protected the left flank and tied the division with the 99th Division, V Corps on the north. The 424th Infantry was on the right flank of the salient.

During the late afternoon of the first day of the German drive, it became evident that the German penetration in the area of the cavalry and the 99th Division was deep, and in danger of becoming much deeper with the American troops folding back rapidly. Since the Schnee Eifel salient now formed the southern shoulder at the penetration, it was desirable to hold this position if possible. Only if the left flank were heavily protected could the position be held. Otherwise, and German envelopment south in the Schonberg area would place the two regiments with their direct supporting artillery in a precarious position.

Concern for the security of these two regiments was transmitted to the commander of the 106th Division during the evening of the 16th, but he felt sure that the situation was in hand and that the salient troops were not in jeopardy. Later that night when it was evident that German pressure was not only continuous but also increasing on the Corps front, the division commander was again called and advised to pull the two regiments out of the exposed position. General Alan W. Jones, the division commander, felt confident of the security of his position, especially since he had information to the effect that the 7th Armored Division was on its way to assist him and scheduled to close by 3:00 p.m. the next day.

During the night of 16–17 December, the Germans continued to move up troops and armor, making extensive use of flares and searchlights to facilitate movement. In the Corps center groups of tanks and infantry sustained their infiltration under cover of darkness. The extent of this infiltration was not fully known, for communication between regiments and subordinate units began to fail during the night. As the penetrations increased, the situation became more obscure because of disruption of wire communications by the Germans.

The first day the magnitude of the German effort manifested itself early through the large number of identified divisions. The pattern of the enemy's attack, however, unfolded more slowly. It was not until the night of the 16th and the morning of the 17th that an estimate of the enemy's intention could be made. From information extracted from captured German documents and the northwest direction of early thrusts, it was evident that the objective was Liege and possibly Namur. The number of enemy divisions currently involved, together with the rate new divisions were being identified, led to the conclusion that the enemy needed a system of roads greater than that in the area under immediate threat, if he were to push successfully such a large number of troops to these objectives. It was also apparent that if the enemy were blocked or delayed in his thrust into the V Corps right flank and if the St. Vith road net were denied to the Germans, they would not hesitate to divert their efforts farther south toward Bastogne to secure the excellent highways radiating from that town. It was therefore assumed that the Germans would direct their efforts toward securing the primary roads and the defensive plan selected was designed to block him in this attempt.

The defensive plan consisted of two distinct phases. The first phase was to defend in place along the original defensive line of VIII Corps in accordance. with the directive received from First Army when the sector was first taken over. This action would afford the maximum delay with the forces available, but it was realized that because of the extensive frontage and the paucity of reserves, any delaying action against the large German forces building up on the Corps front might not be of long duration. The second phase of the defense was to deny the vital road nets to the Germans by building strong defenses in front of St. Vith, Houffalize, Bastogne and Luxembourg as rapidly as possible. Prompt dispatch of assistance from the First and Third Armies would make it possible to build up the defenses of St, Vith and in front of Luxembourg, whereas the attachment of two airborne divisions would make the defense of Bastogne and Houffalize feasible.

On the second day of the attack German pressure revealed a marked increase. In the north the 18th Volks Grenadier Division reinforced with armor renewed its attack against the 106th Division at 6:00 a.m. The 295th Volks Grenadier Regiment supported by armor attacked Schonberg from the north, and the 293rd Volks Grenadier Regiment reinforced with tanks attacked Bleialf from the south. These two German drives linked up at Schonberg at 9:00 a.m. The 422nd and 423rd Infantry Regiments, 106th Division, with the 2nd Battalion, 423rd Infantry which had moved from reserve to Schonberg to protect the left flank, were isolated in the Schnee Eifel positions.

The northern prong of the pincer movement expanded westward and shortly after the capture of Schonberg German armor was proceeding through Heuem toward St. Vith. The southern prong of the pincer likewise expanded westward against the 424th Infantry, and by 10:30 a.m. Winterspelt and Winterscheid were held by the Germans. The attack against Winterspelt was spearheaded by the German 183rd Volks Grenadier and 62nd Volks Grenadier Divisions. To the north American forces were also being forced to withdraw. The 12th German Infantry Division and the 12th SS Division drove against the right flank of V Corps and rapidly pushed back the 99th Division. Elements of these German divisions with some units of the notorious 1st SS Division swept the 14th Cavalry Group back to the Born-Wallerode line by 11:45 a.m.

The encirclement of the Schnee Eifel positions and the expansion of these thrusts to the west constituted a serious threat to St. Vith and necessarily focused all efforts on delaying the onslaught until reinforcements could arrive and a defensive line could be established in front of the city. North and east of the city the 168th Engineers fought a delaying action which hampered the German armored threats, particularly the threat from Schonberg. Combat Command "B" of the 9th Armored began arriving in the St. Vith area at about 10:30 a.m. and was committed in the direction of Winterspelt to stem the German tide surging against the 424th Infantry in that area. The Combat Command reached the outskirts of Winterspelt but was ordered to withdraw to the vicinity of Lommersweiler where it too up a defensive position in the left of the 424th Infantry. By 3:40 p.m. reconnaissance elements of Combat Command "B" of the 7th Armored arrived in St. Vith. Germans had advanced to within one kilometer of St. Vith by 5:00 p.m., but elements of Combat Command "B" of the 7th were committed as they arrived and by 7:30 p.m. held the Germans. In addition to the 168th Engineers, one battalion or armored infantry, one company of medium tanks, and the reconnaissance squadron of Combat Command "B" were disposed north and east of the city. They were tied in with Combat Command "B" of the 9th Armored to the southeast. One battalion of tanks and one battalion or armored infantry were available west of St. Vith for employment. By 10:00 p.m. most of the remainder of the 7th Armored Division had closed into their area.

In the 28th Division sector the Germans continued their heavy thrusts on the 17th. Elements of the 560th Volks Grenadier Division, with tanks from the 116th Panzer Division, renewed their attack against the 112th Infantry. The Germans appeared to be attempting to drive around both the left and right flanks of the regimental position, and actually succeeded in attacking the regimental command post with tanks and infantry, forcing its displacement. Penetrations were made against the 1st Battalion on the north and toward Lieler on the southern flank. The pounding became so severe that plans were made to withdraw under cover of darkness to the west side of the Our River. The move was fairly well completed during the night of 17–18 December.

In the zone of the 110th Infantry, the Germans continued to hammer savagely at the remaining defenses and to exploit the deep penetrations made the day before. At 2:00 a.m. the enemy was reinforcing Marnach by infantry carried in half-tracks. The 2nd Panzer Division and elements of the 26th Infantry Division deepened their penetrations and by 11:00 a.m. a pitched tank battle was in progress in Clerf, threatening the regimental command post located in that town. Defenses in the adjacent area were either by-passed or overrun and at midnight the enemy had elements through to the division rear boundary west of Clerf. The penetration in the Bockholz area was deepened to the southwest and near midnight Wilwerwiltz was threatened. K Company, 110th Infantry was surrounded in Hosingen, and the Germans drove on through the positions of the 3rd Battalion, taking Holzthum at about 11:30 a.m. and approaching the battalion command post during the evening.

The German 352nd Infantry Division and the 5th Parachute Division continued their pressure on the 109th Infantry, 28th Division. From their penetration near Hoscheid the Germans were sliding off to the northwest. In the center they drove through to Brandenburg before being stopped. Eppeldorf was captured during the evening.

At 11:30 a.m. VIII Corps ordered the 44th Engineer Combat Battalion to Wiltz for attachment to the 28th Division. It was originally planned to use the engineers to head off the German penetration from Buckholz toward Wilwerwiltz, but by 9:30 p.m. the Headquarters Company, 707th Tank Battalion at Wilwerwiltz was being thrown back and the engineers were employed in defense of the 28th Division command post at Wiltz. On the front of the armored infantry battalion of the 9th Armored, the 276th Infantry Division and elements of the 212th Infantry Division drove hard against the left and right flanks of battalion positions. In the draw west of Berdorf on the right flank, an estimated German regimental combat team was reported at 9:25 a.m. By 1:30 p.m. this group had taken Mullerthal and Waldbillib before being stopped.

Company E of the 12th Infantry, 4th Division, isolated in Echternach on the first day, remained surrounded. Although attacks against the 4th Division seemed intended to tie down the American forces, penetrations up the draw on the south of the 9th Armored constituted a serious threat to the left flank of thew 12th Infantry. The drive southwest from Echternach was also dangerous, but the Germans were definitely halted in this sector by evening. By 7:25 p.m. the defense in this area was considerably strengthened, and the German groups which had infiltrated beyond were cleaned out.

The 10th Armored Division arrived in the Luxembourg area during the day and Combat Command "A" was concentrated in the rear of the 4th Division zone, materially strengthening the southern flank. Combat Command "R" of the 9th Armored, in Corps reserve at Trois Vierges, was moved during the evening of the 17th to Oberwampach, where roadblocks were established on the Bastogne–Trois Vierges road at the junctions with the Clervaux road and the road to Wiltz.

The end of the second day of the German offensive round the balance tilted in favor of the Germans. They had surrounded two regiments of the 106th Division in the Schnee Eifel and had penetrated deeply in the center of the 28th Division zone. Stubborn defense by the 106th and supporting troops, however, had held the enemy away from the vital road net of St. Vith until the arrival of Combat Command "B" of the 9th armored. The arrival of the entire 7th Armored Division during the afternoon and evening of the second day, 17 December, gave these forces time to execute a planned defense of the St. Vith area. The 10th Armored reached the southern sector of VIII Corps in time definitely to assure defense of that sector. The Corps center, however, was in a critical condition.

On 18 December, the 3rd day of the offensive, the Germans increased the momentum of their drive, especially against the center of the Corps. VIII Corps flank, bolstered by the arrival of reinforcements, held secure throughout the day, but the onslaught against the center was so overwhelming that the thin defenses disintegrated and the enemy achieved a break-through.

In the north the Germans penetrated deeply along the Corps left flank. German armor was in possession of Recht early in the morning, and by 7:40 a.m. German tanks were engaging elements of the 7th Armored southeast of the town. At 9:00 a.m. the German 1st SS Division made a lunge at the left flank and cut the east–west road from St, Vith to Vielsalm at Poteau. This thrust caught a heavy column of traffic moving on the road and the 740th Field Artillery Battalion lost eight of their 8-inch Howitzers in the attack. Farther west the Germans were held off the east-west road but succeeded in penetrating the road leading north out of Vielsalm.

18 December was spent in reinforcing the defenses of St. Vith and meeting the attack of the Germans as they attempted to enter the city. Combat Command "B" of the 7th Armored strengthened its defenses north and east of the town and linked up with Combat Command "B" of the 9th Armored which was defending to the southeast. Farther south the 424th Infantry continued its defense and attempted to regain contact with the 112th Infantry, 28th Division.

At 2:15 a.m. the 106th Division sent a message to the two regiments isolated in the Schnee Eifel, ordering them to fight out of the encirclement of the previous day. They were directed to attack toward Schonberg, clear the St. Vith road, and move to the St. Vith–Wallerode–Weppeler area. Simultaneously plans were made for the 7th Armored to attack eastward and aid in the relief of these two regimental combat teams. Unfortunately German strength and the number of attacks against the St. Vith perimeter precluded assumption of the offensive by the 7th, so assistance to the surrounded troops never materialized. It is known from several survivors of the 423rd Infantry that an effort was made by the two regiments to move on Schonberg on the 18th. This effort was continued on the 19th, but their last reported locations placed them only as far as the vicinity of Oberlascheid and Radscheid. Radio communications with the isolated units, which had never been good, was finally lost with the 422nd on the 19th and the 423rd the following morning.

In the southern part of the Corps sector Combat Command "A," 9th Armored Division, received severe enemy pressure throughout the 18th. The lines held during the morning, but by 1:30 p.m. the reconnaissance troop had been overrun and its vehicles had been captured or destroyed. The Germans pierced the front lines, disrupting communication. The penetration up the valley on the right flank of Combat Command "A" was contained before Waldbillig, but the depth of the penetration on the north flank assumed alarming proportions. Only a hazy picture of events in this breach between Combat Command "A" and the 3rd Battalion, 109th Infantry, 28th Division could be obtained. By nightfall, there were indications that the Germans were approaching Ettelbruck on the left rear of the Combat Command "A" defenses.

South of Combat Command "A" in the zone of the 4th Infantry, the situation was stabilized. The 12th Infantry, assisted by the 2nd Battalion, 22nd Infantry and three task forces shaped up from Combat Command "A," 10th Armored, mopped up German troops who had penetrated behind Osweiler and Dickweiler. The penetration on the left flank was blocked at Mullerthal and Company E, isolated in Echternach was contacted and supplied. During the day additional German attempts at bridging operations east of Echternach were broken up by artillery fire.

The timely arrival of the two armored divisions, the 7th in the north, and the 10th in the south contributed much to the strength of the ends of the Corps sector. For the moment, St. Vith seemed secure and the German path to Luxembourg was definitely blocked. The situation in the center of the Corps, however, was far from encouraging. The 28th Division weakened rapidly during the day under the savage pounding of German attacks and artillery fire. With its reserves committed, there was little left to plug the numerous gaps opened by the Germans. The small Corps reserve added more tanks and armored infantry to the division, but the concentration had negligible influence on such an extended front as the 28th Division was manning.

In the northern part of the 28th Division sector the 112th Infantry pulled back across the Our River the previous night, but because of German pressure it failed to stabilize its lines during the 18th. The 28th Division was directed to have this regiment establish a strong roadblock at the crossroads one and a half kilometers southwest of Malscheid. The Germans had already gained the ridge between the Clerf and Our Rivers, and the purpose of the block was to deny them the use of roads leading north from the ridge to Beho and St. Vith. This roadblock was never firmly set up, for the Germans were on this vital crossroads the next day. Although use of the north bound roads was denied the Germans, possession of this crossroads enabled them to push forces to the southwest over good highway.

With the withdrawal of this regiment, the right flank battalion folded back rapidly to the northwest and created a wide gap between the regiment and the 110th Infantry to the south. Apparently the Germans pushed considerable armor through the gap for by 1:45 p.m. German light tanks were in Trois Vierges and one hour later they were reported two kilometers west of the town. Farther west a few German tanks were on the prowl, shooting up columns on the Houffalize–Bovigny road. On the left flank a gap developed between the regiment and the 424th Infantry to the north went unexploited by the Germans. The separation the 112th Regiment from the 28th Division disrupted communication, and by nightfall little information concerning the location of its battalions could be secured.

Meanwhile the situation of the 110th Infantry caused the gravest concern. Numerous German thrusts between strongpoints encircled companies and destroyed or captured them one by one. Here too the picture was obscure throughout the day because of lost communication, but the appearance of many German columns behind the regimental sector and the tragic tales of stragglers indicated a complete disintegration of the regimental defenses.

As early as 4:40 a.m. tanks were reported in Donnage which is five kilometers west of Clerf, and at 10:30 a.m. Clerf was occupied by elements of the 2nd Panzer Division. Two kilometers northwest of the 28th Division command post at Wiltz a column of German tanks, half-tracks and horse-drawn vehicles was sighted at 11:10 a.m. North of Wiltz a Tiger tank was firing into houses of Eschweiler at 1:25 p.m., and forty-minutes later German armor was in the town itself. During the evening the division reported that it had no contact with the 110th Infantry but remnants of the regimental command post were at Allerborn attempting to establish a straggler line. The division command post was now being threatened and the 44th Engineer Combat Battalion, part of the 447th AAA Battalion and miscellaneous headquarters personnel from the division were defending Wiltz.

In the 109th Regimental sector the German attack became more vigorous and increasing pressure was exerted all along the front. Part of the left flank battalion was overrun and a penetration was made on the right flank between the regiment and the 9th Armored. Elements of the reserve battalion were committed and new attempts were made to relieve E Company which had been cut-off the first day of attack. These efforts were unsuccessful and during the afternoon it was decided to withdraw to the high ground just north-east of Diekirch. Although this regiment received heavy hammering during the day, good communications were maintained and the unit withdrew in good order.

Directly behind the 110th Infantry on the Bastogne–St. Vith Road were roadblocks established by Combat Command "R," 9th Armored early on 18 December. One block at the junction of the Clerf Road was manned by Task Force Rose and consisted of an armored infantry company, a medium tank company and some engineers. At 10:00 a.m. it was attacked by infantry and armor from the direction of Clerf. By 2:00 p.m. this block was overrun and resistance was eliminated. Southwest a similarly composed block, called Task Force Hayze, was established at the road junction with the Wiltz Road. Shortly after the first block was crushed, the second task force was attacked. By 6:15 p.m. it was under heavy fire. The command post and the artillery of Combat Command "R," 9th Armored was located farther down the road at Longvilly and it came under attack with some pressure coming from the southeast. During the night resistance at these two places disintegrated and the remnants fell back on defenses being set up by Combat Command "B," 10th Armored.

Combat Command "B," 10th Armored, which had been ordered north to the Corps center after reaching the Luxembourg area the night before, began arriving in the Bastogne area near 4:00 p.m. Divided into three task forces of equal strength, the team established during the night a sector of roadblocks on the northeast and eastern approaches to Bastogne. Task Force Desobry set up its defense position astride the Bastogne–Houffalize road in the vicinity of Noville. Task Force Cherry attempted to occupy a position near Longvilly and Task Force O'Hara moved to a position about five kilometers east of Bastogne near Wardin.

A secondary set of blocks was established on the eastern and southeastern routes into Bastogne. The eastern blocks were placed behind the defenses established by armor and were located near Mageret and Neffe. The block on the road from Wiltz was on high ground in the vicinity of Marvie. The Mageret position was manned by the 158th Engineer Combat Battalion, a new unit sent in by First Army. The Neffe and Marvie blocks were defended by the 35th Engineer Combat Battalion.

Relentless German pressure on the St. Vith–Bastogne road started when the Germans overran the 9th Armored positions late in the afternoon and evening and continued during the night. Confusion on the road caused by straggling vehicles and men from the overrun units and night attacks coming from all direction forced the 10th Armored to retire from Longvilly. These troops fell back on defenses established by the engineers, and they were fighting here when the 101st Airborne Division came up the next morning.

During the afternoon of the 18th a message from First Army announced a change in plans for employment of airborne troops due to arrive during the night. The 101st Airborne was to remain with Corps but the 82nd was to pass to control of the XVIII Corps for employment in the north near Werboment. It will be recalled that the 82nd Airborne was to be used in the Houffalize area to deny enemy the roads radiating from the town. Establishment of a blocking force in this locality was an essential part of the Corps plan to hold the four road centers of St. Vith, Houffalize, Bastogne and Luxembourg. Consequently the diversion of this division left a gap between Bastogne and St. Vith which could not be filled. At the time, the Germans were making an end run north of the Corps area, and the necessity for blocking the move in the Werboment area with paratroopers was fully realized. Nevertheless, it was regrettable that the Houffalize gap had to be left open to the enemy, for it gave him access to LeRoche and an excellent network of roads to the west. During the night of 18–19 December the 101st Airborne Division closed in its concentration area west of Bastogne and prepared to move out at daylight to defensive positions east the city.

Endnotes

Chapter 1

1 Cole, "The Ardennes: Battle of the Bulge," *The U. S. Army in WWII* (1965), p. 57.
2 *Ibid.*
3 Wagener, "Fifth Panzer Army (2 Nov 1944–16 Jan 1945)," *Foreign Military Studies, MS#A-858. Historical Division.* U. S. Army, Europe (1945), p. 2.
4 Jablonsky, "The Paradox of Duality: Adolf Hitler and the Concept of Military Surprise." Second Annual Conference on Intelligence and Military Operation, May 1987. U. S. Army War College, Carlisle, Pennsylvania.
5 "The Invasion of Poland, Fall 1939," *Holocaust Encyclopedia.*
6 "The Invasion of the Soviet Union, June 1941." *Holocaust Encyclopedia.*
7 Jablonsky.
8 "28th Infantry Division Historical Summary," 28th Infantry Division Archives, p. 87.
9 *Ibid.*
10 Coates, and Pellegrin, *Military Sociology: A Study of American Military Institutions and Military Life* (1965), p. 162.
11 Henderson, *Cohesion: The Human Element in Combat* (1985), p. xi.
12 Shils and Janowitz, "Cohesion and Disintegration in the Wehrmacht in World War II," *Public Opinion Quarterly*, 12: 280-315 (1948).
13 Bartov, "Daily Life and Motivation in War: The Wehrmacht in the Soviet Union," *The Journal of Strategic Studies, 12: 200–214* (1989).
14 Zapotoczny, *Beyond Duty: The Reasons Some Soldiers Commit Atrocities* (2017), p. 50.
15 Herberg, *Protestant, Catholic, Jew: An Essay in American Religious Sociology*, revised (1960), p. 77.
16 von Clausewitz, and Rapoport, *Carl Von Clausewitz on War.* (1968), p. 97.
17 *Ibid*, p. 62.
18 Stouffer, Lumsdaine, A. A., Lumsdaine, M. H., and Williams, Smith, Janis, Star, and Cottrell, *The American Soldier: Volume II: Combat and its Aftermath* (1949), p. 172.
19 Little, R. W., *American Sociological Review 31, no. 6* (1966), p. 870.
20 Shils, E. A., "Primary Groups in the American Army," in *Studies in the Scope and Method of The American Soldier*. Ed. Merton and Lazarsfeld (1950), p. 110.
21 Henderson, *op. cit.*, p. xviii.
22 Rielly, "Confronting the Tiger: Small Unit Cohesion in Battle," *Military Review*, November–December 2000.

23 *Ibid.*
24 Boesch, *Road to Huertgen: Forest in Hell* (2018), p. 231.
25 *Ibid*, p. 232. Note: The word Boesch comes from a French slang phrase *tête de caboche*, which means cabbage head.
26 MacDonald, *Company Commander: The Classic Infantry Memoir of World War II* (1999), p. 219.
27 *Ibid*, p. 256.
28 Ginzberg, quoted in Kennett, *G.I. The American Soldier in World War II* (1987), p. 138.
29 Kennett, *Combat Motivation: The Behavior of Soldiers in Battle* (Boston: Kluwer-Nijhoff Publishing, 1982), p. 159.
30 Henderson, *op. cit.*, p. 63.
31 Gray, *The Warriors: Reflections on Men in Battle* (1959), p. 49.
32 Cooke, *The Moral Warrior: Ethics and Service in the U. S. Military* (1954).
33 Henderson, *op. cit.*, p. 64.
34 Brokaw, *The Greatest Generation* (2001), p. xxxvii.
35 Dorsett, *Serving God and Country: U. S. Military Chaplains in World War II* (2012), p. 144.
36 Wansink, B., and Wansink, C. S., "Are There Atheists in Foxholes? Combat Intensity and Religious Behavior," *Journal of Religion and Health 52* (2013), pp. 768–779.
37 Roosevelt, "Labor Day Radio Address," online by Gerhard Peters and John T. Woolley, The American Presidency Project, www.presidency.ucsb.edu/node/209922. Accessed August 3, 2022.
38 Dorsett, *op. cit.*, p. 145. Note: One line in the 23rd Psalm reads, "Yea, though I walk through the valley of the shadow of Death, I will fear no evil: for thou art with me; thy rod and thy staff they comfort me."
39 Henderson, *op. cit.*, p. 84.
40 Kellett, *Combat Motivation: The Behavior of Soldiers in Battle* (1982), p. 195.
41 Henderson, *op. cit.*, p. 110.
42 Stouffer, *op. cit.*, p. 149.
43 Ambrose, S., *Citizen Soldier: The U. S. Army from the Normandy Battlefields to the Bulge to the Surrender of Germany, June 7, 1944–May 7, 1945* (1997), p. 14.
44 Moskos, *The American Enlisted Man: The Rank and File in Today's Military* (1970), p. 147.
45 Marshall, *Men against Fire: The Problem of Battle Command* (1947), p. 33.
46 *Ibid.*
47 Sarkesian, *Combat Effectiveness: Cohesion, Stress and the Volunteer Military* (1980), p. 244.
48 Ambrose, *op. cit.*, p. 437.
49 Wesbrook, *The Potential for Military Disintegration in Sam C. Sarkesian, Combat Effectiveness: Cohesion, Stress and the Volunteer Military* (1980), p. 255.
50 "Religions in America," *Religious Landscape Studies* (2021).
51 Marshall, *Bastogne: The First Eight Days* (1946).
52 Toland, *Battle: The Story of the Bulge* (1959).
53 Cole, "The Ardennes: Battle of the Bulge," *The U. S. Army in WWII* (1965), p. 57.
54 Crookenden, *Battle of the Bulge 1944* (1980).
55 MacDonald, *A Time for Trumpets: The Untold Story of the Battle of the Bulge* (1985).
56 Ambrose, *op. cit.*
57 Beevor, *Ardennes 1944: The Battle of the Bulge* (2015).

58 Merriam, *Dark December: The Full Account of the Battle of the Bulge* (2017).
59 Wilson, *If You Survive* (1987).
60 Zapotoczny, *op. cit.*, p. 62.
61 Durham, Company "A," 109th Infantry Regiment, Interview by Roger S. Durham, Pontiac, Illinois, August 12, 1996.
62 Haug, *As I Remember It: Courageous Defenders*, unpublished memoir, November 1994.
63 Pocklington, Interview by 28th Division Historical Section, Fort Indiantown Gap, Annville, Pennsylvania, December 1988.
64 Forde, Interview by Katharine Goodloe, *Dallas Morning News, May 29, 2004.*
65 "Interviews of Battle of the Bulge Veterans," *28th Division Historical Section*, Fort Indiantown Gap, Annville, Pennsylvania, December 1988.

Chapter 2

1 Morgan, "The Significance of Citizenship Recognition Day," *Journal of the National Education Association, 28* (1939), p. 257.
2 *Ibid.*
3 Roosevelt, "Annual Message to Congress, January 4, 1939," Public Papers & Addresses of Franklin D. Roosevelt, The American Presidency Project.
4 *Saturday Evening Post*, July 17, 1943, quoted in John Morton Blum, *V Was for Victory: Politics and American Culture During World War II* (1976), p. 67.
5 Roosevelt, 1941 State of the Union Address to Congress, FDR Library and Museum, www. fdrlibrary.org/four-freedoms. Accessed September 17, 2022.
6 "A Special Role," *St. Paul's Church and World War II*, National Park Service, U.S. Department of the Interior, www.nps.gov/articles/st-paul-s-church-and-world-war-ii.htm. Accessed August 20, 2022.
7 Stouffer, *The American Soldier: Adjustment During Army Life*, Vol. 1 (1949), p. 81.
8 *Ibid*, p. 149.
9 Hoopes, *Americans Remember the Home Front: An Oral Narrative of the World War II Years in America* (1977), p. 169.
10 Sostaric, "The American Wartime Propaganda During World War II: How Comic Books Sold the War," *Australasian Journal of American Studies 38,* no. 1 (2019), p. 17.
11 Bohn, *Why We Fight*, film essay (1977).
12 *Ibid.* Note: *Triumph of the Will* is a 1935 German Nazi propaganda film directed, produced, edited and co-written by Leni Riefenstahl. It became a major example of film used as propaganda.
13 *Ibid.*
14 *Ibid.*
15 *Ibid.*
16 *Ibid.*
17 Behringer, "Why We Fight: Prelude to War, America's Crash History Lesson," *The Unwritten Record Blog*, September 1, 2020, the National Archives, unwritten-record.blogs.archives.gov/2020/09/01/why-we-fight-prelude-to-war-americas-crash-history-lesson/. Accessed September 1, 2020.
18 Pfannenstiel, *A Wartime Log*. Note: Eddie was eventually assigned to the 112th Infantry Regiment, 28th Infantry Division.
19 Dick, *Man in the High Castle* (1962).
20 Zietsma, "Sin Has No History: Religion, National Identity, and U. S. Intervention, 1937–1941," *Diplomatic History 31*, no. 3 (2007), pp. 531–565.

Chapter 3

1 Yarbrough and Associated Press, "MacArthur Vows Victory or Death in Freedom Fight," *Lewiston (ME) Daily Sun*, March 27, 1942; *Reports of General MacArthur, vol. 1*, Facsimile Reprint (1994), p. 29.
2 Eisenhower, "D-Day Statement to the Soldiers, Sailors, and Airmen of the Allied Expeditionary Force," *Collection DDE-EPRE: Eisenhower, Dwight D: Papers, Pre-Presidential, 1916–1952*, Dwight D. Eisenhower Library, Abilene, Kansas.
3 D-Day Prayer, President Franklin Roosevelt. The American Presidency Project.
4 Herberg, *Protestant, Catholic, Jew: An Essay in American Religious Sociology*, Revised (1960), p. 77.
5 *Fourth Supplemental National Defense Appropriation Act of 1941*, Public Law 13, U. S. Statutes at Large 55 (1941), p. 34.
6 Dorsett, *Serving God and Country: U. S. Military Chaplains in World War II* (2012), p. 21.
7 Gushwa, *The Best and Worst of Times: The U. S. Army Chaplaincy, 1920–1945*, Vol. IV (1977), p. 79.
8 Dorsett, *op. cit.*, p. 23.
9 Stahl, "Chaplain Jim Wants You!: The Boundaries of Religion in the Warfare State" (presented at the World War II and Religion Conference, Paper presented at the World War II and Religion Conference, Florida State University, Tallahassee, 2012).
10 Belth to Aryeh Lev, January 15, 1941, 000.3 Religion: Religious Ministration in the Army, v. 2, Office Management Division Decimal File 1920–45, Records Relating to Administration and Management, Records of the Office of the Chief of Chaplains 1902–75, Record Group 247.
11 Schultz, *Tri-Faith America: How Catholics and Jews Held Postwar America to Its Protestant Promise* (2011), pp. 44–50.
12 *Ibid.*
13 Dorsett, *op. cit.*, p. 6.
14 *Ibid*, p. 39.
15 Hertz, "The Role of the Laity in American Christianity," *Mid-Stream 22, no. 3–4* (1983), pp. 326-341.
16 *Ibid.*
17 Bennett (ed.), *The Hymnal, Army and Navy* (1941).
18 Bennett (ed.), *Song and Service Book for Ship and Field* (1941).
19 "Bible Bits and Topic Talks," *Link Magazine* (February 1943), p. 37.
20 Jewish Welfare Board, *Prayer Book: Abridged for Jews in the Armed Forces of the United States*, revised (1943), p. iv.
21 Ridgway, *Soldier: The Memoirs of Matthew B. Ridgway* (1956), p. 3. Note: The events at Gethsemane are discussed in the Bible, Matthew 26: 36–56.
22 Blair, *Ridgway's Paratroopers: The American Airborne in World War II* (1985), p. 21.
23 Johnson, "What I Am Fighting For," *Link Magazine* (September 1943), p. 27. Note: *Link Magazine* was a Protestant Devotional magazine designed for U.S. military personnel.
24 Redmann, "Letter to His Mother, February 20, 1944," in *Unfinished Journey: A World War II Remembrance*, ed. Kerry P. Redmann (2006), pp. 117–8. Note: Redmann died in the Battle of the Bulge less than one year after this letter.
25 Gehr, "Letter to the Editor," *Wheaton Alumni* (October 1944), p. 1.
26 Slomovitz, *The Fighting Rabbis: Jewish Military Chaplains and American History* (1999), pp. 92–97.

27 United States, *Report on the Army Chaplain in the European Theater*. Report of the General Board, United States Forces, European Theater Study No. 68 (1945), p. 41.
28 Reid, *General Sacramental Absolution: An Historical, Canonical and Pastoral Perspective* (1998), pp. 18–19.
29 *Ibid.*
30 Houtz to Mabel Houtz, *Personal Correspondence, Dec 1942–Nov 1943*, Roger L. Houtz Papers (May 11, 1943).
31 Houtz to Mabel Houtz (October 3, 1943).
32 Skinner, *Daws: The Story of Dawson Trotman, Founder of the Navigators* (1974).
33 Butler, *Awash in a Sea of Faith: Christianizing the American People* (1990), p. 21.
34 Glasser, *And Some Believed* (1946), p. 109.

Chapter 4

1 Snape, *God, and Uncle Sam: Religion and America's Armed Forces in World War II* (2015), p. 42.
2 Zeiler, *The American Way in World War II from Part III—The Perils of Interdependence*, www.cambridge.org/core/books/cambridge-history-of-america-and-the-world/american-way-in-world-war-ii/879D823F1F695D2F92677D66A5D6AB99. Accessed October 3, 2022.
3 Fussell, *Wartime: Understanding and Behavior in the Second World War* (1989), p. 13.
4 Weigley, *The American Way of War: A History of United States Military Strategy and Policy* (1973), p. 149.
5 Koppes and Black, *Hollywood Goes to War: How Politics, Profits, and Propaganda Shaped World War II Movies* (1987), p. 324.
6 *Ibid*, p. 84.
7 Grinker and Spiegel, *Men under Stress* (1945), p. 450.
8 Stimson quoted in Thomas W. Bohn, An Historical and Descriptive Analysis of the "Why We Fight" series (1977), pp. 92-93.
9 Memo quoted in Carl I. Hovland *et al.*, eds., *Studies in Social Psychology in World War II*, vol. III: Experiments on Mass Communication (1949), p. 24.
10 Girardat, Company C, 112th Infantry Regiment, unpublished diary, 28th Division Archives.
11 Sessoms, Company D, 112th Infantry Regiment, unpublished diary, 28th Division Archives..
12 Smith, Personal History of Robert L. Smith. 28th Division Archives.
13 Holmes, *Acts of War* (1985), p. 301.
14 Cooke, *The Moral Warrior: Ethics and Service in the U. S. Military* (1954), p. 22.
15 Johnson, *Morality and Contemporary Warfare* (1999), p. 18.
16 Greene, *The Infantry Journal Reader* (1944), p. 271.
17 FM 21-100—War Department Basic Field Manual: Soldier's Handbook (July 23, 1941).
18 Fagelson, "Fighting Films: The Everyday Tactics of World War II Soldiers," *Cinema Journal*, Vol. 40, No. 3 (Spring 2001), pp. 94-112.
19 Nay, *Leadership and Transformation of the Army Chaplaincy During WWII* (2020), p. 19.
20 Ickles, "Speech during an 'I am an American Day', May 18, 1941," *Harold L. Ickes Papers*, ID No.: MSS27011 (May 18, 1941).

21 Zeitz, "The Speech That Set Off the Debate About America's Role in the World," *Politico Magazine* (December 29, 2015).
22 *Ibid.*
23 "28th Infantry Division Historical Summary," 28th Infantry Division Archives, p. 22.
24 *Ibid*, p. 35.
25 Burghardt, *My Tour with the 28th Division*, unpublished manuscript.
26 "28th Infantry Division Historical Summary," p. 45.
27 "History of the 112th Infantry Regiment," 28th Infantry Division Archives.
28 Interview of Howard J. Friedman by Virginia Perkins, December 16, 1975. M77-164, *Junior League of Tallahassee, Oral Histories* (1976–1977).
29 Burghardt. Note: Alois Hitler (born Alois Schicklgruber) was an Austrian civil servant and the father of Adolf Hitler.
30 *The Trumpeter*, 110th Infantry Unit Paper, Vol. IV, No. 7. 28th Infantry Division Archives, (May 30, 1942). Note: The unit paper was distributed to every man in the regiment.
31 "28th Infantry Division Historical Summary," p. 23.
32 *Ibid.*
33 Hickman, unpublished diary, 28th Infantry Division Archives. Note: Hickman was a Battalion Scout with the 1st Battalion of the 109th Infantry.
34 "28th Infantry Division Historical Summary," p. 40.
35 *Ibid*, p. 51.
36 *Ibid.*
37 Burghardt, *op. cit.*
38 Brighton, *Patton, Montgomery, Rommel: Masters of War* (2009), p. 262.
39 Burghardt, *op. cit.*
40 Dorsett, *Serving God and Country*. (2012), p. 131.
41 "28th Infantry Division Historical Summary," p. 64.
42 Dorsett, *op. cit.*, p. 39.
43 *Ibid*, p. 41.
44 *Ibid*, p. 43.
45 *Ibid*, p. 45.
46 *The Federalist Papers*, thefederalistpapers.org/current-events/the-fdr-bible. Accessed August 29, 2022.
47 Stifler, "The Scriptures Go on the Assembly Line," *Protestant Voice* (December 10, 1943).
48 Dorsett, *op. cit.*, p. 6.
49 *Ibid*, p. 39.
50 Carpenter and Eiland, *Chappie: World War II Diary of a Combat Chaplain* (2007), p. 1.
51 Pellegrino, "Embattled Belief: The Religious Experiences of American Military Combatants during World War II and Today," *Journal of Military Experience*: Vol. 3: Issue 2, Article 10 (2013).
52 Brokaw, *The Greatest Generation* (2001), p. xxxvii.

Chapter 5

1 28th Division Historical Summary, p. 79.
2 Downey, Company C, 112th Infantry, letter to his mom and dad, July 30, 1944, 28th Infantry Division Archives.
3 28th Division Historical Summary, p. 92.

4 Blumenson, "Breakout and Pursuit." CMH Pub 7-5-1. *The European Theater of Operations* (1993), p. 302.
5 Tauchert, staff sergeant, Company L, 110th Infantry Regiment, 28th Infantry Division, Distinguished Service Cross.
6 *Ibid.*
7 Schroder, PFC, Company D, 1st Battalion, 112th Infantry, 28th Infantry Division, *Personal History of the Men Who Marched in the Paris Parade* (1945).
8 Blumenson, *op. cit.*, p. 452.
9 "109th Infantry Regiment Historical Data," 28th Infantry Division Archives.
10 Blumenson, *op. cit.*, p. 300.
11 *Do You Remember—The Olympic Games in Berlin?* German propaganda flyer 081144/8c.
12 "U. S. Army K-Rations, 1941–1945," *Minnesota's Greatest Generation*, Minnesota Historical Society, www.mnhs.org/mgg/artifact/k_rations. Accessed September 1, 2022. Note: The K-ration was an individual daily combat food ration. The K-ration provided three separately boxed meal units: breakfast, lunch, and dinner.
13 28th Division Historical Summary, p. 100.
14 Buckler, Company C, 112th Infantry, *Personal History of the Men Who Marched in the Paris Parade* (1945).
15 28th Division Historical Summary, p. 103.
16 *Ibid.*
17 Burghardt, *My Tour with the 28th Division*, unpublished manuscript.
18 28th Division Historical Summary, p. 112
19 *Ibid.*
20 *Ibid.*
21 Stewart, captain, "A Tall Texan Assigned to the 28th Division, 110th Regiment in France," 36th Infantry Division, San Antonio Chapter Newsletter, February 25, 1991.
22 28th Division Historical Summary, p. 121.
23 *Ibid.*
24 Kemp, *The Regiment: Let the Citizens Bear Arms! A Narrative of an American Infantry Regiment in World War II* (1990), p. 112.
25 *Ibid*, p. 113.
26 MacDonald, *The Siegfried Line Campaign (United States Army in World War II: The European Theater of Operations)* (1977), p. 41.
27 28th Division Historical Summary, p. 124. Note: Dragon's Teeth were square-pyramidal fortifications of reinforced concrete used to impede the movement of tanks and mechanized infantry.
28 Clark, Congressional Medal of Honor, Medal of Honor Monday, U.S. Department of Defense, August 26, 2019, www.defense.gov/News/Feature Stories/story/Article/ 1942575/medal-of-honor-monday-army-tech-sgt-francis-j-clark/. Accessed August 29, 2022.
29 *Ibid.*
30 *Ibid.*
31 *Ibid.*
32 110th Infantry Regiment, Unit History. Headquarters, 110th Infantry, APO Europe (1945).
33 Dalton, staff sergeant, Company L, 110th Infantry Regiment, 28th Infantry Division, Bronze Star Award, APO 28, U. S. Army.
34 Combat Interviews, 28th Division Siegfried Line, interviews conducted by 1Lt John S. Howe. U.S. Army, European Theater, Historical Section (1944).

35 110th Infantry Regiment, Unit History.
36 *Ibid.*
37 *Ibid.*
38 Ciccone, PFC, Company M, 110th Infantry Regiment, 28th Infantry Division, Silver Star Award.
39 Leff, Company K, 3rd Battalion, 110th Infantry, 28th Infantry, Silver Star Award, APO Europe (1945).
40. MacDonald, *op. cit.*, p. 48.
41 Hark, PFC, Company B, 630th Tank Destroyer Battalion, unpublished memoirs.
42 Schroder, *op. cit.*
43 Jordan, sergeant, Company C, 1st Battalion, 112th Infantry, 28th Infantry Division, *Personal History Of the Men Who Marched in the Paris Parade* (1945).
44 MacDonald, p. 51.
45 Cole, *The Ardennes: Battle of the Bulge.* The U.S. Army in WWII (1965), p. 1.
46 *The Fort Point Salvo Newsletter* of the Fort Point and Army Museum Association, Volume 5, No. 2 (1980).
47 *Ibid.*
48 U. S. Army, Headquarters, V Corps, G-3 After-Action Report (1944), pp. 3-4.
49 U. S. Army, Headquarters, V Corps, G-1 After-Action Report (1944), p. 11.
50 Hark, *op. cit.*, p. 14.
51 *Historical and Pictorial Review of the 28th Infantry Division* (1946), p. 29.

Chapter 6

1 Atkinson, *The Guns at Last Light: The War in Western Europe, 1944–1945* (2014), p. 44. Note: The Third Battle of Ypres also known as the Battle of Passchendaele was a campaign of the First World War, fought by the Allies against the German Empire.
2 9th Infantry Division, Report of Operations, September 1–30, 1944, October 1, 1944; Report of Operations, October 1–31, 1944, November 1, 1944.
3 Headquarters, U.S. V Corps, After-Action Report for November 1944, G-3 Summary (1944), p. 2
4 *Ibid.*
5 Kensler, Private, Company B, 112th Infantry Regiment, unpublished diary.
6 Whiting, *Siegfried: The Nazis' Last Stand* (1982), pp. 58-59.
7 *Ibid.*
8 *Ibid.*
9 Drapeau, *Dark November*, unpublished manuscript (1993).
10 Headquarters, U.S. V Corps, After Action Report for November 1944.
11 *Ibid.*
12 *Ibid.*
13 *Ibid.*
14 *Ibid.*
15 Unit Report Number 5, 28th Infantry Division, December 6, 1944 for period November 1–30, 1944 inclusive, p. 28.
16 "28th Division Historical Summary," p. 149.
17 "112th Infantry Regiment Awards and Decorations, Kauffman," 28th Infantry Division Public Affairs Office (1945).
18 "28th Division Historical Summary," p. 99.

19 Hickman, unpublished diary, p. 40. Note: Hickman was a Battalion Scout with the 1st Battalion of the 109th Infantry.

20 Curry, *Follow Me and Die: The Destruction of an American Division in World War II* (1984), p. 97.

21 *Ibid*, p. 98.

22 "110th Infantry Regiment Awards and Decorations, Welc," 28th Infantry Division Public Affairs Office (1945).

23 Johnson, staff sergeant, Company D, 1st Battalion, 112th Infantry, 28th Infantry Division. *Personal History Of the Men Who Marched in the Paris Parade* (1945).

24 Esterly, Company I, 112th Infantry, Silver Star Award. Press release for First Army by 28th Division Public Relations Office (1944).

25 Unit Report 5, 110th Infantry Regiment (1944), p. 2.

26 Currey, *op. cit.*, p. 17.

27 "28th Infantry Division Historical Summary," p. 157.

28 Gary M. Dix, Company M, 109th Infantry, Silver Star Award (March 6, 1945).

29 Drapeau, *op. cit.*

30 *Ibid.*

31 Kensler, *op. cit.*

32 "112th Infantry Regiment Awards and Decorations, Kauffman," 28th Infantry Division Public Affairs Office (1945).

33 *Ibid.*

34 Morrison, *Report of medical evacuation* (1944).

35 *Ibid.*

36 Buckler, tech sergeant, Company C, 1st Battalion, 112th Infantry Regiment, 28th Infantry Division. *Personal History Of the Men Who Marched in the Paris Parade*, 28th Infantry Division Public Relations Section (1945).

37 *Ibid.*

38 "109th Infantry Regiment Awards and Decorations, Topping," 28th Infantry Division Public Affairs Office (1945).

39 *Ibid.*

40 Wells, interview by Cecil B. Curry, Washington, Pennsylvania (1979).

41 *Ibid.* Note: Eleanor was President Roosevelt's wife. Fala was his dog.

42 Fuller, interview by Cecil B. Curry, Washington, Pennsylvania (1979).

43 Nikola, Private, 110th Infantry Regiment, 28th Infantry Division, Silver Star Award.

44 Unit Report 5, p. 15.

45 Hubner, *op. cit.*

46 Kensler, *op. cit.*

47 112th Infantry Regiment, Unit Report (1944).

48 *Ibid.*

49 "28th Division Historical Summary," p. 172.

50 Corbett, private, Company B, 109th Infantry, 28th Infantry Division. Letter to his wife, November 8 (1944).

51 109th Infantry Regiment, Unit Report (1944).

52 Setliffe, lieutenant colonel, 1340 Combat Engineer Battalion, After-Action Report (1944).

53 "112th Infantry Regiment Awards and Decorations, Hackard," 28th Infantry Division Public Affairs Office (1945).

54 "28th Division Historical Summary," p. 200.

55 *Ibid.*

56 "28th Division Surgeon's Report of Casualties," November 1, 1944 to April 30, 1945 (1945).

57 Meyer, *The Shadow of Death. The Hürtgen Forest, Luxemburg, Battle of the Bulge, Stalag XIIA, Stalag IIA, Arbeit Kommandos* (1999), p. 59.
58 28th Division G3 Report to VIII Corps G3 (1944).
59 *Ibid.*
60 28 Signal Company Unit History, November 1, 1944 to January 1, 1945.
61 28th Division G1 Documents, November 1–30, 1944.
62 "The Battle of the Hürtgen Forest," DOCFILM. Deutsche Welle, www.dw.com/en/the-battle-of-hürtgen-forest/av-53307984. Accessed September 4, 2022.
63 28th Division G3 Report to VIII Corps G3.
64 Bruckner, lieutenant colonel, "Tab J to Appendix 1 to Advanced Sheet, Lesson 1," *The Battle of Hutgenwald* (1982), p. 80.
65 28th Division G1 Documents, November 1–30, 1944.
66 Peterman, "Great Unsung Battle of the 28th Division: Pennsylvanians on the Western Front," *Philadelphia Inquirer*, January 1944.
67 McDaniel, Company A, 1340th Engineer Battalion, unpublished journal.
68 Skains, Company M, 112th Infantry, unpublished journal, 28th Infantry.
69 Arford, Company G, 110th Infantry, unpublished journal.

Chapter 7

1 Dials, "Send up the Yardstick," *Army* (1973), p. 27. Note: Captain George E. Dials notes that FM 61-100 (Division) does not explicitly specify what a division frontage was to be, but he notes that by June 1944 8 miles was the accepted figure.
2 Zapotoczny, *Beyond Duty: The Reasons Some Soldiers Commit Atrocities* (2017), p. 82.
3 Steis, Captain. Service Company, 112th Infantry Regiment, interview by 28th Division History Detachment (1988).
4 Crosby, *Battlefield Chaplains: Catholic Priests in World War II* (1994), p. 129.
5 Perret, *There's a War to be Won* (1991), p. 404.
6 Meyer, *The Shadow of Death. The Hürtgen Forest, Luxemburg, Battle of the Bulge, Stalag XIIA, Stalag IIA, Arbeit Kommandos* (1999), p. 69.
7 Luxembourg, *Society and Culture—History*, luxembourg.public.lu/en/ society-and-culture/history/battle-bulge.html. Accessed August 20, 2022.
8 McManus, *Alamo in the Ardennes: The Untold Story of the American Soldiers Who Made the Defense of Bastogne Possible* (2007), p. 8.
9 O'Neill, reprinted from his 1950 essay, "The True Story of The Patton Prayer," *Review of the News* (1971).
10 *Ibid.*
11 *Ibid.*
12 *Ibid.*
13 Bull, Company B, 110th Infantry Regiment, interview by Walter A. Zapotoczny Jr., Bourscheid, Luxembourg (2019.
14 Brandenberger, "Seventh Army, 16 December 1944–16 January 1945," European Theater Historical Interrogations, Foreign Military Studies, MS#A-934, Historical Division (1945), p. 12.
15 *Ibid.*
16 Bergström, *The Ardennes 1944–1945: Hitler's Winter Offensive* (2016), p. 81.
17 *Ibid*, p. 83.
18 "After Action Report for period 13–20 December 1944," 112th Infantry Regiment, 28th Infantry Division (1945).
19 *Ibid.*

20 Olsen, Company A, 1st Battalion, interview by 28th Division History Detachment (1988).
21 "S-3 Journal, 150001A December 1944 to 162400A December 1944," 112th Infantry, 28th Infantry Division.
22 *Ibid.*
23 Haug, *As I Remember It: Courageous Defenders*, unpublished memoir, November 1994, p. 17.
24 "28th Division Historical Summary," p. 236.
25 *Ibid.*
26 *Ibid.*
27 *Ibid*, p. 18.
28 112th After-Action Report.
29 Train, lieutenant colonel, Silver Star Award, 112th Infantry Regiment, 28th Infantry Division. (1945).
30 *Ibid.*
31 *Ibid.*
32 Warrant Officer Donald H. Wadsworth, communications officer, 1st Battalion, 109th Infantry Regiment, After-Action Interview, Montfaucon, France (1945).
33 112th Infantry, Presidential Unit Citation (1947).
34 "28th Infantry Division Historical Summary," 109th Infantry Regiment.
35 "G-3 Journal, 160001A December 1944 to 162400A December 1944."
36 28th Infantry Division Public Relations Press Releases (1944-45).
37 *Ibid.*
38 Katz, first lieutenant, 108th Field Artillery Battalion, Bronze Star Award. Boston port of debarkation (1945).
39 *Ibid.*
40 "Battle Record of Company D," 109th Infantry Regiment, 28th Infantry Division.
41 "109th Infantry Regiment Historical Record," *Period of German Counterattack in Luxembourg, December 16–18, 1944 Report.*
42 *Ibid.*
43 *Ibid.*
44 28th Infantry Division Historical Record, *Period of German Counterattack in Luxembourg, and Belgium, 109th Infantry Regiment Report.*
45 *Ibid.*
46 VIII Corps After-Action Report (1945), p. 3.
47 Bergström, *op. cit.*, p. 81.
48 DeVore, "Armor Under Adverse Conditions," *Committee and Officers Advanced Course* Journal (1948–1949), p. 2.
49 Zapotoczny, *op. cit.*, p. 45.
50 *Ibid*, p. 50.
51 Bergström, *op. cit.*, p. 81.
52 Kokett, *The 26th Volksgrenadier Division in the Ardennes Offensive* (1946).
53 28th Infantry Division Historical Record, *Period of German Counterattack in Luxembourg, and Belgium, 110th Infantry Regiment Report.*
54 *Ibid.*
55 3rd Battalion, 110th Infantry After-Action Report (1945).
56 Zapotoczny, *op. cit.*, p. 92.
57 Welc, second lieutenant, Headquarters Company, 3rd Battalion, 110th Infantry Regiment, 28th Infantry Division, Bronze Star Award (1945).
58 28th Infantry Division Historical Record, 110th Infantry.
59 *Ibid.*

60 Obuchowski, 103rd Engineer Battalion, 28th Infantry Division, unpublished memoirs, pp. 2-3.
61 *Ibid*, p. 4.
62 *Ibid*, p. 6.
63 von Manteuffel, *Fifth Panzer Army (Ardennes Offensive Preparations, 16 Dec 1944–25 Feb 1945)*, European Theater Historical Interrogations, Foreign Military Studies, MS# 151A, Historical Division (1946), pp. 29-31.
64 Zapotoczny, *op. cit.*, p. 51.
65 MacDonald, *A Time for Trumpets* (1997), p. 144.
66 *Ibid*, p. 145. Note: Infiltration tactics was an idea developed by German General Oskar von Hutier in 1917. Instead of following preliminary bombardment with a massed infantry attack, small forces of experienced troops were sent forward to slip between enemy strong points on the front-line.
67 Johnson, *A Soldier's Story (1941–1946)*, unpublished manuscript, p. 11.
68 28th Infantry Division Historical Record, 110th Infantry.
69 Phillips, *To Save Bastogne* (1996), p. 135.
70 *Ibid.*
71 Maddox, Headquarters Company, 2nd Battalion, 110th Infantry, 28th Infantry Division, Silver Star Award.
72 Bull interview.
73 *Ibid.*
74 *Ibid.*
75 Johnson, *op. cit.*
76 *Ibid.*
77 *Ibid.*
78 *Ibid.*
79 Ridenour, Company L, 3rd Battalion, 110th Infantry, 28th Infantry, Silver Star Award (1945).
80 *Ibid.*
81 28th Infantry Division Historical Record, 110th Infantry.
82 Pizzo, first sergeant, Headquarters Company, 3rd Battalion, 110th Infantry, 28th Infantry Division, Silver Star Award (1945).
83 28th Infantry Division Historical Record, 110th Infantry.
84 Perry, "Recommendation: Unit Citation, 110th Infantry Regiment" (1945), pp. 1-3.
85 *History of the 630th Tank Destroyer Battalion* (1945), pp. 5-6.
86 "Certificate of special recognition of the 28th Infantry Division." Note: A certification given to the division by the secretary of the army on May 19, 1979, commemorating the 100th anniversary of the 28th Infantry Division.
87 112th Infantry Regiment, Presidential Unit Citation (1947).
88 103rd Medical Battalion Unit Report (1945).

Chapter 8

1 Ambrose, *D-Day: June 6, 1944. The Climatic Battle of World War II* (1994), p. 473.
2 Flynn, *The Heroes of Hosingen: Their Untold Story* (2016).
3 Cassidy, "The Week of a Thousand Battles," *The Kansas City Star* (1945).
4 Peterman, "Great Unsung Battle of the 28th Division," *Philadelphia Inquirer* (1944).
5 Ambrose, *op. cit.*, p. 14.
6 Crosby, *Battlefield Chaplains: Catholic Priests in WWII* (1994), p. 150.
7 "The Malmédy Massacre," *Holocaust Encyclopedia.*

8 "Hobo, December 17, 1944," 28th Division G-2 News Flyer.
9 *Ibid*, Crosby, *op. cit.*.
10 *Ibid.*
11 Goodloe, "War veterans, survivors reflect on faith in God," *The Spokesman Review, May 29, 2004*, www.spokesman.com/stories/2004/may/29/war-veterans-survivors-reflect-on-faith-in-god/. Accessed September 10, 2022.
12 *Ibid.*
13 *Ibid.*
14 Merriam, *Dark December: The Full Account of the Battle of the Bulge* (1947), p. 75.
15 *Ibid.*
16 *Ibid.*
17 Cedric W. Foster papers, 1903–1975. American Heritage Center, University of Wyoming.
18 Hark, PFC, Company B, 630th Tank Destroyer Battalion, unpublished memoirs.
19 *Ibid.*
20 *Ibid.*
21 *Ibid.*
22 *Ibid.*
23 *Ibid.*
24 Jurosek, Company A, 1st Battalion, 110th Infantry Regiment, unpublished diary.
25 *Ibid.*
26 *Ibid.*
27 Leech, captain, Company D, 109th Infantry Regiment, 28th Infantry Division, unpublished journal.
28 *Ibid.*
29 *Ibid.*
30 *Ibid.*
31 Puryear, *The 107th Evacuation Hospital*, unpublished journal.
32 *Ibid.*
33 Johnson, p. 1. Note: Written from the notes of a diary kept by Johnson during his service during the war.
34 *Ibid.*
35 *Ibid.*
36 *Ibid*, p. 12.
37 *Ibid.*
38 Waldrup, Company K, 110th Infantry Regiment, unpublished memoir (1989).
39 *Ibid.*
40 *Ibid.*
41 *Ibid.*
42 Snedden, Service Company, 110th Infantry Regiment, unpublished memoir (1989).
43 *Ibid.*
44 *Ibid.*
45 *Ibid.*
46 Richard G. Gooley, Company C, 112th Infantry, Distinguished Service Cross (1945).
47 Studs Terkel, *The Good War: An Oral History of World War Two* (1984), p. 236.
48 *Ibid.*
49 *Ibid.*
50 Pfannenstiel, *A Wartime Log*, unpublished memoir.

51 *Ibid.*
52 *Ibid.*
53 Robert Pocklington, interview by 28th Division Historical Section.
54 *Ibid.*
55 *Ibid.*
56 *Ibid.*
57 Katz, first lieutenant, 108th Field Artillery Battalion, Bronze Star Award. Boston port of debarkation (1945).
58 *Ibid.*
59 Henschen, 3rd Battalion, 110th Infantry Regiment, unpublished journal.
60 *Ibid.*
61 *Ibid.*
62 Kusnir, staff sergeant, 110th Infantry Regiment, interview by 28th Division Historical Section (1988).
63 *Ibid.*
64 *Ibid.*
65 *Ibid.*
66 *Ibid.*
67 *Ibid.*
68 *Ibid.*
69 *Ibid.*
70 *Ibid.*
71 David Y. Hurwitz, Headquarters, 28th Division, Public Affairs Office Release (1945).
72 Chernitsky, Anti-tank Company, 110th Infantry Regiment, interview by 28th Division Historical Section (1988).
73 *Ibid.*
74 *Ibid.*
75 *Ibid.*
76 Rudder, lieutenant colonel, 109th Infantry Regiment, interview by the 3rd Information and Historical Services, Headquarters III U. S. Corps (Washington, D.C.: National Archives, 1945).
77 *Ibid.*
78 Marshall, letter (1945).
79 Macsalka, lieutenant colonel, 2nd Battalion, 112th Infantry Regiment, interview by the 3rd Information and Historical Services (1945).
80 *Ibid.*
81 *Ibid.*
82 Allen, commander of the 1st Battalion, 112th Infantry Regiment was interviewed by the 3rd Information and Historical Services, Headquarters III U. S. Corps on January 16, 1945 at Montfaucon, France.
83 Strickler, After-Action Report (1945).
84 Colbaugh, first lieutenant, 108th Field Artillery Battalion, interview by Gus Hickock, 28th Division Association Historian (1985).
85 *Ibid.*
86 *Ibid.*
87 *Ibid.*
88 Slanger, F. Y., editorial for *Stars and Stripes* (November 7, 1944).
89 Ogborn, "Gentlemen From Hell," Poem.

Bibliography

Primary Sources

Archived

28th Infantry Division Archives (Fort Indiantown Gap: Pennsylvania National Guard Military Museum)

"28th Infantry Division Historical Record, Period of German Counterattack in Luxembourg, and Belgium, 110th Infantry Regiment," World War II Unit Records, Record Group 407, Box 8596. (College Park: National Archives and Records Administration II)

"28th Infantry Division Public Relations Press Releases, 1944–45" (Fort Indiantown Gap: Pennsylvania National Guard Military Museum)

"28th Division Surgeon's Report of Casualties," 1 November 1944 to 30 April 1945 (Washington, D.C.: U.S. Army Center of Military History, 1945)

"3rd Battalion, 110th Infantry After Action Report," RG 407, Box 8586 (Washington, D.C.: National Archives)

"109th Infantry Regiment Awards and Decorations, Topping," 28th Infantry Division Public Affairs Office, 12 July 1945 (Fort Indiantown Gap: Pennsylvania National Guard Military Museum)

"110th Infantry Regiment Awards and Decorations, Welc," 28th Infantry Division Public Affairs Office, 12 July 1945 (Fort Indiantown Gap: Pennsylvania National Guard Military Museum)

"112th Infantry Regiment Awards and Decorations, Kauffman," 28th Infantry Division Public Affairs Office, 12 July 1945 (Fort Indiantown Gap: Pennsylvania National Guard Military Museum)

"112th Infantry Regiment Awards and Decorations, Hackard," 28th Infantry Division Public Affairs Office, 12 July 1945. (Fort Indiantown Gap: Pennsylvania National Guard Military Museum)

"Certificate of special recognition of the 28th Infantry Division," a certification given to the division by the secretary of the army on May 19, 1979 (Fort Indiantown Gap: Pennsylvania National Guard Military Museum)

Ciccone, T. J., PFC, Company M, 110th Infantry Regiment, 28th Infantry Division, Silver Star Award (Fort Indiantown Gap: Pennsylvania National Guard Military Museum)

"Combat Interviews, 28th Division Siegfried Line, 11–16 September 1944," interviews conducted by First Lieutenant John S. Howe, U.S. Army, European Theater, Historical Section (Carlisle Barracks: U. S. Army History Institute)

"Corbett, Elliott R. II, Private, 109th Infantry, 28th Infantry Division," letter to his wife, November 8, 1944, Elliott R. Corbett II commemoration website, the Netherlands, www.elliott-r-corbett-ii.com/publications

Dalton, R. A., Staff Sergeant, Company L, 110th Infantry Regiment, 28th Infantry Division, Bronze Star Award, APO 28, U.S. Army Europe (Fort Indiantown Gap: Pennsylvania National Guard Military Museum)

"Downey, Milton R., Company C, 112th Infantry. Letter to his mom and dad, July 30, 1944," 28th Infantry Division Archives (Fort Indiantown Gap: Pennsylvania National Guard Military Museum)

"Durham, George, Company A, 109th Infantry Regiment," interview by Roger S. Durham, Pontiac, Illinois, August 12, 1996

Esterly, R. J., Company I, 112th Infantry, Silver Star Award, press release for First Army by 28th Division Public Relations Office, November 20, 1944, 28th Infantry Division Public Relations Section, APO 28, U. S. Army, Europe, September 28, 1945, 28th Infantry Division Archives (Fort Indiantown Gap: Pennsylvania National Guard Military Museum)

"FM 21-100 - War Department Basic Field Manual: Soldier's Handbook, July 23, 1941," Western History and Genealogy, Jack L. Kuhl Papers (TMD96) Box 1, 1941–1944 (Denver: Denver Public Library)

Fourth Supplemental National Defense Appropriation Act of 1941, Public Law 13, U.S. Statutes at Large 55 (1941): 34

"Friedman, Howard J. interview by Virginia Perkins, December 16, 1975," M77-164, Junior League of Tallahassee, Oral Histories, 1976–1977 (Tallahassee: Florida State Archives)

"History of the 630th Tank Destroyer Battalion. Headquarters," 28th Infantry Division, APO #408, 1945 (Fort Indiantown Gap: Pennsylvania National Guard Military Museum)

Ickles, H. L., "Speech during an 'I am an American Day', May 18, 1941," Harold L. Ickes Papers, ID No.: MSS27011 (Washington, D.C.: Library of Congress)

Katz, M., First Lieutenant, 108th Field Artillery Battalion, Bronze Star Award, Boston port of debarkation, 1945 (Fort Indiantown Gap: Pennsylvania National Guard Military Museum)

Kokett, H., Generalmajor A.D., "The 26th Volksgrenadier Division in the Ardennes Offensive," European Theater Historical Interrogations, Foreign Military Studies, MS# B-040, Historical Division, U. S. Army Europe, 1946 (Washington, D.C.: U. S. Army Center of Military History)

Leff, H. B., Staff Sergeant, Company K, 3rd Battalion, 110th Infantry, 28th Infantry, Silver Star Award, APO Europe, April 1945 (Fort Indiantown Gap: Pennsylvania National Guard Military Museum)

Maddox, K. G., Headquarters Company, 2nd Battalion, 110th Infantry, 28th Infantry Division, Silver Star Award, Individual Deceased Personnel File (Fort Knox: U. S. Army Human Resources Command, Casualty & Memorial Affairs Operations Division, Department 450)

"Marshall, John F. Letter, January 5, 1945" (Fort Indiantown Gap: Pennsylvania National Guard Military Museum)

Morrison, H. W., "Report of Medical Evacuation, November 11, 1944," sent to 28th Division Surgeon, 28th Division Archives (Fort Indiantown Gap: Pennsylvania National Guard Military Museum)

"Olsen, Frank, Platoon Sergeant, Company A, 1st Battalion," interview by 28th Division History Detachment, December 1988 (Fort Indiantown Gap: Pennsylvania National Guard Military Museum)

"Personal History of the Men Who Marched in the Paris Parade," 28th Infantry Division Public Relations Section, APO 28, U. S. Army Europe, September 28, 1945, 28th Division Archives (Fort Indiantown Gap: Pennsylvania National Guard Military Museum)

Pizzo, S. J., First Sergeant, Headquarters Company, 3rd Battalion, 110th Infantry, 28th Infantry Division, Silver Star Award, March 30, 1945 (Fort Indiantown Gap: Pennsylvania National Guard Military Museum)

"Pocklington, Robert," interview by 28th Division Historical Section, Fort Indiantown Gap, Annville, Pennsylvania, December 1988 (Fort Indiantown Gap: Pennsylvania National Guard Military Museum)

Roosevelt, F. D., "Annual Message to Congress, January 4, 1939," *Public Papers & Addresses of Franklin D. Roosevelt* (Santa Barbara: The American Presidency Project, University of California)

Roosevelt, F. D., "Labor Day Radio Address," online by Gerhard Peters and John T. Woolley, The American Presidency Project, www.presidency.ucsb.edu/node/209922

Roosevelt, F. D., "1941 State of the Union Address to Congress," FDR Library and Museum, www.fdrlibrary.org/four-freedoms

Ridenour, E. E., Staff Sergeant, Company L, 3rd Battalion, 110th Infantry, 28th Infantry, Silver Star Award, APO Europe, April 1945 (Fort Indiantown Gap: Pennsylvania National Guard Military Museum)

"S-3 Journal, 150001A Dec 1944 to 162400A Dec 1944," 112th Infantry, 28th Infantry Division (Fort Indiantown Gap: Pennsylvania National Guard Military Museum)

"Steis, Bernard, Captain, Service Company, 112th Infantry Regiment," interview by 28th Division History Detachment, December 1988 (Fort Indiantown Gap: Pennsylvania National Guard Military Museum)

Strickler, D. B., Action Report of the German Ardennes Breakthrough, Record Group 407, Records of the US Army Adjutant General, World War II Records, 110th Infantry Regiment, 28th Infantry Division, History, Box 8596 (Washington, D.C.: National Archives and Records Administration)

Train, W. F., Lieutenant Colonel, Silver Star Award, 112th Infantry Regiment, 28th Infantry Division, 28th Division Press Release, March 21, 1945 (Fort Indiantown Gap: Pennsylvania National Guard Military Museum)

"V Corps, After Action Report, 2 December 1944 for period 1–30 November 1944 inclusive" (Washington, D.C.: U. S. Army Center of Military History)

"VIII Corps After Action Report, 6 April 1945" (Washington, D.C.: National Archives and Record Administration)

Welc, J. P., Second Lieutenant, Headquarters Company, 3rd Battalion, 110th Infantry Regiment, 28th Infantry Division, Bronze Star Award, April 19, 1945 (Fort Indiantown Gap: Pennsylvania National Guard Military Museum)

Unpublished

Arford, R., Company G, 110th Infantry, unpublished journal, 28th Infantry Division Archives (Fort Indiantown Gap: Pennsylvania National Guard Military Museum)

Burghardt, A. W., *My Tour with the 28th Division*, unpublished manuscript (Fort Indiantown Gap: Pennsylvania National Guard Military Museum)

Drapeau, A. E., *Dark November*, unpublished manuscript (Fort Indiantown Gap: Pennsylvania National Guard Military Museum)

Hark, R. M., PFC, Company B, 630th Tank Destroyer Battalion, unpublished memoir (Fort Indiantown Gap: Pennsylvania National Guard Military Museum)

Haug, C., *As I Remember It: Courageous Defenders*, unpublished memoir, November 1994 (Fort Indiantown Gap: Pennsylvania National Guard Military Museum)

Henschen, R. H., 3rd Battalion, 110th Infantry Regiment, unpublished journal (Fort Indiantown Gap: Pennsylvania National Guard Military Museum)

Hickman, T. W., unpublished diary, 28th Infantry Division Archives (Fort Indiantown Gap: Pennsylvania National Guard Military Museum)

Johnson, R., *A Soldier's Story, 1941–1946*, unpublished memoir (Fort Indiantown Gap: Pennsylvania National Guard Military Museum)

Jurosek, L., Company A, 1st Battalion, 110th Infantry Regiment, unpublished diary (Fort Indiantown Gap: Pennsylvania National Guard Military Museum)

Kensler, O. A., Private, Company B, 112th Infantry Regiment, unpublished diary (Fort Indiantown Gap: Pennsylvania National Guard Military Museum)

McDaniel, D., Company A, 1340th Engineer Battalion, unpublished journal, 28th Infantry Division Archives (Fort Indiantown Gap: Pennsylvania National Guard Military Museum)

Obuchowski, R., Private, 103rd Engineer Battalion, 28th Infantry Division, unpublished memoir (Fort Indiantown Gap: Pennsylvania National Guard Military Museum)

Ogborn, R. G. "Gentlemen from Hell," poem (Fort Indiantown Gap: Pennsylvania National Guard Military Museum)

Perry, B. H., "Recommendation: Unit Citation, 110th Infantry Regiment," Headquarters, 28th Infantry Division, APO #26, 1945 (Washington, D.C.: U. S. Army Center of Military History)

Puryear, R., 107th Evacuation Hospital, unpublished journal (Munshausen, Luxembourg: Cercle D'Etudes Sur La Bataille Des Ardennes)

Skains, C., Company M, 112th Infantry, unpublished journal, 28th Infantry Division Archives (Fort Indiantown Gap: Pennsylvania National Guard Military Museum)

PUBLISHED

Belth, N. C., to Aryeh, L., January 15, 1941, 000.3, Religion: Religious Ministration in The Army, v. 2, Office Management Division Decimal File 1920-45, Records Relating to Administration and Management, Records of the Office of the Chief of Chaplains 1902–75, Record Group 247 (College Park: National Archives)

Bennett, I. L., (ed.), *The Hymnal, Army and Navy* (Washington, D.C.: Government Printing Office, 1941); *Song and Service Book for Ship and Field* (Washington, D.C.: Government Printing Office, 1941)

Blumenson, M., "Breakout and Pursuit, CMH Pub 7-5-1," The European Theater of Operations (Washington, D.C.: Center of Military History, 1993)

Brandenberger, General der Panzertruppen E., "Seventh Army. 16 December 1944–16 January 1945," European Theater Historical Interrogations, Foreign Military Studies, MS#A-934, Historical Division, U. S. Army Europe, 1945 (Washington D.C.: National Archives)

Cole, H. M., *The Ardennes: Battle of the Bulge (U.S. Army in World War II)* (Washington, D.C.: Office of the Chief of Military History, U. S. Army, 1965)

"Do You Remember—The Olympic Games in Berlin?" German propaganda flyer 081144/8c (Fort Indiantown Gap: Pennsylvania National Guard Military Museum)

Eisenhower, D. D., "D-Day Statement to the Soldiers, Sailors, and Airmen of the Allied Expeditionary Force," Collection DDE-EPRE: Eisenhower, Dwight D: Papers, Pre-Presidential, 1916–1952 (Abilene, KS: Dwight D. Eisenhower Library)

Headquarters, U.S. V Corps, After Action Report for November 1944, G-3 Summary, dated 5 December 1944 (Fort Leavenworth: Combined Arms Research Library)

Houtz, R. L., to Houtz, M., May 11, 1943, personal correspondence, December 1942–November 1943, Roger L. Houtz Papers (Carlisle: U. S. Army Military History Institute)

Jablonsky, D., "The Paradox of Duality: Adolf Hitler and the Concept of Military Surprise" in *Leaders and Intelligence*, Second Annual Conference on Intelligence and Military Operation, May 1987 (Carlisle: U.S. Army War College)

MacDonald, C. B., *The Siegfried Line Campaign (United States Army in World War II: The European Theater of Operations)* (Washington, D.C.: U. S. Army Center of Military History, 1963)

Marshal, S. L. A., *Bastogne: The First Eight Days* (Washington, D.C.: Infantry Journal Press, 1946)

Meyer, P. O., *The Shadow of Death: The Hürtgen Forest, Luxemburg, Battle of the Bulge, Stalag XIIA, Stalag IIA, Arbeit Kommandos*, as told to her by Robert W. Meyer Jr., Company A, 109th Infantry Regiment (Self-published, 1999)

Nay, R., *Chaplain. Leadership and Transformation of the Army Chaplaincy During* WWII (Washington, D.C.: Office of the Chief of Chaplains, Department of the Army, 2020)

Redmann, M. B., "Letter to His Mother, February 20, 1944," in *Unfinished Journey: A World War II Remembrance*, ed. Kerry P. Redmann (Guilford: Lyon's Press, 2006)

"The Trumpeter," *110th Infantry Unit Paper*, Vol. IV, No. 7 (Fort Indiantown Gap: Pennsylvania National Guard Military Museum)

U.S. Army, Headquarters, V Corps, After Action Report for September 1944, G-1 Summary, Dated 7 October 1944 (Fort Leavenworth: Combined Arms Research Library)

U.S. Army, Headquarters, V Corps, G-3 AAR for September 1944 (Fort Leavenworth: Combined Arms Research Library)

United States, "Report on the Army Chaplain in the European Theater," Report of the General Board, United States Forces, European Theater Study No. 68 (Bad Nauheim, Germany: The General Board, U.S.F.E.T, 1945)

von Manteuffel, General Der Panzer A.D. H., Fifth Panzer Army Ardennes Offensive Preparations, 16 Dec 1944–25 Feb 1945, European Theater Historical Interrogations, Foreign Military Studies, MS# 151A, Historical Division, U. S. Army Europe, 1946) 29-31 (Washington, D.C.: National Archives and Record Administration)

Wadsworth, Warrant Officer D. H., Communications Officer, 1st Battalion, 109th Infantry Regiment, After Action Interview, Montfaucon, France, January 15, 1945 (Fort Indiantown Gap: Pennsylvania National Guard Military Museum)

Wagener, C., "Fifth Panzer Army (2 Nov 1944–16 Jan 1945)," Foreign Military Studies, MS#A-858, Historical Division, U.S. Army, Europe, 1945 (Washington, D.C.: National Archives and Record Administration)

Secondary Sources

Books

Ambrose, S., *Citizen Soldier: The U. S. Army from the Normandy Battlefields to the Bulge to the Surrender of Germany, June 7, 1944–May 7, 1945* (New York: Touchstone, Simon, and Schuster, 1997)

Atkinson, R., *The Guns at Last Light: The War in Western Europe, 1944–1945* (New York: Picador, 2014)
Beevor, A., *Ardennes 1944: The Battle of the Bulge* (New York: Viking Adult, 2015)
Bohn, T. W., *Why We Fight. Film essay, 1977* (Washington D.C.: Library of Congress)
Bergström, C., *The Ardennes 1944–1945: Hitler's Winter Offensive* (Havertown: Casemate Publishers, 2016)
Blair, C., *Ridgway's Paratroopers: The American Airborne in World War II* (Garden City: Doubleday, 1985)
Boesch, P., *Road to Huertgen: Forest in Hell* (Independently published, 2018)
Brighton, T., *Patton, Montgomery, Rommel: Masters of War* (New York: Crown Publishing Group, 2009)
Brokaw, T., *The Greatest Generation* (New York: Random House, 2001)
Bruckner, Lt-Col. P., "Tab J to Appendix 1 to Advanced Sheet, Lesson 1," *The Battle of Hutgenwald* (Fort Leavenworth: U.S. Army Command and General Staff College, 1982)
Carpenter, A. E., and Eiland, A. A., *Chappie: World War II Diary of a Combat Chaplain* (Mesa: Mead Publishing, 2007)
Coates, C. H., and Pellegrin, R. J., *Military Sociology: A Study of American Military Institutions and Military Life* (University Park: Social Science, 1965)
Cooke, M. L., *The Moral Warrior: Ethics and Service in the U. S. Military* (New York: State University of New York, 1954)
Crookenden, N., *Battle of the Bulge 1944* (New York: Charles Scribner's Sons, 1980)
Crosby, D. F., *Battlefield Chaplains: Catholic Priests in World War II* (Lawrence: University Press of Kansas, 1994)
Curry, C. B., *Follow Me and Die: The Destruction of an American Division in World War II* (Briarcliff Manor: Stein and Day Publishers, 1984)
DeVore, J., "Armor Under Adverse Conditions," Committee and Officers Advanced Course (Fort Knox: The Armored School, 1948–1949)
Dorsett, L. W., *Serving God and Country* (New York: Berkley Caliber, 2012)
Flynn, A., *The Heroes of Hosingen: Their Untold Story* (CreateSpace Independent Publishing Platform, 2016)
Fussell, P., *Wartime: Understanding and Behavior in the Second World War* (New York: Oxford University Press, 1989)
Ginzberg, E., quoted in Kennett, L., *G.I. The American Soldier in World War II* (New York: Charles Scribner's Sons, 1987)
Glasser, A. F., *And Some Believed* (Chicago: Moody, 1946)
Gray, G. J., *The Warriors: Reflections on Men in Battle* (Lincoln: University of Nebraska, 1959)
Greene, J., *The Infantry Journal Reader* (New York: Doubleday, Doran & Company, Inc., 1944)
Grinker, R. R., and Spiegel, J. P., *Men under Stress* (Philadelphia: Blakiston Books, 1945)
Gushwa, R. L., *The Best and Worst of Times: The U. S. Army Chaplaincy, 1920–1945, Vol. IV* (Washington, D.C.: Chief of Chaplains Office, 1977)
Henderson, W. D., *Cohesion: The Human Element in Combat* (Washington D.C.: National Defense University Press, 1985)
Herberg, W., *Protestant, Catholic, Jew: An Essay in American Religious Sociology*, revised (Garden City: Anchor Books, 1960)
Historical and Pictorial Review of the 28th Infantry Division (Atlanta: Love Press, 1946)

Holmes, R., *Acts of War* (New York: The Free Press, 1985)
Jewish Welfare Board, *Prayer Book: Abridged for Jews in the Armed Forces of the United States*, revised (New York: Press of the Jewish Publication Society, 1943)
Kellett, A., *Combat Motivation: The Behavior of Soldiers in Battle* (Boston: Kluwer-Nijhoff Publishing, 1982)
Kemp, H., *The Regiment: Let the Citizens Bear Arms! A Narrative of an American Infantry Regiment in World War II* (San Francisco: Nortex Publishers, 1990)
Koppes, C. R., and Black, G. D., *Hollywood Goes to War: How Politics, Profits, and Propaganda Shaped World War II Movies* (New York: University of California Press, 1987)
MacDonald, C. B., *Company Commander: The Classic Infantry Memoir of World War II* (Ithaca: Burford Books, 1999)
MacDonald, C. B., *A Time for Trumpets: The Untold Story of the Battle of the Bulge* (New York: William Morrow and Company, Inc., 1985)
Marshall, S. L. A., *Men against Fire: The Problem of Battle Command* (Norman: University of Oklahoma Press, 1947)
McManus, J. C., *Alamo in the Ardennes: The Untold Story of the American Soldiers Who Made the Defense of Bastogne Possible* (New York: Penguin Group, 2007)
Memo quoted in Carl I. Hovland *et al.*, eds., "Studies in Social Psychology in World War II," vol. III: *Experiments on Mass Communication* (Princeton: Princeton University Press, 1949)
Merriam, R. E., *Dark December: The Full Account of the Battle of the Bulge* (Mount Pleasant: Arcadia Press, 2017)
Morgan, J. E., "The Significance of Citizenship Recognition Day," *Journal of the National Education Association*, 28 December 1939
Moskos, C. A., *The American Enlisted Man: The Rank and File in Today's Military* (New York: Russell Sage Foundation, 1970)
Perret, G., *There's a War to be Won* (New York: Random House, 1991)
Phillips, R. E., *To Save Bastogne* (Burke: Borodino Books, 1996)
Sarkesian, S. C., *Combat Effectiveness: Cohesion, Stress and the Volunteer Military* (London: Gage Publications, 1980)
Schultz, K. M., *Tri-Faith America: How Catholics and Jews Held Postwar America to Its Protestant Promise* (New York: Oxford University Press, 2011)
Skinner, B. L., *Daws: The Story of Dawson Trotman, Founder of the Navigators* (Grand Rapids: Zondervan, 1974)
Slomovitz, A. I., *The Fighting Rabbis: Jewish Military Chaplains and American History* (New York: New York University Press, 1999)
Shils, E. A., "Primary Groups in the American Army" in *Studies in the Scope and Method of The American Soldier*, eds. Robert K. Merton and Paul F. Lazarsfeld (Glencoel: The Free Press, 1950)
Snape, M., *God, and Uncle Sam: Religion and America's Armed Forces in World War II* (Rochester: Boydell Press, 2015)
Stahl, R., "Chaplain Jim Wants You!: The Boundaries of Religion in the Warfare State," paper presented at the World War II and Religion Conference (Tallahassee: Florida State University, 2012)
Stimson, H., quoted in Bohn, T. W., *An Historical and Descriptive Analysis of the "Why We Fight" Series* (New York: Arno Press, 1977)
Stouffer, S. and Suchman, E., *The American Soldier: Adjustment During Army Life* (Princeton: Princeton University Press, 1949)
Stouffer, S. A., Lumsdaine, A. A., Lumsdaine, M. H.,. Williams, Jr., R. M., Smith, M. B., Janis, I. L., Star, S. A., and Cottrell, Jr., L. S., *The American Soldier:*

Volume II: Combat and its Aftermath (Princeton: Princeton University Press, 1949)
"The Invasion of Poland, Fall 1939," *Holocaust Encyclopedia* (Washington D.C.: The United States Holocaust Memorial Museum)
"The Invasion of the Soviet Union, June 1941," *Holocaust Encyclopedia* (Washington D.C.: The United States Holocaust Memorial Museum)
Toland, J., *Battle: The Story of the Bulge* (London: Bison Books, 1959)
von Clausewitz, C., and Rapoport, A., *Carl Von Clausewitz on War* (Harmondsworth: Penguin, 1968)
Weigley, R. F., *The American Way of War: A History of United States Military Strategy and Policy* (Bloomington: Indiana University Press, 1973)
Wesbrook, S., *The Potential for Military Disintegration in Sam C. Sarkesian, Combat Effectiveness: Cohesion, Stress and the Volunteer Military* (London: Gage Publications, 1980)
Whiting, C., *Siegfried: The Nazis' Last Stand* (New York: Stein and Day, 1982)
Wilson, G., *If You Survive* (New York: Ivy Books, 1987)
Zapotoczny, Jr., W. S., *Beyond Duty: The Reasons Some Soldiers Commit Atrocities* (Stoud, U.K.: Fonthill Media, 2017)

Journals and Magazine Articles

"A Special Role," St. Paul's Church and World War II, National Park Service, U. S. Department of the Interior, www.nps.gov/articles/st-paul-s-church-and-world-war-ii.htm. Accessed August 20, 2022
Bartov, O., "Daily Life and Motivation in War: The Wehrmacht in the Soviet Union," *The Journal of Strategic Studies,* 12 (1989): pp. 200-214
Behringer, A. S., "Why We Fight: Prelude to War, America's Crash History Lesson," *The Unwritten Record Blog*, September 1, 2020, The National Archives, unwritten-record.blogs.archives.gov/2020/09/01/why-we-fight-prelude-to-war-americas-crash-history-lesson/
"Bible Bits and Topic Talks," *Link Magazine*, February 1943, p. 37
Dials, G. E., "Send up the Yardstick," *Army*, May 1973
Fagelson, W. F., "Fighting Films: The Everyday Tactics of World War II Soldiers," *Cinema Journal*, Vol. 40, No. 3 (Spring 2001)
Gehr, L., "Letter to the Editor," *Wheaton Alumni*, October 1944
Hertz, K. H., "The Role of the Laity in American Christianity," *Mid-Stream* 22, no. 3–4 (1983): pp. 326-341
Johnson, H., "What I Am Fighting For," *Link Magazine*, September 1943
Little, R. W., *American Sociological Review 31*, no. 6 (1966): pp. 870–870
Luxembourg, Society and Culture—History, luxembourg.public.lu/en/society-and-culture/history/battle-bulge.html. Accessed August 20, 2022
O'Neill, Father J. H., reprinted from his 1950 essay "The True Story of The Patton Prayer," Review of the News, October 6, 1971, *The Imaginative Conservative*, theimaginativeconservative.org/2022/03/true-story-patton-prayer-james-hugh-o-neill.html
Pellegrino, N., "Embattled Belief: The Religious Experiences of American Military Combatants during World War II and Today," *Journal of Military Experience* (2013)
"Religions in America," *Religious Landscape Studies* (Washington, D.C.: Pew Research Center, 2021)
Rielly, R. J., "Confronting the Tiger: Small Unit Cohesion in Battle," *Military Review*, November–December 2000

Sostaric, M., "The American Wartime Propaganda During World War II: How Comic Books Sold the War," *Australasian Journal of American Studies 38*, no. 1 (2019): p. 17

Shils, E. A., and Janowitz, M., "Cohesion and Disintegration in the Wehrmacht in World War II," *Public Opinion Quarterly*, 12 (Summer, 1948): pp. 280-315

Stewart, Capt. A. W., "A Tall Texan Assigned to the 28th Division, 110th Regiment in France," *36th Infantry Division, San Antonio Chapter Newsletter*, February 25, 1991 (Fort Indiantown Gap: Pennsylvania National Guard Military Museum)

The Federalist Papers, thefederalistpapers.org/current-events/the-fdr-bible. Accessed August 20, 2022

The *Fort Point Salvo Newsletter* of the Fort Point and Army Museum Association, Vol. 5, No. 2, May 1980

"The Malmédy Massacre," *Holocaust Encyclopedia* (Washington, D.C.: The United States, Memorial Holocaust Museum)

"U.S. Army K-Rations, 1941–1945," Minnesota's Greatest Generation, *Minnesota Historical Society*, www.mnhs.org/mgg/artifact/k_rations. Accessed July 23, 2022

Yarbrough, T., and Associated Press, "MacArthur Vows Victory or Death in Freedom Fight," Lewiston, ME, *Daily Sun*, March 27, 1942; *Reports of General MacArthur*, vol. 1, facsimile reprint (Washington, D.C.: Center of Military History, 1994)

Wansink, B., and Wansink, C. S., "Are There Atheists in Foxholes? Combat Intensity and Religious Behavior," *Journal of Religion and Health 52*, 768–779 (2013)

Zeiler, T. W., "The American Way in World War II from Part III" The Perils of Interdependence, *Cambridge University Press Online*, www.cambridge.org/ core/ books/american-history-of-america-and-the-world/american-way-in-world-war-ii/879D823F1F695D2F92677D66A5D6AB99

Zeitz, J., "The Speech That Set Off the Debate About America's Role in the World," *Politico Magazine*, December 29, 2015

Zietsma, D., "Sin Has No History: Religion, National Identity, and U. S. Intervention, 1937–1941," *Diplomatic History 31*, no. 3 (2007)

Newspaper Articles

Cassidy, M., "The Week of a Thousand Battles," *The Kansas City Star*, January 28, 1945

"Forde, Norman, interview by Katharine Goodloe," *Dallas Morning News*, May 29, 2004

Goodloe, K., "War veterans, survivors reflect on faith in God," *The Spokesman Review*, May 29, 2004, www.spokesman.com/stories/2004/may/29/war- veterans-survivors-reflect-on-faith-in-god/. Accessed August 16, 2022

Newman, L., "A Saga of Gallant Men; How Heroic 28th Halted Nazis And Saved Our Armies," *International News Service*, January 6, 1945

Peterman, I., "Great Unsung Battle of the 28th Division: Pennsylvanians on the Western Front," *Philadelphia Inquirer*, January 1944, Robert H. Henschen Collection, Series #272.99, Manuscript Group 272 (Harrisburg: Pennsylvania Military Museum Collection, Pennsylvania State Archives)

Peterman, I. H. (Cy), "Great Unsung Battle of the 28th Division," *Philadelphia Inquirer*, November 16, 1944, Robert H. Henschen Collection, Series# 272.99, Manuscript Group 272 (Harrisburg: Pennsylvania Military Museum Collection, Pennsylvania State Archives)